155 LEGAL DO'S

(and Don'ts)

for the
SMALL BUSINESS

PAUL ADAMS

JOHN WILEY & SONS, INC.

New York • Chichester • Brisbane • Toronto • Singapore

This text is printed on acid-free paper.

ISBN 0-471-13161-X (paper)

Printed in the United States of America

10 9 8 7 6 5 4 3 2 1

CONTENTS

Introduction

1 Types of Businesses

2 Financing

Litigation and the Alternatives

Intellectual Property

Patents

Trademarks

5   Commercial Transactions

6   International Transactions

7 Employment

INTRODUCTION

I have written one book, reviewed a few, read quite a number, and skimmed through many, many books relating to legal matters for the small businessperson. One problem seems endemic—they are simply too boring (including, in retrospect, the one I wrote a number of years ago for this publisher). Not that the legal issues involving small business are uninteresting, it is that the law in the abstract is like those math word problems we had in high school. Someone left the drain open in the swimming pool and we are asked to find how many hours it will take to fill the pool if the water enters at a rate of thirteen gallons per second. . . . Who cares? That wasn't real-world stuff. It was boring because we couldn't relate to the abstract, mathematical principles in that contrived context. Most small-business legal books produce the *War and Peace* syndrome. The reader believes, with good intentions, that he or she will like it if he or she can only get by the first fifty pages. Legal books are simply too hard to get into.

On the other hand, I have always liked encyclopedias (don't classify me as a nerd yet). When I have a specific topic I want to address, I can quickly find it, and in a relatively small bite, digest the subject matter. There is another appeal to the encyclopedia. I start on a topic only to find that it leads to something related, equally interesting, and more pertinent to my inquiry, and soon I am flitting from subject to subject, chasing down paths that I never would have otherwise been exposed to. It's entertaining because *I* am in control, not the author. *I* decide where the story ends. I have found the same type of satisfaction on the Internet. And I believe that is what leads to its current popularity as much as its interactive capability. Each Web site is a new treasure trove of information—and if I find one boring, I can speed away to a new location. (Unfortunately, there is a great deal of junk on the Net to wade through to find the pearls.)

This book is organized into ten chapters according to subject matter. A reader may traverse the book either sampling the law in small portions for fun or looking for a specific topic of immediate interest. With the related topics tied to one another, the reader could then follow the thread as desired. Of course, one may feel up to reading all of the items within a single subject—employment law, for example. Each item (an item is a single DO or DON'T, such as **#117**) within a single topic is related to a subject number. I wager that few readers will read the book in the traditional mode. Since an item may refer to another item entirely outside the subject being pursued, the reader will soon be drawn down another lane. A way back can always be found by returning to the table of contents.

Let me give you an example. One fundamental decision for you as a businessperson is the form of the entity through which you operate. In other words, will you do business as a sole proprietor, a partnership, a corporation, or a limited liability company (a relatively new form of business entity that is highly recommended)? To find your way through this quandary start with an overview at Item **#1.** It points out three or four very important decision factors and directs you to an item for more information regarding corporate formation or forming a limited liability company. But if you want to follow the subject in full, you can follow the Types of Business Entities entries that will take you to more discussion of the rights of ownership (Item **#2**). Then the subject splits into a corporation path or a limited liability company path. Yet even where there is information about the share structure of a corporation, there are pointers to the types of situations that use these instruments—family business succession planning (Item **#149**) and venture capital financing (Item **#37**). One of the advantages of a corporation is that you can use stock options to reward key employees and thereby compete with larger corporations that offer higher pay and more benefits. Item **#13,** in the Corporation path, discusses stock options. But methods for compensating employees is also a subject under Employment, so Item **#13** points you to retirement plans (Items **#115** and **#116**) and ESOPs (Item **#117**). Of course, retirement plans depend on the type of business entity you choose, so Item **#116,** DON'T, points you to the discussion of the differences between the C corporation and the S corporation (Item **#5**) that are part of the Corporation path under the general heading Types of Business Entities. In other words, you have come full circle. But it was your choice to follow the Types of Business Entities path from start to finish or to go off and consider if employee benefits and compensation were so important that you needed to visit the employment subject right then and there.

It is this feature of the Item structure of the book that makes it unique because it puts *you* in control.

The Subject Matter

I have tried to select subjects that are current and relevant to most small businesses. In truth, there is also a bias toward intellectual property subjects in which I have had the most experience and interest: patents, trademarks, copyrights, software, computers, trade secrets, and so on. But I also believe that in this world where manufacturing is drawn by the magnet of low labor costs, the products of the mind are where the opportunities of the future lie. If we recapture, or at least resist the migration of manufacturing from this country, it will be because we are intellectually capable of creating the machines, processes, and new products that overcome the cost disadvantage. This is good because cost advantage means a higher standard of living for the worker. We must invent and discover how to accomplish the same function and goal without so much labor. These advantages of the intellect must be preserved and protected. And to do so we must have a grasp of what these basic property rights are all about—and how to use them to gain the competitive advantage over not merely the foreign competitor, but the competitor down the street.

Intellectual property has also been thrust on the scene by the strange directions in which our culture sometimes heads. If Donna Karan had asked your grandmother, or surely your great-grandmother, to wear her brand of blouse or shirt with DKNY emblazoned on the front in bold letters, your grandmother would have given the salesperson the same look that she reserved for a petty thief. If she were more enterprising, she may have asked Ms. Karan to pay her for advertising her brand each time she wore the blouse. The Adidas craze she would *never* have understood! The time may come when Walt Disney will show movies without charge, for the money will be made instead on T-shirts and lunch pails bearing a likeness of the animated star. To put the matter more directly, trademarks and copyrights now assume as much importance in many businesses as any hard assets on the balance sheet. (It will take the fuddy-duddy accounting profession awhile to figure this out, but it doesn't escape the notice of the stock market analysts.) Furthermore, the rules relating to real estate and personal property (cars, boats, computers, desks, etc.) are old and stale. Intellectual property law is newer because there are new types of property that did not even exist fifty years ago—such as software. And fifty years is a wink in the life of the law.

Another subject matter of interest has developed from the leviathan proportions the central government has now assumed. Early on, employment law was about contracts between a company and a worker. Later it subsumed the development of unions and the contentious relations between organized workers and management. After the depression in the 1930s, the New Deal ushered in many laws regulating that relationship including: child labor laws, minimum wage laws, maximum hours laws, and social security law. The government became a partner of the worker to level the playing field in bargaining for division of the fruits of labor and capital. When the Americans with Disabilities Act (ADA) was passed, I had a vision of Samuel Gompers and John L. Lewis dancing a jig on the coffin of Henry Ford. This was not leveling the playing field—this was creating a *new* field where the management team was playing the worker team *and* the referee. I am not passing judgment here on whether this is good for the country and the common welfare. I am commenting on the fact that the area of employment law has become vast, changeable, and complex. The penalties for running afoul are not trivial. You cannot run a business today, and keep out of trouble, without some fundamental understanding of the laws and regulations relating to employment.

In the event you haven't noticed, there are a lot of lawyers around today: When the Warren Court, during the 1960s, proclaimed to the populace that all the problems of the country could be solved in the courtroom, we believed it. Today judges run schools and prisons. There is hardly a scurrilous phrase that is not protected by the First Amendment. Voting districts are regerrymandered by courts to achieve the goal of one man one vote. And at the time of this writing, the O.J. Simpson trial threatens *Dallas* as one of the all-time great dramatic TV programs. All this power and attention attracts ambitious and bright young people into the study of law. The net effect of these changes in society is to bring the court system to its knees. There are too many laws, too many lawyers, and too many cases. Court dockets are packed. And since persons accused of crime have priority access to the courts, it is nearly impossible to get to trial in a civil case while the litigants are still alive.

It did not take long—but some say too long—before dispute resolution was not the exclusive province of the courts, at least if the parties agreed. In the last ten years a variety of Alternative Dispute Resolution (ADR) mechanisms have been invented: mediation, arbitration (binding or nonbinding), mini trials, and so on. It is not merely the delay in receiving justice from a regular court that has encouraged ADR, it is also the cost and complexity. The fact is, you need to be aware that there are alternatives to high-noon shoot-outs where only one party, if any, survives.

The world is getting smaller. (How can a cliche that has gained such prevalence be so illogical?) Of course, we mean that advanced transportation and communication have made social and business intercourse easier. Not only are the large multinational corporations striding across the earth sowing and reaping, but small businesses that were previously foreclosed by ignorance and timidity are also on the move. Knowledge of legal rights and obligations is clouded primarily by the difference in the laws of the countries whose citizens can enter into a transaction with a company 12,000 miles away as easily as one 200 miles away. Yet ease of communication between two persons who are 12,000 miles apart does not erase a thousand years of cultural differences that have shaped entirely different legal systems. To succeed, international business must still cope with those years of barriers embodied in custom tariffs and transaction protocols. An attempt to introduce you to these problems is included here.

There is only slight coverage of the basics. Some fundamentals are included, but they are of specific areas of the law, not the broad outlines. I do open the Pandora's box of handing the reins to the next generation in your family business (the professionals call it *succession planning*)—a thicket of tax law and estate planning. But the portion served is only an appetizer, which leads me to an important matter.

Can You Throw Away Your Lawyer Now?

Of course not. You may be able to do a few things for yourself that you would otherwise have shied away from. But by and large, you will learn here how much more there is to learn. At first it may be frustrating, but that is the nature of gaining knowledge. It is unlikely that you will find the specific answer to your specific problem in these pages. You may very well find that the answer that you thought was correct is in error because the law is not always logical, and you simply assumed that logic would lead you to the correct solution. You may also find that the common wisdom is *not* that. There are people who, by virtue of their occupation (accountants and real estate agents come to mind), are exposed to the law in specific transactions and who then assume that the applicable law in the situation is *the* law, when in fact the applicable law may have been a narrow exception to the general rule. They then profess to know the law and pass that knowledge to others. Soon there is a coterie of professionals who all believe they know the law on that subject. They are wrong, but the myth persists. This book will disabuse a few of these misconceptions.

The main intent of the book, however, is to create a background, a foundation, in the subjects of the law covered here. This will assist you in recognizing problems, which, surprisingly, is one of the most important parts of being legally prepared: to know the law enough to know that you have, or may have, a legal problem. For instance, there are two terrible things about not being paid a large accounts receivable. The worst, of course, is that you may *never* be paid, but the more immediate is that you planned your cash outflow on that collection. The former may well be outside your control. The latter is something you could have prepared for if you had been alert—calling the customer to find out the status, checking credit more carefully, requiring a security interest in the goods. Legal problems, in this sense, are similar to cash flow problems; there is a part you cannot control, yet there is a part you can be prepared for if you are vigilant. That is the aim of this book—to make you vigilant.

And yet there is more to it than being alert. It is developing that sixth sense: being "street legal savvy," sensing an impending problem—an intuition that there will be potential legal difficulties if you continue on a particular path—before it is too late to turn back. You may not know exactly *why,* but you know that something is going wrong. That antenna is what this book tries to create. Forewarned is forearmed. When you are negotiating, if an answer sounds too pat, too glib, then probe. Press for the information that is being avoided or delayed. Write the letter that confirms that "the party said that the. . . ." Insist that "the agreement in principle includes. . . ." Explain to the employees that he or she "may do this, but not that." There are endless things you can do in a wide variety of matters, if you know you should be doing them.

Think of the benefit of this book in that sense, rather than as an answer to specific problems that arise in your business. It may address the existing problem, but knowing that you have a potential problem may be much more valuable. Then you have a choice: to find a specific answer to your problem on your own, or to seek legal advice that will resolve your question. If you choose to seek legal advice, you will be much more prepared to properly use your legal consultant to your advantage. Get to the point. Know which facts are relevant and even determinative of the problem. Ask probing and insightful questions, rather than putting yourself in the hands of your lawyer. Present your ideas on what you are planning to do, then obtain confirmation or correction. Provide a list of deal points, rather than have your lawyer laboriously and expensively draw out these elements of the deal from you.

Know your limitations. A good lawyer respects a knowledgeable client but is frightened by a client who presumes superiority in the field of law. If you can't read a balance sheet, you are probably headed for disaster; but if you can't prepare one, you are probably spending your time and money intelligently. (Unless, of course, you are the controller of the company!) In short, you can learn a lot about how to fly comfortably and inexpensively without being a pilot or a travel agent. You must learn how to use your lawyer. And the priorities are to be able to carry on an intelligent conversation about the subject matter, to understand your options in the particular circumstances, and to grasp the risks and the benefits of your position. You can do this only by having a rudimentary understanding of the applicable law. With such a foundation, you can advance and protect your interests with the help of your lawyer. Or, if you decide that the cost-benefits weigh in favor of representing yourself, you will not be running off believing the law to be one way—when it is in fact, the opposite.

Where Do You Go from Here?

Since this book admittedly is not likely to answer your specific question, where do you go to increase your general knowledge of the subject of interest? Fortunately, there are many books dealing with specific areas of the law that are accessible and readable. Between these sources and the judicious question to your lawyer, you will develop a fair working knowledge of certain areas of the law that clearly affect your business on a day-to-day basis. That is all you need. When you collide with a new area of the law that is only peripheral, pay your lawyer for advice and spend time building your business.

I would hope this book will also demystify the law, which is no more complex than many areas of intellectual endeavor. There was a time, hundreds of years ago, when the practice of law was beyond the ability of most people who, generally speaking, could not read and were not educated. The ability to read and write with skill and to reason and argue with force was admired, if not esteemed. Those possessing such abilities occupied a position of respect and conducted themselves accordingly. Now we have enlarged faces of lawyers on billboards and on TV, and the amount of education lawyers receive is surpassed by most technologists. The subject matter of technology dwarfs the law in complexity. Except for trial lawyers, the lawyer today is a legal consultant, no different from a consultant who has mastered any other field of expertise. I predict that within the next ten to twenty-five years, law offices will merge with accounting firms, real estate firms, and other personal service organizations. They will offer advice in areas where the legal issues will be only a part of the problem to be resolved. There will be firms that specialize in entertainment, including lawyers, accountants, talent agents, and producers. There will be firms that specialize in environmental matters, including lawyers, zoologists, remediation experts, biologists, and public relations people. There will be start-up financiers who will include lawyers, financial advisers, technologists, and personnel recruiting specialists. The only obstacles to these mergers today are the archaic laws for maintaining separate professions—fostered by the people who make a living in these organizations and their pompous pronouncements that they protect the people from the professional miscreants.

Most important, lawyers will be unnecessary in many transactions in which they now participate. The level of education of the average citizen will allow those willing to solve their own problems to do so simply because the gap between the lawyer's knowledge and that of the average citizen is closing, at least in comparison to the last few hundred years. More important, the ability to access information on legal issues will be commonplace and the capability of structured query information databases to find specific answers through intelligent dialog will be at your computer's fingertips. The same process is taking place, and will continue to take place in the medical field. An intelligent populace coupled with advanced technology is a great leveler of knowledge disparity. All of the learned professions exist for just that reason—a superior knowledge of one group in relation to another. The law is now so specialized that no one lawyer practices in any but a small area of expertise. While this would appear to widen the gap between the law expert and the layperson, access to that narrower area is quicker with a powerful search system and requires less accumulated breadth of knowledge.

In this changed environment, the edge in business will still go to the people who are most willing to avail themselves of the information for solving problems and narrowing down the questions that require more specialized expertise. This book will assist you in that process.

CHAPTER

1

TYPES OF BUSINESSES

DO *consider the various forms of business organization—sole proprietorship, partnership, corporation, or limited liability company (LLC).*

There are various advantages and disadvantages in the type of organization you choose for your business. While there are many factors involved and there is some variation depending on the type of business (how long it has been in operation if at all, etc.), there are still two dominant considerations in the choice.

1. *Limited liability.* To insulate your personal assets from creditors of the business is obviously sound advice. Basically, there are two forms of entities that can be used for such a purpose: a corporation, or a limited liability company (LLC). Ignore limited partnerships for the moment. These entities divorce your personal assets from the business because they create a new entity, that is, one other than the natural persons who invest in the business. These entities can be created only with the approval of the state. So the state grants limited liability to investors in a business, but only on certain terms and conditions.

2. *Taxes.* Once you create this new entity, you attract the attention of another agency of the government—the taxing authorities. If the entity makes a profit, the various tax agencies want tax filings and payments. The difference between a corporation and an LLC lies at this juncture. Are there two entities to be taxed or one? If you form a corporation, there are two; if you form an LLC, there is one. This explains, very roughly, the popularity of the LLC.

DON'T *totally ignore the sole proprietorship or partnership forms of business—but they rarely can be justified.*

There are two, and only two, positive things that can be said for the sole proprietorship: It is very quick (zero time) and inexpensive to form (zero dollars). If you are a freshly minted school graduate what assets do you have to protect anyway? It is hard to justify doing business as a sole proprietorship except at the very early stage of a start-up.

The partnership has some advantages, but considering that all your assets are at risk, even for an act of another partner, ownership rarely weighs in favor of this form. At one time, partnerships were useful to prevent disclosure of sensitive matters because you did not have to comply with state disclosures required when you filed a corporation. But now you can have that same benefit with an LLC and keep your assets safe. LLCs also replace limited partnerships (LPs), which were used to protect the limited partners' assets from liability. LPs have two downsides: (1) A limited partner that gets too active loses his shield, and (2) there must be one general partner.

After considering some of the idiosyncrasies of corporations and LLCs we can summarize better the pros and cons. Look to **#8** for corporation formation and the details of this entity, and to **#19** for formation of an LLC and its many facets. It is recommended that beyond the simple tax advice in this guide you discuss the forms of entity—from a tax perspective—with a good accountant. For some salary/dividend considerations relating to taxes in the corporate context see **#15**.

2

DO *understand what you own when you own a part of a company.*

Regardless of the type of entity that you choose for operating your business, you need a primer on what ownership means in the context of a business.

Ownership of almost everything is a *bundle* of rights. We ordinarily think first of possession as the primary right of ownership and, indeed, it is in many cases. But it may also encompass other rights that are attendant to or implement the possession right. In a business entity, a corporation for example, a share of common stock represents your right to a proportionate amount of the profit and loss of the corporation. This is undoubtedly the reason that you purchased the share. The profit may be distributed annually as a dividend or, when the corporation retains the profit and reinvests it, the value of the share will increase (capital appreciation). Do you own any of the assets of the company? You do not own assets in the sense that you can demand a wheelbarrow, a microscope, or your share of the cash in the corporate bank account. If the company is liquidated, after financial failure for example, you are entitled to a proportionate share of the remaining assets. But you are not entitled to sell your stock back to a corporation when you wish, at any price; this is not true with a partnership or a limited liability company where a buyback may be forced.

These broad generalizations of company ownership are, as we will see, subject to innumerable variations. But there are also other, more minor in most contexts, ownership rights.

DON'T *overlook the other important right in company ownership.*

The right to your piece of the pie, standing alone, may be in jeopardy if not complemented by other rights. Voting or governance rights are necessary to protect your share. Every *interest* (i.e., a unit of ownership) has rights to influence the operation of the business. In a partnership this voting right may be exercised directly at a partnership meeting. In a corporation it may be exercised at an annual shareholder's meeting (usually to vote for directors who represent your rights, hopefully more faithfully than your representative in Congress).

Voting rights may be significantly altered from the norm. Such variations may appear in the description of the corporate share (nonvoting Class B shares) or in the partnership or limited liability company (LLC) agreement, that must therefore be read very carefully. See **#8** and **#18.** Even where voting rights are materially decreased there is always protection that the right may not be attenuated further without your approval.

In some states, for closely held corporations (only a few shareholders—the term *closely held* is widely used to distinguish the corporation owned by a few persons from a publicly owned corporation), there is also a *minority shareholder* right that protects against oppression by the majority. This right forces the corporation to buy out the interest of the minority shareholder. Because it involves a long, drawn out, and expensive court proceeding, the relief to the minority interest may be less than satisfactory. When entering into a business with others, understand your rights *before* you invest.

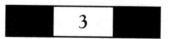

DO *separate your status as an employee from that as an owner.*

In most, if not all small businesses, the owners toil daily as the employees. Indeed, many small businesses are simply jobs with no boss. As explained in

#1, there are several popular types of business entities—corporation, sole proprietorship and partnership. And the limited liability company (LLC) will prove to be the most popular, in time, for the reasons set forth in **#17.** But regardless of the type of entity, the distinction between owner and employee must be observed. We will look at the distinctions as they apply to each type of entity.

In a corporation that you form, you will assume many roles: shareholder, member of the board of directors, and officer to operate your business. The services you render as a director (there really are no services performed as a shareholder) are not performed as an employee. If for some reason you wish to compensate yourself (or more likely, if you wish to compensate a family member shareholder who worked elsewhere) you will pay them as an independent contractor and report the payment to the IRS on a Form 1099.

As an officer of your corporation, you can technically be either an independent contractor (IC) or an employee. But for the reasons set out in **#105,** you are probably going to be classified as an employee. However, if you own several small businesses, each being a separate corporation, you may be an IC for one and an employee for another.

DON'T *ignore your employee status as the corporation owner.*

Assume, as previously suggested, that you are an independent contractor (IC) for your own company. (For a discussion of how to properly classify a worker as an employee or an independent contractor, see **#105.**) As such, the company will not pay any social security taxes for you, withhold any federal income taxes, or pay any medicare or federal unemployment taxes for you. It will file a Form 1099 at year end, and you will pay self-employment taxes including social security and medicare. You will also be responsible for paying estimated income taxes during the course of the year. Conversely, if you are an employee, the company must withhold income taxes from each paycheck, pay the social security taxes, and pay federal unemployment taxes. From the state's point of view, the company must also pay worker compensation insurance premiums and state unemployment insurance premiums.

The employee/owner problem that is unique to a corporation (a regular corporation called a C corporation, see **#5** for the two different kinds of corporations from the tax perspective) is the classification of payments from the company to you. What you classify as salary may be challenged by the IRS because it is too high (based on the pay level in comparable companies, among other factors). The IRS will call it a *dividend,* namely, a payment based on your stock ownership rather than for the services you performed as an employee. Salaries are deductible; dividends are not! Additionally, some fringe benefits (see **#115**) are measured by salary.

4

DO *compare the limited liability company (LLC) with a limited partnership (LP).*

The LLC was first approved for use in the United States in the late 1970s. But not until the IRS agreed that the LLC could be taxed as a partnership in the late 1980s did the LLC bandwagon begin to roll. Now nearly every state has adopted an LLC law that permits this entity to be formed. The popularity stems from the simple fact that an LLC offers limited liability (like a corporation) but has a tax status like a partnership (pass-through of income), so it is taxed only once.

Perhaps the closest form of entity to the LLC is the limited partnership (LP). This device has been used in many investment partnerships because it insulates liability of the limited partners from losses of the partnership and yet is taxed as a partnership. There are two serious limitations to the LP. First, all state laws require at least one general partner who is fully liable for the losses of the partnership. To avoid liability, the general partner is often a corporation. However, this creates a tax problem because the IRS requires that a corporate general partner's net worth must be at least equal to 10 percent of the total contributions of the partners to the partnership. This ties up capital unnecessarily. Second, a limited partner who participates in management of the partnership risks losing his or her limited liability status. A limited partner must be truly passive.

DON'T *fail to understand the reason an LLC can be taxed as a partnership.*

As noted, the IRS treats a corporation, for tax purposes, entirely differently from a partnership. It is true that one hallmark of difference between a corporation and a partnership is that the latter does not offer limited liability. What else, if anything, does the IRS use to distinguish a corporation from a partnership? (1) Continuity of life—does the entity go on even though a member dies? If it is a corporation, sure. If it is a partnership, death (or resignation, or sale of an interest) threatens termination. (2) Free transferability of interest—a corporate share can be freely traded. Ordinarily, a partnership agreement forbids a partner from selling his or her interest in the partnership. (3) Centralization of management—one partner in a partnership can bind the partnership to third parties. A corporation shareholder, of course, has no such power. These three factors, plus limited liability, are the four factors used by the IRS to classify any entity—corporation or partnership. Only the latter is granted favorable tax status. Thus, when approaching the LLC for the first time, the IRS uses this same test. If an entity lacks two or more of the corporate characteristics, it is a partnership. Since the LLC is intended to be a limited liability entity, one characteristic of a corporation is always present. To achieve favored tax status, an LLC must at least either threaten to terminate its life if a member dies, forbid transfer of an LLC interest, or decentralize its management.

5

DO *weigh the advantages and disadvantages of "C" and "S" corporations.*

Before discussing the formation of a corporate entity, you must become familiar with the two types of corporations from a tax perspective.

A *C corporation* is a standard corporation that is an independent taxable entity. Thus, when a C corporation has income, it owes a corporate tax. When you wish to obtain the remaining income after such taxation, as a shareholder (not as an employee, which, within bounds, you may do if you are actively working for the company, see **#15**), you are receiving a dividend. You must then pay personal income tax on that dividend money. The net effect is that money earned and distributed by a C corporation is taxed twice, once at the corporate level and once more at the personal level. (The matter is considerably complicated by many factors, but this basic framework applies.)

With the creation of the *S Corp*, Congress tried to provide relief for small companies by treating corporation income as passing through directly to the shareholder and thus subject only to personal income tax. To qualify, certain conditions must be met (see **#6**), and if these are complied with, the corporation can elect *Subchapter S* status, now commonly referred to as an S Corp. You should understand, if you are familiar with partnership tax matters, that the S Corp is *not* the same as a partnership, though it is similar.

DON'T *entirely ignore the C corporation as a vehicle if you can zero out.*

The tax problems of the S Corp, in addition to the qualification problems discussed at **#6,** have led some businesses to consider the use of a regular C corporation in a unique manner.

One approach for reducing or eliminating C corporation taxes is to limit income. That is, to *zero out* the income each year. If all shareholders, or at least the major shareholders, are employees of the company, the simplest method for doing this is to pay these employees salaries and bonuses that consume any year-end profit. But the IRS will look suspiciously on this tactic if done entirely at year end.

The IRS will become aroused if the salaries and bonuses are out of proportion to the services rendered. This determination may be based on comparisons of the salary levels in public companies that are similar in size and type of business with those you are claiming. If the business is capital intensive, the IRS assumes that there should be some return on this capital investment and will insist that part of the salaries must be treated as a dividend. The use of salaries to zero out will also look suspicious if the bonuses are proportional to shareholdings rather than to the positions or contributions of the employee shareholders. In other words, if your spouse is the secretary and receptionist at a modest salary, but a 30 percent shareholder, and she gets 30 percent of the excess income as a bonus, you are heading for trouble.

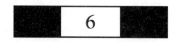

DO *carefully consider whether you can qualify for S Corp status.*

There are limits to the number and type of shareholders in an S Corp. The number is limited to 35 shareholders. If you have a family business or a business that does not require a great deal of equity from investors this should not be a problem. Each shareholder must be a U.S. citizen or a resident alien and must be a natural person. This rules out not only many foreign individuals but also foreign entities. And it rules out other corporations and partnerships. Only certain types of trusts and estates may be shareholders.

A particular problem for tax planning in connection with succession in a family business (see **#149**) is that an S Corp cannot have more than one class of stock. So preferred stock as a vehicle for separating ownership from control is not possible. This is also one reason why an S Corp is not typically used for a venture capital backed business. A disqualified salary of an officer shareholder can be reclassified as a dividend, thereby creating a separate class of stock and spoiling the election.

An S Corp cannot own more than 80 percent of another corporation, such as a subsidiary. It therefore precludes division of a segment of the business with high-financial exposure from the core business. Probably of less concern to the typical small business is the fact that there are also types of businesses, such as insurance and financial companies, that cannot qualify for S status.

DON'T *overlook the other potential tax problems with an S Corp.*

Even assuming that you can qualify as an S Corp, that you have not botched the election (sometimes tricky), and that you have not inadvertently spoiled your election, an S Corp is still not the tax equivalent of a partnership—which is the sought-for tax entity form.

Generally, the tax implications for most events in the formation, operation, and termination (sale) of an S Corp are the same as for a limited liability company (LLC). There are several pitfalls, however, in the formation of an S Corp relating to the issuance of stock in exchange for services; the rule for partnerships (and LLCs) is less severe. Partnerships (and LLCs) have great discretion in the allocation of losses between partners for purposes of taxation; S Corps are tightly limited in allocation to the number of shares and days' losses of the shareholder. Allocation allows high-bracket members of an LLC or partnership to benefit from the losses; however, there must be a substantial economic effect to the arrangement between the members.

S Corps with passive income (rent, royalties, etc.) that exceeds 25 percent of gross receipts may also be hit with the so-called sting tax. When an S Corp is the successor to a C corporation, there are also a number of problems that can crop up on the transfers of assets previously owned by the C corporation. The message here is that good tax advice is invaluable.

DO *understand the legal structure and operation of a corporation.*

Before addressing the formation of a corporation, you should appreciate the legal organizational structure of the corporate entity. As noted in **#2,** the corporation is an entity entirely separate from its shareholders. When a corporation owns an asset (or owes a debt) the shareholder does not own some part of that asset (or owe some part of that debt). The shareholder owns a share of stock (equity) in the company. It can be bought and sold as an asset in itself. The shareholder has no right to participate in the business decisions of the corporation, except as described below. In small, closely held corporations, where the shareholder is also a director, officer, and employee, it is sometimes easy to confuse the separate roles, but the distinctions are very important.

Shareholders elect a board of directors. The board appoints the officers. The officers employ the other persons working for the company. Shareholders act through shareholder meetings, and they have certain rights to call such meetings when they feel it is necessary. They may hire and fire the board members, depending on the restrictions in the incorporation documents (which are called articles in some states, or charter, etc.) as explained in **#8.** The board is normally a small group of individuals who meet periodically to oversee the affairs of the company. They set the broad direction for the company, decide when to sell stock and how much to sell it for, limit the officers' scope of authority, and have fiduciary duties to act in the best interest of the company.

DON'T *mix up the respective powers of corporate shareholders, directors, and officers.*

Directors are normally elected for a period of one year by the shareholders at an annual meeting. They may be compensated—normally a modest amount.

The officers are elected by the board, usually once a year, and they may be terminated by the board at any time. It may seem confusing, but an officer with an employment contract can be fired. The officer's recourse is to sue for damages on the contract (which is why there is usually a negotiated resignation). Officers have the power to bind the corporation; in fact, because an officer usually has the authority to bind a company, a third party may usually rely on the status of that person as assurance of the power to bind. That is why the board should deliberate carefully before electing an officer.

The devolution of power in a corporation is therefore (1) the state allows the corporation to be formed on certain terms and conditions; (2) the shareholders within the company have the ultimate power, but are largely confined to exercising such power through the board of directors; (3) the board of directors is given broad power, but it is confined to exercising its power through the officers; and (4) the officers have the day-to-day responsibility and authority to run the company. The powers of shareholders, directors, and officers are defined in a series of documents prepared in the formation of the corporation. See **#8.**

8

DO *form a corporation to limit your business liability.*

As seen in **#1,** a principal motive in forming a corporation is to limit your liability for your business dealings. While other entities can, more or less, provide limited liability, the corporation is the traditional vehicle used in the United States. The one chink in the limited liability armor is discussed in **#11.**

A corporation is a creature of the state in which you live. So corporate law varies from state to state. The comments here are of general applicability. A document, called a charter (or various other names) is filed with a state official by *incorporators.* They may not be the owner or in any way associated with the company after formation, or they may be the key members of the new entity. A fee, naturally, must be paid. The charter document is usually very brief—a name, a statement of the purpose of the business (usually very broad), the name of an agent (the firm or person who is served with a complaint, see **#46,** in a lawsuit), and an address.

The charter may include many other features of the corporation but this is a matter of choice; succinct charter provisions are favored. The documents that control a corporation include the charter, by-laws, and in closely held corporation (a corporation with only a few shareholders), a shareholders agreement. Certain control devices may be put into any of these documents. For completion of formation, see **#9.**

DON'T *place control devices for a corporation in the wrong document.*

A *control device* is used to define the scope of the action that may be taken by officers, directors, or shareholders of a corporation. For example, the directors may limit the power of the officers to purchase capital equipment that costs more than a certain amount. This control would ordinarily be placed in the by-laws. The shareholders may limit the directors' powers in many ways: prescribing a short term during which the director serves, having removal power over the directors, requiring a supermajority (meaning more than 51 percent) vote for certain transactions. The shareholders, or one faction of the shareholders with common interests, also may enter into a separate agreement that they will vote together on certain issues at any shareholder meeting.

There are several considerations for deciding in which document to put the control device. One obvious factor is privacy; if the device is part of the charter, it is available for the general public to see. If it is in the by-laws, the public is excluded, but all shareholders and directors have free access. The greatest privacy can be obtained by a separate agreement among only the shareholders that have a common interest. There are some limitations that must be put into the charter, if they are to be valid; for example, a limitation on the types of business in which the corporation may engage can bind outsiders only if in the charter. Use of control devices should be done only after consultation with a lawyer.

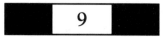

DO *properly complete the formation of your corporation.*

After the charter has been approved by the state agency, the incorporator buys a fancy leather-bound book with blank stock certificates and a blank set of by-laws. An organization meeting is called by the incorporator for the purpose of electing directors and adopting by-laws. Typically, the persons for whom the corporation was formed will attend.

Take the case of a small, family-held corporation involving two children and their parents. The parents may decide to be the directors of the company to control its affairs. They will be nominated and elected as directors at this meeting. The directors will then consider the form by-laws and decide if they would like some special provisions, such as control devices. See **#8.**

Then officers are elected, including one or more of the parents and the children. Officers are usually employees of the company, and if the children are employed in positions of responsibility, or will be as the company grows, they may be officers.

Ironically, there are still no shareholders of the corporation at this time. That is because shares in most states may not be sold, even to the family members in our example, without complying with state securities laws. (*Securities* is a generic term for shares of stocks, bonds, and other financial instruments.)

DON'T *sell stock in a new corporation without compliance with state rules.*

Before the sale of stock, a corporation is truly a *paper* entity. Without money or assets, it cannot operate. Of course, it could borrow money, but would you lend money to an entity without assets and with completely limited liability? So the directors must sell stock.

They may sell the stock for cash. Or they may sell it in return for the transfer of a preexisting business to the corporation (this may be done without, generally speaking, any tax implications). The stock may be sold for the ownership of a patent, a piece of real estate, or for services that were performed prior to incorporation or that are to be performed in the future. Although this latter consideration (remember that the sale is a contract and that every valid contract must have consideration, see **#130**) may raise problems. All states have rules regarding the issuance of shares. These are referred to as *blue sky* laws. In some states, such as California, the state requires not only full disclosure (the goal of the SEC rules) but also that the share price is "fair, just, and equitable" in the infinite wisdom of the state enforcement bureaucrats. The state is particularly watchful over offers to sell stock to the general public. Many states, like California, have created exemptions for the sale of stock to a limited group of purchasers, such as officer investors, and most closely held corporations, such as our hypothetical family corporation, will qualify for such exemption. See **#11.**

DO *complete the formation of your corporation.*

Once shares in a new corporation have been validly issued, ironically, the shareholders may then fire the directors, even if they are the incorporators! The shareholders now own the corporation. They may modify the charter (within limits set by the state) and the by-laws. If a date for annual stockholders meetings was not established in the by-laws, the shareholders will want to set such a date. Rules by which any special shareholder meetings may be called should be established. It is more likely, in a close corporation, that the meetings of shareholders will be special (i.e., called irregularly to settle a particularly important matter—issue more stock, change the number of directors, or sell the company).

The by-laws similarly set the dates for directors meetings (usually set for once a quarter, in sync with the preparation and distribution of financial results). They typically approve the establishment of a corporate bank account (the bank will want a copy of the resolution authorizing the account).

What sometimes is confusing in a closely held corporation is that the shareholders are often the directors and also the officers, as in our hypothetical family corporation (see **#9**). Indeed, the officers may be the *only* shareholders of the company. But each of these participants (officers, shareholders, and employees) in the corporation have defined powers and obligations that cannot be mixed willy-nilly. See **#11.**

DON'T *disregard other formalities after forming your corporation.*

Remember that the formation of your corporation created a new legal person. You will need to comply with a number of other laws, beyond corporate law, for this person. Most important, you will need to obtain a federal taxpayer ID number from the IRS as an identifier. This is the equivalent of your personal social security number. Your accountant should be able to assist you in this regard.

If you had a state license for operating your business, such as a liquor license, it must be changed to the new entity. If you had existing contracts in your business while you were operating as a sole proprietor or partnership, these must be reassigned. Ordinarily, license transfers or contract assignments are easily accomplished. However, there are instances where such transfer is closely scrutinized, or flatly prohibited. For example, a liquor license may require reinvestigation of persons added to the corporation as shareholders who were not equity owners previously, even if they had made substantial loans to the entity. A contract may require you to be a minority-owned business to qualify for a contract set-aside, and such status may be changed if you allow other persons to become shareholders of the company. It will pay to consider these matters before you convert your existing business into a corporation.

You may wish to consider the sharing of equity in the corporation with key employees now that the ownership in the company is more easily divisible. See **#12.**

11

DO *form your corporation as a close corporation.*

As set forth in **#8,** it is easy to form a corporation to protect your assets. However, the corporation form was designed as an all-purpose limited liability vehicle, capable of use by a billion-dollar company *or* by the corner convenience store. The complexity of the rules to govern a large company can be extremely burdensome for a small organization with only a few employees and limited funds to spend on lawyers. Many states, therefore, have created special corporations in which the stock is closely held by a small group of shareholders as in the family corporation mentioned in **#9.** These close corporations may have certain relaxed privileges to operate their companies more like a sole proprietorship or a partnership without jeopardizing their limited liability status. You should investigate what your state has done for you in this regard. Be careful not to become too casual in treating your corporation as identical to yourself.

Aside from the law, it is recommended that the directors meetings be used to step outside of the company, at least once a quarter, putting day-to-day matters aside, to consider the direction of the business. It is convenient to do this in conjunction with the receipt of a quarterly financial statement from the company's accountant. Review the financial results, establish near-term goals for the next quarter, and ponder the future. Also face reality—review the goals that were made for the last quarter. Ask *why* they were not achieved if that is the case.

DON'T *lose your liability shield through sloppy operation of your corporation.*

Even after you have validly formed your corporation to protect your personal assets from liabilities of your business, you must act like a corporation. When a small corporation is operated as if the company and the sole shareholder, director, officer, and employee (yes, this is possible) are one and the same, your creditors will agree and will ask a court to ignore the corporate entity and your liability shield. Courts have come up with a colorful phrase to do this—*pierce the corporate veil!*

To place this in perspective, the piercing doctrine is not applied in the ordinary case where the corporation is insolvent and the creditor has no way to recover. Indeed, that is the essence of the corporation. The piercing doctrine applies when the creditor is deceived into believing that there was no such entity because the operator of the business ignored it, perhaps to fool the creditor into believing that assets existed that could be counted on as security for the extension of credit when, in fact, such assets were owned by another. The doctrine is vague at best, but here are some factors the courts use to pierce: the formalities of corporation structure or control are disregarded, the company is undercapitalized, there is one shareholder and one operator and they appear indistinguishable, and assets are commingled. The courts are looking for fraud and chicanery. You can smell it, but you can't always describe it.

12

DO *use different classes of stock as necessary to reach the right financial structure for your venture.*

A corporation may have different classes of stock to meet its financial and other needs. The subject is too lengthy for discussion here, but a rudimentary understanding of classes of stock may come to your assistance as a tool at some later time. For example, different classes of stock are used often in succession planning for closely held corporations (see **#150**) and in venture capital financing of start-up companies (see **#37**).

Common stock is one class, while a typical second class of stock is a *preferred stock.* A preferred share is one with advantages over common stock (common stock is the usual class of shares that small companies issue). From a financial point of view, a preferred share is between a common share and a bond. It pays a fixed yearly dividend *if* the board of directors declares such a dividend. Thus, unlike a bond, on which interest must legally be paid, a preferred dividend is discretionary, but it must be declared before any dividend may be declared on the common. The second major financial advantage of a preferred share is its preference on liquidation (voluntary or involuntary). A bond (which is a debt) is paid on liquidation before all shares, but the preferred is second in line. In many cases, after the debts and the preferred are paid, there is nothing left for the common.

A nonfinancial feature of a preferred is that it may have voting rights that are superior to the common.

DON'T *underestimate the power gained by venture capitalists with preferred shares in regard to control, priority to funds, and so on.*

In a venture capital (VC) investment there are at least two groups: investors and doers (sarcasm intended). Money controls deal structure. The concerns of the VCs that steer them toward preferred stock are safety and control if an investment turns sour. Most venture investors do not want control of the company (i.e., the board of directors). They want to influence and participate in policy and strategy, but not control. (One wag thinks VC stands for voyeurs' control.) If the company is failing, the preferred shares may provide that the voting rights per share increase to the point that the preferred shares may take over the board and directly manage the business, including terminating management. Separating shares into two classes, common and preferred, accomplishes this end.

If the investment *fails,* the preferred shareholder investors have first claim on the remaining assets (assuming the bank debt is nominal). They claim this privilege on the grounds that management has been getting paid salaries, and so the preferred should have a priority to any remaining assets since they have received no return to that point. Management's common shares are always valueless when a liquidation occurs.

There are a number of other share features used in venture capital financing for other purposes. Unlike common, preferred shares are issued with a wide variety of provisions tailored to a particular financial transaction. See **#37.** Professional assistance is required.

DO *use stock options for incentives, if appropriate.*

Stock options should be a relatively straightforward tool for rewarding employees who make major contributions to a corporation's success. There are two complexities, however, which must be dealt with: taxes and securities laws.

A *stock option* is a right to purchase corporate stock at a certain price for a certain period of time. Sometimes referred to as "golden handcuffs," an option usually cannot be exercised for a period of time, thus inducing the employee to remain with the company until he or she can cash in. Typically, an option is granted in one year with exercise dates that are staggered over three, four, or five years. As each date passes, the employee can, but need not, immediately exercise the option; these options are referred to as *vested,* meaning that they can be exercised at the discretion of the employee. For example, an employee receives an option to purchase 10,000 shares of a corporation for a period of ten years so long as employment continues. The options vest on the next four anniversary dates, 2,500 shares each year. If the employee stays three years and then decides to leave, he or she may exercise the option, before leaving, for 7,500 shares. Of course, the motivation is that the shares will have risen in price, above the exercise price, at the time of exercise. The employee presumably has an impact on such a result and is therefore induced to work hard and increase the profit of the corporation and the value of the stock. The reward may then be collected through exercise of the option and sale of the shares.

DON'T *grant corporate stock options without fully understanding the tax aspects.*

Incentive stock options are securities—as that term is defined in most states—and thus the state regulates the use of options, since they may become stock. In a close corporation, state rules may permit the grant of options to employees since they are presumably fully apprised of the financial and operating condition of the company. But options are used more typically in a company that intends to *go public* (sell shares to the public that are traded through a stockbroker). See **#40.** They are used in high-tech start-up companies because these companies usually have a high potential for increase in stock value; therefore, it is a real incentive. If public, the shares may be sold in the open market (with certain restrictions) later. There is liquidity for the employee's shares. Other incentive schemes for a *private* company are available. See **#155**.

If an option is granted in conformance with the rules of the IRS, there may be favorable tax treatment. Options are referred to as *qualified* incentive stock options or simply qualified ISOs if they meet the test of Section 422 of the Internal Revenue Code. The basic rules are as follows: The exercise price at time of grant must be substantially equal to the price of the stock at that date; the total grant must be limited in value as of that date to $100,000 of stock exercisable in any one year; if the employee owns more than 10 percent of the corporation stock, the price must be 110 percent or more of the current stock price and limited to a five-year term; the employee must be employed at time of exercise; and the total term (for a less than 10 percent shareholder) is limited to ten years. You need a lawyer here.

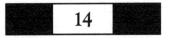

DO *use the proper tools for preventing strangers from becoming your business partner.*

One of the most important characteristics of a small, closely held business is that the key persons in the business work closely together and usually complement one another. No one welcomes a stranger who approaches a key person and offers to buy additional shares or the shares of one of the inner circle. Yet unless you take specific steps to prevent one of the circle from selling the shares, *they are freely salable.* Prohibition is achieved by placing restrictions on transferability of the shares.

The typical stock restriction agreement (although the restriction may also be placed in the formation documents) provides not an absolute prohibition against transfer, but a qualified one. It allows such transfer only after the shareholder intending to sell the shares first offers the shares for sale to the company or the other shareholders. (Similar options are available for partnerships or limited liability companies.) This right of first refusal operates to allow the other shareholders the option to buy-in the stock or accept the intended buyer as a new member of the inner circle. The mechanics may be simple. When a shareholder voluntarily elects to sell, he or she gives notice to the company (or the individual other shareholders) and gives them, say, ninety days to purchase the shares at the price offered by the stranger. The shareholders may place the restriction on sales to outsiders, or any sale, thereby preventing one of the group from purchasing another member's stock and altering the balance of power.

DON'T *use a stock restriction agreement that is not practically effective to maintain your closely held business.*

A common technique for restricting the transfer is to provide that if one of the shareholders in the group decides not to buy his or her pro rata share of the selling shareholder's total shares, the other shareholders may purchase the shares not picked up, on a pro rata basis.

The payment of the share price can be a problem, and the restriction may provide that the shares may be paid for in installments over a period of as much as ten years. This then becomes a part of the withdrawing shareholder's retirement plan. But care must be taken that the selling shareholder, who no longer has a voice in the business, is assured that the payments are made—that is, that the company is financially viable. A personal guarantee from the other shareholders is the very least security that should be obtained. Other rights may arise only when a payment is missed, such as a voting right in the business.

The restriction may also be triggered by involuntary transfers such as in a divorce or marital separation agreement or even a court order. How about death and the transfer to the heirs of the deceased's shares? Clearly the agreement should provide that the heir can take the stock only if he or she signs the restriction agreement. This succession of shares to heirs can be prevented only if the agreement goes further and provides what is referred to as a Buy-Sell agreement—an arrangement that forces the heirs to sell upon the death of the original shareholder. This agreement is discussed in **#154.**

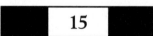

15

DO *plan the payment of your corporate salary so that it withstands challenge from the IRS.*

Employee shareholder compensation is one of the most significant tax issues for the closely held corporation. As stated in **#5,** one of the disadvantages of the corporate form of business is that profits are subject to a corporate tax and then when distributed to the shareholder (who may be the sole shareholder of the corporation) are taxed again as income. Of course, if the corporation paid a higher salary to that employee shareholder, and could deduct that salary from corporate profits, there would be no tax at the corporate level, yet the employee shareholder would have received the same amount. With only one tax!

The IRS has figured this out too. It may challenge a salary of an employee shareholder as unreasonable compensation. To avoid the challenge, you must first understand that the IRS will look at total compensation, in whatever guise—salary, bonuses, commissions, fringe benefits, retirement benefits, deferred compensation—and in whatever form—property, stock, or cash. Nor does it matter what you label the payment. A dividend is a dividend is a dividend.

What does the IRS look at? It examines the nature of your duties, the responsibilities of your position, your knowledge and experience in the business, time spent, contribution to profit, size of the business, times during the year in which the payments are made (see **#5**), comparable salaries of other executives in similar companies, and economic conditions.

DON'T *allow your salary in your closely held corporation to be characterized as a dividend by the IRS—plan and record your justification.*

As the parameters used by the IRS to test for reasonableness of compensation clearly exhibit, there is no safe harbor in this area of the tax law. So marshaling the facts and constantly making your decisions with an eye on the tax collector is very important. At meetings, board members should record decisions for a bonus with strong details of why the performance of the individual was particularly meritorious, note all changes in responsibility, and record efforts to obtain major contracts or reductions in cost. In other words, demonstrably and flagrantly pat yourself on the back. Because contingent formulas are so convincing, they should be used extensively, but they must be entered into *before* the year begins.

The IRS may take the position that as a shareholder you would not invest in the company unless there was some return on investment, so it may take 8 percent or 9 percent of the equity in the company as the normal return and argue that *at least* that amount was a dividend, not salary. If the equity is low, accept that deal.

For family corporations, justifying salaries for younger family members is very important. One well-accepted consideration is showing that a family member was offered a comparable salary in the open market.

If you set a salary for yourself during the early days and there is not enough cash to pay that salary, may you pay it years later and take a deduction? Yes. The IRS will resist, but there is good court precedent to justify payment and deduction.

16

DO *treat yourself as a self-employed person with respect to taxes and fringe benefits when you work for your own limited liability company (LLC).*

Your status as a self-employed person is quite different from that of an employee of a regular C corporation with respect to income taxes for your earnings, withholding, and many of the fringe benefits that you have as an employee in such a corporation. As an employee of an LLC, you are in the same position as a sole proprietor of the business, or a partner in a partnership.

For example, in a regular corporation, you may participate in an Employee Stock Purchase Plan as an employee, even if you are one of the owners. Your medical benefits are excludable as income in a C corporation, but not as a partner, sole proprietor, or LLC member. You may also receive, without being taxed, life insurance up to $50,000 as an employee of a C corporation who participates in a group medical plan. But the most significant loss of benefits is with respect to retirement.

The corporate owner may borrow from his or her retirement plan, but a self-employed person may not. If a contribution made by a corporation results in a net operating loss, it is permissible, but not if you are self-employed; this allows the corporate owner to continue funding his or her retirement plan during both good and bad years (the operating loss is used later to reduce taxes) but not a self-employed person. There is no rational basis for this difference; corporations simply have more clout with Congress.

DON'T *overlook the possibility that a challenge by the IRS to your salary in your closely held corporation can be met with a hedge agreement.*

Remaining with the issue of corporate employee shareholder compensation (see **#15**), the concept of hedging your salary against a charge of unreasonable compensation should be mentioned. If the IRS proved that your corporate salary as an owner/employee was excessive because there was no arms-length determination of amount, you could agree to repay any such unreasonable amount to the corporation. You would then be able as an individual taxpayer to take a deduction for such repayment. If the agreement to repay was made prior to taking the salary, a deduction will be allowed. But the deduction will be available only in the year of repayment, which may not have the same tax effect. (You could have been earning zero in the year that the deduction was available, but were taxed at the maximum rate in the year taken.) There is a fair argument that the IRS position (the deduction is only good in the year taken) is wrong and the taxpayer may choose the year in which the deduction may be taken (filing an amended return in the latter case).

The most difficult decision is whether to enter into such a hedge agreement at all. Many tax practitioners believe that the very existence of the agreement will call attention (the "red flag" argument) to the salary. Others feel that a high salary will be challenged in most events anyway, so why not protect yourself. This is not a legal question. You must always remember that the final decision is yours. Your lawyer will likely recommend the safest course, but you may be more willing to take the risk of an IRS challenge.

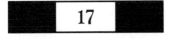

DO *form a limited liability company (LLC) correctly.*

As set forth in **#1**, a prime advantage of the LLC is to avoid the double taxation of a corporation while providing liability protection. You must understand the basis on which the IRS distinguishes a corporation from a noncorporation to see why an LLC is structured as it is.

The IRS has a four-factor test to decide if an entity is a corporation; if an entity has three or more of the following factors, it is a corporation, regardless of what you call it. First, does it have limited liability? Of course, it will—this is the very object of forming the LLC. (Therefore, only one of the remaining three factors may be "corporate-like.") Second, does it have "centralized management"? This is a controllable factor. There are various ways to structure the management—from nonowner hired managers (similar to a corporation) to member management (similar to a partnership). Third, does it have unlimited life. The LLC must be structured so that it will end if one of the members withdraws, as discussed at **#22.** Fourth, are the ownership interests freely transferable? Defeating free transferability is easy—indeed, in a closely held business, it is usually *desirable* to prevent interests from being transferred to another person. In many small, closely held corporations there are separate agreements restricting transfer. In an LLC this may be done directly in the operating agreement, as discussed at **#21.**

DON'T *incorrectly structure the management, transferability of interests, or life of an LLC if you want the right tax result.*

An LLC may have centralized management if you desire to restrict transfer of the membership interests and limit the life of the company.

What is *centralized management?* According to the IRS, if the LLC elects to be member managed, it will always avoid centralized management because each member can bind the company. But if you elect a manager-managed structure (see **#19**), you will have centralized management. Unless the IRS softens the rules regarding manager-managed LLCs, LLCs will not replace all limited partnerships. For the small business, it is recommended that you choose a manager-managed structure unless you are confident that your other members will not bind the company to a bad deal. Alternatively, you may create a member-managed structure but limit the power of some members in the operating agreement.

With a limited-life structure, the LLC must dissolve on the occurrence of death, insanity, bankruptcy, retirement, resignation, or expulsion of a member. This does *not* mean that the company cannot continue in existence; it must simply be a different entity. An LLC may provide that upon occurrence of any of the six events, the remaining members may vote to continue the company. This does not jeopardize the limited-life characteristic and therefore the tax status. See **#22.**

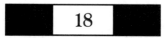

18

DO *adopt an operating agreement—the heart of a limited liability company (LLC).*

An operating agreement is like a partnership agreement in that it sets forth the rights and obligations between the members (see **#21**), which is highly recommended in forming a correct LLC. To understand the importance of the operating agreement, it is beneficial to compare the structure of an LLC with a corporation and a partnership.

Since a corporation is a creature of the state, the state is active in supplying the rules through statutes by which the corporation is operated. It supplies many of the rules that the company presumably would adopt—referred to as default rules. If the articles, charter, or the by-laws are silent, these rules apply. By contrast, a partnership is a creature of the citizens, with no involvement by the state. If a rule is not in the agreement, expressly or by implication, it is not part of the parties' agreement. Most LLC statutes fall in around the middle—there are some default rules but these are not as complete as the corporation statutes. It is strongly recommended that every LLC adopt an operating agreement.

There are two important decisions to be made immediately upon LLC formation that affect the operating agreement. First, should the LLC be run by the members ("members" are how the participants in the LLC are referred to as compared to "stockholder" in a corporation and "partner" in a partnership) or should it be run by managers (see **#19**)? Second, should the financial rights and the governing rights be handled separately or combined (see **#21**)?

DON'T *confuse managers and members in an LLC.*

It isn't easy. Remember when we discussed the three roles (shareholder, director, and officer) that a participant in a corporation can hold? See **#3.** Well, in an LLC you may be a member, manager, and an officer. The word manager is not used in the same sense with which you are familiar. LLC statutes (except in Colorado) require you to elect either a manager-managed or member-managed structure. "Member-managed" is best thought of as the way a partnership operates—all partners have an equal voice in the decision making. (This power can be limited by an agreement between the partners.) If you select a "manager-managed" structure, the members give up almost all of their power by delegation to the managers. This is similar to shareholders delegating power to the directors. The analogy between a member-managed LLC and a partnership and a manager-managed LLC and a corporation is generally true—but one of the benefits of an LLC is that hybrids can be tailored to specific needs.

Can a manager be a member? Not just yes but almost always some members will be managers, particularly in a small entity. Are there officers? Yes, if the structure is member-managed, the members appoint officers; if it is manager-managed, the managers appoint the officers.

Then why all this fuss? Because the power to bind the LLC depends on status. See **#19.**

DO *consider the exposure of the assets of a member-managed limited liability company (LLC).*

In selecting the form of business entity (see **#1**), it was pointed out that the primary advantage of the limited liability company was, in fact, the protection of your personal assets. A closer look at this concept is warranted. We will look first at partnerships in which partners have equal tax advantages but are subject to the exposure of loss of personal assets.

A partner is personally liable for all the debts of a partnership. That is the biggest problem. But that problem is aggravated by the fact that each partner can bind the partnership. Your partner can borrow money for the partnership without your knowledge and the debt is binding. In an LLC you are not personally liable for any of the debts of the company, but *if* you elect the member-managed structure, any member may bind the LLC just as any partner can bind a partnership. In other words, you have solved only part of the problem.

If you and the other members of the LLC build up the company to substantial value, which is what you hope to do, an errant member could enter into a foolish deal on behalf of the LLC and you could lose the company. There are methods for limiting the power of the other members to bind the LLC in an operating agreement, but only between the members. You *cannot* bind third parties by such an arrangement. See **#78**. You may be able to sue the member who breaches your operating agreement by acting outside the scope of his or her authority, but is that member capable of satisfying the judgment?

DON'T *choose a management structure for a limited liability company (LLC) that increases exposure to third parties.*

In the operating agreement, under most state statutes, you may elect that the LLC be member- or manager-managed. Because of the agency rules that allow an LLC to be bound by any member (see **#78**), if there are members who are not part of the day-to-day management of the business, or there are simply many members, it could be unwise to choose a member-managed structure.

By electing a manager-managed structure, you can control the size of the group that can bind the LLC. You choose a limited number of the members to be the managers. When filing your Articles of Organization, you elect the manager-managed structure. This gives constructive notice to all third parties dealing with the LLC that member signatures and representation of authority as a member are of no value. Since you may not wish to delegate all of your member powers to the managers, you may reserve some powers; for example, the power to admit new members to the LLC.

One disadvantage of choosing the manager-managed structure is that you have, for tax purposes, added a centralized management characteristic. Thus, the LLC is closer to being taxed as a corporation than a partnership. However, this should not be a problem in most closely held LLCs. See **#78**.

20

DO *comply with the rules in your state when filing a charter for a limited liability company (LLC).*

If you have selected the LLC as the form of business under which you will operate, you must file certain papers with an official in your state. Although many states have adopted the Uniform Limited Liability Company Act (uniform laws are model legislative enactments that are prepared by an independent commission of lawyers, professors, and judges and made available for adoption by any state that may wish to enact comprehensive laws regarding any subject—the most popular, adopted by forty-nine states is the Uniform Commercial Code, which you probably know as the UCC), not all have and those that have usually modified the model before enactment.

To form an LLC you will need to contact the proper government agency in your state. Try contacting the official who regulates the formation of corporations.

If your state has an annual maintenance fee or minimum tax on corporations, you won't avoid this tax by forming an LLC. In California, for example, it is $800 per year. Similarly, you will need a federal tax ID number as does a corporation or any other business with employees.

DON'T *form a defective limited liability company (LLC).*

An LLC is created by filing papers that are usually referred to as the articles of organization. Most states require only one person to file. Some states require that the LLC have at least two members. The persons filing the articles are referred to as the organizers. The rules will state the number of members necessary to file in terms of organizers, but they mean members. Although some states allow only natural persons to be LLC members, most allow members to be corporations, partnerships, or other LLCs.

Most likely, the only serious problem you will have in filing the articles is the approval of the name—most states will not allow two entities with the same or similar name to be created. See **#67** for advice on choosing names.

Most states require minimum information, which is consistent with one of the advantages of forming an LLC—maintaining secrecy. Usually, only name, address of the principal office, registered agent name (the person on whom a complaint in a lawsuit is filed), and the duration or life of the LLC (say fifty years) are required. Some require the purpose (be brief and broad) and the management structure (see **#19**). Some states allow you to add any other information that may be lawful. Don't. Put it into the operating agreement. See **#21.**

21

DO *create a sound operating agreement after you form your limited liability company (LLC).*

To form an LLC, see **#20.** After formation, you must prepare and have all members sign a written operating agreement for the reasons set forth in **#18.** The operating agreement is the charter or rule book for running the company as an LLC. The law in your state may or may not specifically define what may be included in the operating agreement, but all states allow, even anticipate, that an operating agreement will be entered into.

There are four basic areas that the operating agreement should cover: membership, management, financial structure, and dissolution (see **#22**). The management issue is discussed in **#19.**

Membership deals with the fundamental issue of who may be a member and how new members are admitted. You may provide for any level of approval by existing members for admission of a new member—a unanimous vote may be desirable in a small, closely held LLC. Of course, a member may also be admitted by purchase of an existing member's interest—but again you may have the transfer depend on the approval of all the members. Indeed, this restriction on transfer is recommended in order to obtain favorable tax treatment of the LLC (see **#17**). As a person planning to join an LLC, you should examine the operating agreement to see what transfer restrictions exist, since this controls the liquidity of your investment.

DON'T *fail to cover the necessary issues in your operating agreement for a limited liability company (LLC).*

The financial structure of the LLC may be tailored to meet your needs—as simple or complex as the circumstances dictate.

The primary factor that distinguishes the simple from the complex is whether the financial aspect of the interest is separate from the voting or governance aspect. If the financial interest is separate, then the transfer of interests is easier to accomplish. For intramember transfers, separation greatly simplifies administration; a member may transfer the financial right to profit while maintaining the voting rights. Since these transfers do not jeopardize the favorable tax status (the IRS rule that free transferability characterizes the LLC as a corporation applies only to transfers to nonmembers), the ease of keeping track of separate voting and financial rights is welcome. Because transfers to nonmembers should be subject to a high level of consent, fewer transfers should occur.

The operating agreement should also provide that (1) the LLC may not require additional contributions by members (otherwise a majority of wealthy members may change the balance of power in the LLC) and (2) the members have no right to redemption (unless the LLC has excess capital) nor any rights to interim distributions which would occur if a member withdraws (to prevent one member from forcing a distribution that the company cannot afford).

22

DO *provide in the operating agreement of a limited liability company (LLC) that dissolution can be avoided after dissociation.*

Before explaining the fourth essential element of an LLC agreement, some understanding of terms is required. First, recall that it is necessary that the

LLC have a limited life in order to characterize the LLC as a partnership that has favorable tax treatment (see **#17**). This IRS rule is based on the fact that in all states, partnerships terminate upon withdrawal of a partner. But termination does not mean what you may think it means.

If a member of an LLC (this discussion applies to partnerships, too) dies, is insane, resigns, is expelled, retires, or is bankrupt, he or she has withdrawn (also called dissociated) from the LLC. Unless some event intercedes, the dissociation results in a process that ends the business of the LLC. This process includes dissolution, winding up, and termination. Dissolution results from dissociation and ends the ordinary business of the company. After dissolution, the LLC can settle accounts with third parties, such as creditors and the members. This settling process is called winding up. Once everything is wound up, the LLC terminates its life.

Consequently, an LLC (or a partnership) would be a cumbersome if not impossible entity from which to conduct business, since, at any moment, the death of a member could cause immediate termination, a disastrous result.

DON'T *allow your limited liability company (LLC) to terminate upon death, resignation, withdrawal, expulsion, etc. of a member.*

If an LLC ends, the remaining members could start another LLC. However, this would allow all members to renegotiate their position. No business could be done in the interim and existing LLC contracts (that could be very lucrative) would be lost. Therefore, this result is unacceptable.

The cure is to allow the remaining members to consent to avoid the dissolution. In other words, the enabling statutes in most states allow the LLC to intervene in the process after dissociation and allow the members to avoid the next step in the process, dissolution. The avoidance does not undo the dissolution; it actually prevents it from happening (even though it *did* happen). Such is the imagination of the law!

To achieve this avoidance, the statutes in most states require a unanimous consent of the remaining members. Dissolution avoidance consent in many states must be permitted in the operating agreement. It is therefore highly advisable to include this provision regardless of the state in which you live. Note that what is allowed under the operating agreement is a vote of members to avoid dissolution after dissociation takes place. It should not provide such avoidance in advance because it may spoil the favorable tax classification (see **#17**). An agreement to prevent termination even if a dissolution cannot be avoided is called a business continuation agreement. Discuss this with your lawyer and tax adviser.

DO *convert your corporation to a limited liability company (LLC), if appropriate.*

There are potential tax difficulties if you simply dissolve an existing corporation and transfer the assets to a new LLC. When you liquidate a corporation, if the assets have appreciated, there is a tax due from the corporation on the increase in value. Worse, there is then a second tax due from the shareholders on the increase in value of their shares. There are several alternatives available (see facing page).

Should you convert if you are an S Corp? See **#5** and **#6.** Well, certainly there is less reason to do so than if you are a C corporation, since you already have many of the benefits of partnership taxation. But there are disadvantages of the S Corp that you may need to overcome—for example, if you wanted to allow a foreign investor to become a shareholder, you could not do so and remain an S Corp. If you do decide to convert an S Corp, there is less tax danger than with a C corporation.

Any conversion will involve a valuation. This can be costly. The IRS will require that the valuation be proper—a professional appraisal, which is not a trivial expense. Yet if the cost is unacceptably high, conversion must be ruled out.

If you choose to convert, it is the tax effects that are critical.

DON'T *ignore the tax effects of a conversion from a corporation to a limited liability company.*

The best approach, from a tax perspective, for converting a corporation to an LLC is to liquidate the corporation into the LLC. Here is how it works.

An LLC is formed. The shareholders of the corporation sell/transfer their shares to the LLC in exchange for LLC membership units. There is no tax impact at this point. The corporation liquidates, distributing all of its assets to the single shareholder, the LLC. The assets in the hands of the LLC have a cost equal to the fair market value of such assets as of that time. The bad news is that the LLC members will now be taxed on the difference in value between the shares that they transferred (in exchange for their LLC units) and the value of the assets received by the LLC (when the LLC exchanged its shares for the corporation's liquidated assets). This may be uneventful or disastrous, depending on whether these assets have appreciated during the time the corporation held them.

If the adverse tax effects are too great, there may be solace in other techniques that are commonly used in situations where relief is required from a large gain. You need expert tax advice.

CHAPTER

2

FINANCING

DO look for financing in the right place (i.e., appropriate for a small business).

The financing needs of the small business, if not unique, are at least quite different from those of the larger, more mature organization. The sources are both narrower and shallower. Before we can discuss the types of financing that may be available to a small enterprise, you must first understand the fundamental difference between debt and equity.

Capital is available from lenders and investors. Lenders lend a sum of money that must be repaid with interest, generally after a fixed period. Lenders do not own any part of the business. If the business grows, they will not receive any more than the return of their money with interest. They may be able to charge a higher interest rate from you than from a mature and successful business, but the premium hardly offsets the risk. It follows that lenders are very cautious and look not to the success of the business as the assurance that the loan will be repaid, but to guaranties from the owners (see **#26**) or to security.

Investors, on the other hand, are much more risk receptive. However, they want to share in the growth if the business succeeds. Investors are more difficult to find. For larger companies or those that are in exciting new fields, the company can sell stock to the public. For a small company there is a threshold issue as to whether you want outside investors (that is, those who do not work directly for the business) or you want to keep the ownership within a small group. This decision may be based on the nature of the business or the people.

DON'T put growth and the need for capital before your personal and business strategy unless necessary—then, find capital wherever you can.

Some small start-up businesses can expand at a rate comfortable to the risk aversion of the owners. You may wish to grow more quickly, but there is nothing that forces that growth. On the other hand, some business ideas are perishable. Either you invest in new technology, capture a new trend in a market, or be left in the dust. Thus, the decision on raising capital—debt or equity—is only partly within your grasp. It is clear that you are the only person capable of making that decision. If you decide that the business requires new capital to be a success, where will you find equity money?

The only institutional source is venture capital. This route involves the quintessential equity investors. They operate in high technology and new marketing-concept businesses. As explained in **#35,** they are typically interested in businesses with the potential to go public, that is, reach a size and need for capital that will make an offering of stock to the public possible and even likely. But prior to seeking venture capital, where do you find equity money? In truth, the bulk of entrepreneurs find seed capital in their own pocket or from friends and relatives. It is usually not very much, but may be enough to get the ball rolling to convince the next level of investors that the business warrants more investment. Perhaps a large customer will be willing to provide some financing, or a large supplier who sees the opportunity of gaining a new customer. But make no mistake—when you are looking for money and you are small—you must scramble, overturn every rock, and consider the details later.

25

DO *decide if you are to remain closely held; if so, recognize the need to retain earnings and that debt will be your best source of capital.*

To explain the use of debt and equity we will assume that you have a business that can be expanded at a pace with which you are comfortable. You also decide that you do not want outside investors such as venture capitalists or angels. You want the business to be financed by the resources of the owners, who comprise a small group working in the business. This is a typical model for a family-owned business, or for a group of unrelated persons with complementary skills and dispositions. The owners must be resigned to the heavy reinvestment of profits into the business. These retained earnings may be the primary source of capital to finance growth of the business.

There must be a strong delayed-gratification ethos that the owners agree on. This may be one of the most serious areas of future disagreement. It should be discussed carefully and often.

The principal noninternal source of capital for this business will be debt. To obtain debt, the owners must be willing and ready to personally guarantee the debt. See **#26.** Your ability to finance growth with debt will depend on the nature of the capital requirements. If it is equipment, as in a trucking company or a machine shop, equipment leasing may be the most important source of capital and must be fully exploited. See **#27.** If the money is required for inventory and accounts receivable financing, the most likely source is the bank or the Small Business Administration (SBA), although there are others. See **#29.** But do not overlook your suppliers and customers as sources of capital. See **#34.**

DON'T despair if your business strategy requires more money than you have; if the opportunity is attractive, venture capital may be available.

In contrast to assuming that you can expand your business at a comfortable rate, an alternate assumption is that you must raise capital as equity from other sources. This may be due to the nature of the business. For example, if you intend to develop a new software program or a new drug, you need money for research and development. R&D is too risky for anyone who lends money. If you are successful, they will receive no more than their interest payments. If you fail, they bear the entire loss. You must find equity money, and the amount is not likely to be trivial—so friends and relatives are out. Furthermore, the time to reach a positive cash flow (where the amount of cash each month exceeds the payments made) is long, and this heightens the risk.

Your options here include primarily venture capital. See **#35.** This will require that the business potential is significant, so that the payback on the investment is substantial enough to warrant the risk. It also requires that there is a good possibility that the company can go public, since this constitutes the investor's best exit strategy. If not a potential candidate for a public offering, there must be a good chance that the company can be sold. A public offering is not only a point that allows the venture capitalist to liquidate his investment but may also be the logical next source for additional capital to feed the growth of the business—the private sources being too limited. But there are sources for capital other than the VC. Large corporation partnerships may be possible. These run the gamut from a part ownership in the technology to a minority investment in the company. Equipment leasing (see **#27**) may be important too.

DO *carefully consider the personal financial implications of signing a guaranty.*

As noted above, if you attempt to obtain a loan from a bank or other financial institution and cannot offer collateral owned by the business, you will be asked to execute a personal guaranty. Simplified, the personal guaranty provides that if the business defaults on the note signed by the business, you are personally responsible. As noted in **#1,** the advantage of a corporation or LLC is the protection of your assets from debts of the business. The personal guaranty destroys this advantage.

Banks typically justify the personal guaranty by stating that they are testing management's faith in the business (as if your risking your career and living on a shoestring was a triviality) and making certain that management is devoting its entire efforts to the business. The truth of the matter is that it puts enormous pressure on the signing officers to be conservative and to kowtow to the lending officer's vicarious CEO decisions.

There are several things to look for in the standard guaranty used by banks. First, if there are several owners, the bank will ask that all of them guaranty the loan and that they each be "jointly and severally" liable. What this means is that if the loan amount in default is $100,000, the two owners (guarantors) will each be liable for $50,000. But if your co-owner is not as solvent as you, you will be liable for the entire amount. The bank need not sue you both, they can choose you. Then you must sue your co-owner for contribution.

DON'T *sign a guaranty without carefully considering the terms.*

Another hidden problem in a guaranty is that it is typically made *continuing,* which means that so long as the loan is outstanding, you remain liable. Even if that loan is paid off and a new loan is extended, the continuing guaranty carries over, sometimes for years, long after you have forgotten about signing it. It lies in wait. You should insist that the guaranty expire when the loan is paid off. Or, when the loan is paid off, send a certified letter revoking the guaranty. If a new loan is taken, you can consider the advisability of a guaranty at that time.

The standard guaranty also provides that the bank (or other creditor) may extend the time of payment of the loan or vary other terms without the guarantor's consent. Negotiate for the right to approve such actions. Otherwise, the guaranty could be extended by one of your co-owners and you might never be aware of it. Forewarned is forearmed.

Because a guaranty is an obligation to pay if the debtor fails to pay, you have a claim against the debtor (your own corporation) if you are liable on the guaranty. While that may seem worthless, in bankruptcy it may have some value, although the bankruptcy code may have the same subordination effect. However, a bank standard guaranty will require you to subordinate *any* claim against the company as part of the guaranty. If you attempt to bail out the company at a later time with new debt, be careful, since the subordination will apply to the new debt.

27

DO *use equipment financing as a supplement to straight debt or equity.*

Many small businesses must purchase one or two pieces of expensive equipment to start the business. You can borrow the money from a bank or other source, or you can consider leasing. To simplify, the products (leases) available are capital and operating leases. While both are leases, their purposes are entirely distinct. A *capital lease* is a financial product and as such, an alternative to the loan. It is long term and available even if the equipment is specialized. An *operating lease* is offered for standard and common equipment and is usually short term. It is desirable, not for its financial effect but for the fact that it allows the lessee flexibility in the future to switch to newer equipment that may be required for growth. We discuss here only the capital lease.

One characteristic of capital equipment leases is the availability of certain tax advantages. In fact, there is an entire industry that engages in structuring leases to obtain the tax advantages. Because these companies can use the tax benefits more advantageously than the lessee (you), the financial terms of the lease are more favorable than a loan to buy the equipment. That makes the lease beneficial as a financing tool. But do not be fooled into believing that the equipment lease is always better than the depreciation and interest deductions you will get if you purchase the equipment. On the other hand, if you have no revenue (typical of many start-ups) from which depreciation and interest may be deducted, they are wasted (except as a loss carryforward).

DON'T *use a loan if an equipment lease will improve your finance potential.*

There are several reasons to use capital leasing of equipment, but these must be weighed against other available financing terms. First, an operating lease will only show up in a footnote in the company's balance sheet. Neither an asset or a liability would be recorded. The company's financial condition may be viewed more favorably than if an asset and debt were booked. It is also possible that a loan agreement of the lessee that precludes the acquisition of additional debt without the bank's approval may be avoided by an operating lease. Capital leases may be used in a sale and leaseback transaction for equipment already owned by the lessee and thereby serve as a loan. The principal concern here is the FASB (Financial Accounting Standards Board) rules for characterizing a lease as capital (in which event the tax benefits mentioned above are lost). Structure is all important, as explained in **#28.**

Second, the capital lease will almost certainly relieve cash flow. An outright purchase of equipment will require a down payment of at least 10 percent to 20 percent. A capital lease provides 100 percent financing (the security deposit and advance rent is usually small compared to the typical down payment). If you purchase equipment, there is the sales tax, possibly permits, and other incidental acquisition costs that are capitalized in the lease.

Third, the payments under a lease and the integrated interest that is part of the payment are fixed, which may be preferable to a floating rate that is typically required of a small company.

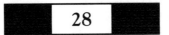

28

DO *require that an equipment lease be characterized as an operating lease if you are seeking off–balance sheet financing.*

Characterization of an equipment lease as a capital lease or an operating lease is complicated by the fact that the characterization is different for tax, accounting, and commercial law purposes. Each has its own test. Because the characterization for tax purposes is of concern to the lessor, not you, we ignore that here.

The characterization for accounting purposes is important because it affects the potential for future financing. Following is a four-part test laid down by Financial Accounting Standards Board Statement No. 13, which helps to determine the characterization of an equipment lease. If ownership is transferred when the last lease payment is made, it is a capital lease, not an operating lease. (See **#27** for the advantage of an operating lease from the point of view of the lessee.) If the lease gives the lessee an option to purchase the equipment at a price less than the fair market value, it is a capital lease. If the leased equipment has a life of, say, 10 years, then the lease term cannot be greater than 7.5 years (75 percent of the useful life). The last test is more complicated. If the present value of the minimum lease payments is more than 90 percent of the value of the equipment measured by the fair market value, less any investment tax credit retained by the lessor, it is a capital lease. Note that with a little care, each of these tests may be met while the lease still has many of the advantages of a capital lease for both parties. If your primary motivation in using equipment leasing is the advantageous future effects of off–balance sheet financing, you must examine, with the aid of your accountant, the structure of the lease to see that it qualifies as an operating lease.

DON'T *sign an equipment lease that is not an operating lease, for commercial law purposes, if there are any signs of imminent financial difficulty.*

The second important characterization of an equipment lease is from the point of view of the commercial law. This is usually more important to the lessor in a bankruptcy proceeding than the lessee, but you should be aware of the implications if you get into financial trouble. If a lease is an operating lease, then the lessor owns the equipment. In the event of bankruptcy, the owner of equipment in the hands of the bankrupt lessee is subject to expedited recovery by the lessor. But if the lease is a capital lease (i.e., the equipment is security for a financing), the lessor is simply a secured creditor. Moreover, the lessor will not even have the advantages of a secured creditor, compared to a general creditor, unless it has perfected its lien by filing a UCC 1 financial statement. The advantage of the secured position of the lessor is to avoid the automatic stay of the bankrupt trustee and to be able to seize and sell its equipment long before the bankruptcy is closed. This may be to your *dis*advantage.

The commercial law test, unlike the accounting test, focuses heavily on the relationship of the term of the lease to the useful life of the equipment and the rights of the lessee to keep the equipment for the whole life. If the lease cannot be terminated before its expiration, is the term greater than the useful life of the equipment? If the lease is shorter, is the lessee bound to renew? Does the lessee have an option to renew? Does the lessee have the option to purchase the equipment at the expiration of the lease for a nominal consideration? If any one of these questions can be answered in the affirmative, it is probably a capital lease.

29

DO *understand the documentation typically used in a bank financing.*

As explained earlier, you may choose to finance growth of your business through debt or equity. If you choose debt, the most common form of debt is the unsecured loan, usually evidenced by a promissory note. Larger companies may issue debentures, but as a small business don't bother to study these. (You may find the term "issue" odd in conjunction with a discussion of borrowing money, but you issue debt (notes) as you do stock; all the sophisticated financing people like to refer to issue as if a promissory note was a bond or other public debt instrument. Play along.) Let us first talk about bank financing.

A debt may be set forth in writing that is a simple contract. We refer to such writing as notes because they are a particular type of contract. Their distinguishing feature is simplicity. They recite the lender name, the borrower name, the date, the date on which the payment is due, and the interest rate. This may be all that you sign when you borrow money from a bank, especially if both the bank and the amount of the loan are small. As the amount increases, the bank will require more documentation. For a loan that is still fairly small, the bank may prepare a term sheet (i.e., a short description of the terms agreed upon) but may not require that it be signed in addition to the note. The term sheet is an informal statement of the parties' expectations and is not binding. Only a note will be signed. If the bank wants such terms built into the loan agreement, it will incorporate the term sheet by reference in the note. As the size of the loan increases, a loan agreement will be required.

DON'T *allow a revolving loan agreement to lure you into believing that it is permanent capital to be invested in inventory and receivables.*

A loan agreement is a contract that includes a note. Sometimes the note is attached and is in the familiar short form; other times it is part of the body of the loan agreement. The agreement is a promise by the bank to lend the money that may be funded on execution or at some later time in whole or in part. In a *revolving loan* the agreement provides that the bank will lend money up to a certain amount, over time, and the borrower may repay and borrow again as it wishes as long as the maximum is not exceeded. Each time the borrower requests more funds a new note is signed. Notes are destroyed or reissued in new amounts as the situation dictates. This process is often simplified by the use of a master note that records each advance and repayment, or an account may be established that similarly records each transaction and renders a monthly statement to show the activity and the current balance.

The nemesis of the revolving loan transaction is that the agreement provides for a full repayment at some point in time. The bank may roll this over on a number of occasions, then one day decide that it does not have the funds to continue the loan. It demands full payment. Meanwhile you are using these funds as working capital—tied up in inventory and accounts receivable that are not immediately able to be liquidated. Therefore, you must negotiate either a substantial grace period to repay or the right to convert the loan to a fixed-term loan (i.e., the equivalent of a grace period with a definite expiration date).

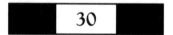

30

DO *examine the true interest (or loan cost) of your bank loan, considering any compensating balances and commitment fees.*

Interest in a note or loan agreement appears to be a simple thing: Set a rate and there it is. Not quite. The most obvious problems are the floating rates that are tied to a wide variety of bewildering indexes that you have no real way to measure or evaluate. Combine the rate base changes with the dates on which the rate is adjusted (you need a computer to keep track of the amount). Fine. But if presented with several alternatives, how do you compare? Still the problem is visible and therefore tractable.

Loan agreements may also require a compensating balance to be maintained. That is, so long as you have a loan outstanding, you must keep a balance in your checking account in a specified amount. The effect is that you are paying interest not on the amount borrowed but on that amount less the balance required, since under a revolving loan (see **#29**) both amounts are fluctuating from time to time. Still, with a good accountant and a basic computer, the rate is determinable.

The loan agreement may also provide, for a revolving loan, that a commitment fee must be paid for the amount not drawn down at any time. In other words, you are paying a fee for the privilege of being able to increase the amount used up to the loan limit. This may be viewed as a cost other than interest. But if you are comparing this loan to another with only interest as stated, a fair comparison is to adjust the interest rate to account for the fee.

DON'T *tie up your assets in a bank financing as security if possible—you may need them as collateral at a later time.*

We previously described the secured loan transaction in connection with equipment lease financing (see **#27**). Other security such as a personal guaranty was discussed at **#26**. In a bank financing, either of these types of security may be encountered. But the most common security is inventory and/or accounts receivable. For the small business, it is standard fare for the bank to demand that you collateralize the loan with these assets. The security may be included in a separate agreement that is incorporated into the loan agreement by reference. Many revolving loans are, in fact, based on the level of these assets. That is, the loan may provide that the maximum amount available is the sum of the receivables (usually 80 percent of the face value) on a certain date and the inventory (usually much less than the receivables percentage because of the lower liquidity of inventory). There are a variety of formulas as well as words used to describe this loan base.

The overriding concern, from your point of view, is that committing these assets to the bank lessens your overall borrowing strength in the future. If you run into difficult times and require an emergency short-term loan, the bank will never release the collateral. Yet the types of lenders that may make money available for the emergency (and will take their pound of flesh for it) will insist on some asset security. For example, a factor (a lender who requires liquid collateral) may lend on accounts receivable but will not be a junior secured party to the bank. Whenever you have the bargaining strength, obtain a release of the working capital assets from the security.

DO *expect the bank to require you to make representations and warranties in the bank loan agreement—understand what these mean.*

Bank loan agreements, like mergers and acquisitions and other major corporate actions, typically include representations and warranties made by the company. It is usual to give these obligations little attention, but doing so may be perilous. The nature of the representations and warranties is an assurance that the facts related during the negotiations are accurate. A false representation will give rise to an immediate breach of the agreement. Thus, the bank will use the representations and warranties for two reasons. First, many people will play fast and loose with facts during discussions, but when faced with a statement that must be signed will understandably balk. The bank therefore may use the reps to smoke out the real facts, and simultaneously measure the honesty of the signer. Second, if you are constantly in breach, you will be at a disadvantage later in pressing your position—since the bank will raise the breach as a basis for termination of the loan. They will have the leverage in the discussion. So don't take the reps and warranties too lightly (although you can be too punctilious and cost yourself a lot of time).

What will you be representing and warranting? Always, the bank will require assurance that the company was duly formed and is operating validly; that you have the requisite authority to borrow—for example, did the board (if you are a corporation) approve the loan?—and that you have taken the proper corporate steps to make the loan; and additionally, that the agreement has been properly executed and is therefore a binding legal agreement. (This is why these are so boring.)

DON'T *ignore all representations and warranties in bank loan agreements—some, like threatened litigation or contingent liabilities, can be serious.*

A few representations and warranties are more substantial. For example, the company will be required to disclose if any litigation is pending or, to your knowledge, is threatened. Of course, pending litigation is easy enough to identify, but what does *threatened* mean? Here you must use some judgment.

Every little dispute with a supplier could blossom into a lawsuit. But is it material—that is, will it seriously affect your financial condition? Is it more likely that this dispute will result in suit or not? Unless a disagreement has progressed so far as to involve written accusations and perhaps face-to-face meetings, it is probably too tentative. It is a call where a good business lawyer would be helpful.

Another troublesome warranty is that the financial statements have been prepared properly (usually easy enough to make—a good place, however, to test the borrower's truthfulness) and that there are no contingent liabilities. This is usually qualified by a requirement that the contingent obligation must be material in amount. But still, what is contingent? If you have returned a substantial shipment of components because they did not meet your specifications, but the supplier disagrees, is this a contingent claim? If a customer has threatened to return one of your major pieces of equipment unless you can bring it up to specification within the next seven days, is this a contingent liability? No one can answer this question, except with hindsight. If you believe that a reasonable businessperson would disclose it, you make the decision while you are still in negotiations and casually disclose it. It's safer.

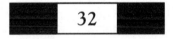

DO *review carefully the affirmative covenants in a bank loan agreement and resist any interference in the business.*

Loans typically have affirmative and negative covenants. A *covenant* is simply a promise. So an affirmative promise is something you agree to do and a negative promise is something you agree not to do. These promises last as long as the credit is outstanding (i.e., they are continuing). The bank generally has a laundry list of covenants that are inserted into the agreement. Common affirmative ones include ratio of debt to net worth, level of net worth and working capital, information that must be provided (principally, financial statements, possibly including how these financial statements are prepared), payment of insurance premiums (especially if the loan is secured by equipment or buildings), timely payment of taxes, and sometimes such internal matters as a notice of change in management, use of the proceeds, salaries of owner officers, payment of dividends, and so on.

You should be aware that the bank walks a fine line between requiring you to take certain actions, while not controlling your activities. If you get in financial trouble, the bank could be liable to other creditors, or to you, if it has interfered to the point that it can be blamed for the difficulty. Since banks have a heavy fear of this possibility, you can use it to object to some terms, arguing that the provision will cause you to relinquish control over the business. Certain affirmative covenants, such as financial ratios, are almost exempt from a charge of interference. However, internal matters, particularly, may be a basis for liability. Therefore, when negotiating the loan terms, be vocal about any interference.

DON'T *allow bank loan negative covenants to hamstring you from future financing.*

The negative covenants (understand that any negative covenant can be written as an affirmative covenant and vice versa) usually relate to assets and debts. Of obvious importance to the bank is the existence of other outstanding loans (typically allowed if the loan is not intended to be used for consolidating debts or retiring debt with a more onerous interest rate, but usually restricted as to any further borrowing against the loan) and the right to take on other debt. This may be prohibited entirely or a maximum amount of other borrowing may be stated. The bank may provide that its security interest be senior (i.e., come before). The likely troublesome point is the use of nontypical debt. For example, as discussed in **#27,** equipment leasing may be the equivalent of financing if it is a capital or finance lease. If it were clear what constituted a finance lease and what constituted an operating lease, the loan agreement could easily proscribe the former. But as noted, the line is not so easily drawn.

It is well to think out your future financing needs and whether they will all be met by the bank—which is not likely. You may want to use not only equipment leasing but also accounts receivable financing. Even major purchases on credit from a large supplier may have some security interest in the inventory that could violate the bank loan. The prohibition against loans will typically include any guaranty that may be important if you have a subsidiary corporation. (Having a subsidiary does not mean that you are a large business; it may be advantageous to separate your risks into two or more corporations to prevent the spread of adversity.)

DO *resist any overly strict limitations in your bank loan agreement on the future purchase of assets.*

As pointed out in **#32,** bank loans generally have negative covenants that may interfere with future financing needs. Similarly, the negative covenants in a loan may affect your future decisions regarding assets, unless you speak up. First, the covenant may provide that you may spend only a certain maximum amount (per year or some other defined time period) for capital equipment. The amount should be defined for this purpose as the excess of the payment above any credit or repurchase of equipment that is being replaced. You might add that the new equipment may provide additional functions to the replaced equipment, as is usually the case. This will foreclose any argument that the net amount should exclude the value of the new features. The clause will usually refer to purchase or lease. But, as pointed out in **#32,** you should exclude any operating lease. (See **#27** for the distinction.)

Second, the negative covenant may preclude you from selling an asset, at least without applying a part of the proceeds to the loan. The prohibition will be total for any sale that is at less than fair market value. But note that this term is vague and could result in a donnybrook. The negative covenant will also proscribe the creation of a security interest on any asset. This will prevent you from purchasing an asset on credit then using that asset as security for payment. This completes the bank's protection against your purchase of assets beyond a certain amount. As to all of these restrictions, you should look ahead and try to determine if any will seriously hamper your future financing plans. If so, fight them off.

DON'T *expect to successfully resist the bankruptcy default provisions in your bank loan agreement, but closely review others.*

A bank loan agreement also defines the events that constitute default. This will obviously include nonpayment and the breach of warranties (see **#31**). It will also include bankruptcy. As noted in **#80,** a bankruptcy trustee (or creditor in possession) may avoid any executory contract. However, an exception exists for bank loan agreements that include a provision for future financing (the typical revolving loan—see **#29**). The exception applies if the agreement was to extend credit or other financing assistance for the benefit of the debtor (you), but not anyone else. That includes any promissory note itself, because if the sole obligation of the debtor is to pay back the money, the contract is considered executed on one side and therefore not entirely executory.

There are a few other default points of note. If you have other loans, the new loan may provide that if you default in the payment of those loans, the payments under the new loan may be accelerated. This is unfair and should be rephrased to state that the default on old loans will accelerate the new loan only if the old loans accelerate on default. As for acceleration of the new loan on default of the payments thereunder, if you go into bankruptcy, an acceleration clause is effective if it automatically accelerates notwithstanding the automatic stay (see **#79**). If it simply gives the bank the *right* to accelerate, exercisable *after* the petition in bankruptcy is filed, it may be avoidable by the trustee. The acceleration clause will also apply to nonbankruptcy default.

34

DO *use your suppliers as a source of borrowing by extending your credit terms.*

There is credit available in your supplier relationships. You probably don't think in terms of the credit policy when selecting your suppliers, but you should. If you have a bank loan outstanding, you are paying interest to pay your supplier on its terms. If your supplier is large and financially well-heeled, its credit terms are better than yours. If you are a good credit risk, the differential that you are paying between your supplier's terms and yours *can* be captured. The supplier's assessment of you as a credit risk will be more liberal than your bank's, simply because your business is at stake. Your purchasing agent is accustomed to ranking suppliers on price, quality, and delivery. But price is directly related to credit terms. Obviously, the fact that a supplier gave you one year to pay your invoices would get your accountant's attention. You would price out such credit and factor it into the price of the goods. The same is true for sixty- versus thirty-day terms. There was a time in which the calculation of this interest was cost justified only in large corporations making huge purchases, but the same calculation can now be done with a good accountant and a mediocre computer.

Then there is the darker side of supplier credit. That is, not paying your bills on time; or, more nicely, applying pressure on your supplier to extend credit terms—or else. Consider paying your bills twice a month or simply stringing them out. It will reduce your costs in preparing the bills and reduce the borrowing costs by extending the time. You will be surprised how long large corporations take to cut you off. However, be fair with your small suppliers.

DON'T *overlook your customers for credit.*

Can you obtain credit from your customers? Well, not as such. But if you are in the fortunate position (gained by BS&T) of having a unique product or service that is greatly needed by large customers, perhaps they can help you reach a mutual goal. If you have a long-term contract involving a substantial volume of business, given your size, you may want to consider negotiating with the customer to advance payments. This may be done by simply requiring, in the contract, a predelivery payment of some portion of the total order size (or first shipment). Or ask that the customer advance the cost of the raw materials for the first order. Then go to your supplier and promise payment before its first shipment in exchange for sixty-day credit terms on each subsequent shipment.

If you are supplying a product that is being sourced by a large customer from several separate suppliers, ask the customer to purchase the critical (expensive) components for all of the suppliers and deduct it from the price. They will get a better price, you will be able to meet your inventory needs without borrowing so much, and everyone (save the critical component supplier) will be happy.

Don't think that these deals are easy to do. There is resistance everywhere. But if there are financial benefits, get to the controller. If there are assurances of supply benefits, get to the purchasing agent. You might even try the PR department; they love showing kindness to small companies in the community.

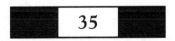

DO *negotiate a fair term sheet with venture capitalists, if possible.*

The venture capital game begins with an assessment of the opportunity and management and ends with the structure of a deal. After the "oohs" ("We financed XYZ that grew to $2 billion in size in eighteen months and now controls the world market for nano-bezakzis") and "aahs" ("We have developed a new neural-network CPU that has the power of a 3080 within a macromolecule and will sell for $0.15 per terahertz; our first order is from Microsoft for 2 billion units") are over, you arrive at the negotiation of an investment agreement that is as badly leveraged as a parking-lot ticket contract. We arrive at the term sheet.

The *term sheet* is a brief summary of the terms of the investment contract. It packs a lot of substance in a very short space. As noted in **#12,** the VC investment is usually structured with convertible preferred shares (explained below) for the investors, and common shares for the entrepreneurs. Because preferred shares can contain such a wide variety of terms, the term sheet is an investor's sandbox. It is impossible to cover all the land mines that may be threatening for entrepreneurs, but some highlights are considered below.

Even prior to the term sheet proposal and negotiation, the investors may insist on a lock-up agreement. It essentially provides that management will not negotiate with any other investor for a fixed period of time (usually thirty to ninety days) without any commitment on their part to invest. This will be argued as necessary for the investors to perform their due diligence in reasonable fashion and cost. Resist it entirely or limit the time to as short a period as possible.

DON'T *count on a single round of financing; take shares that vest over the shortest possible time and as many as possible that vest immediately.*

Understand that venture investors will contemplate multiple rounds of investment. No matter how confident you are about reaching positive cash flow from the first round, negotiate as if there will be multiple rounds. Trust me. Often the amount you seek will not be doled out at the closing; it will be staged and it may be based on reaching certain milestones. This is not the time for bravado. Set damn reasonable milestones. If they are not high enough for the investors, go elsewhere.

Let's look at the common stock that you receive. It is what you are there for. Unless it will materialize, you will be better off seeking financial reward at a job. Only you can determine what level of reward will be satisfying. But you don't want to be surprised. Why are you taking common stock at all? Because it has the best tax implications. The investors put in money. That establishes the value of their shares. If you received the same shares and were granted stock for nothing, this would be taxed immediately. Without any cash, you would not be able to meet your tax obligation. But if your stock is of a different class and the other class has advantages (preferences), your stock can be valued at a fraction of the preferred class shares. As you will see, these advantages are not illusory. Furthermore, you will be asked to take shares that vest only over a period of time. In other words, while you nominally own them, unless the conditions that vest the shares occur, you don't own them. These conditions may be as simple as continued employment or company-based performance measures.

36

DO *expect to give up all of your proprietary rights to the corporation and allow the venture capital firm to hold at least one board position.*

A standard feature of all term sheets (see #35) is the requirement that you and your associates will assign all of your proprietary rights to the company. This includes the ownership of all inventions, patent applications and patents, as well as copyrights. There normally will not be any trademark rights in a new entity, but with a going business, it is required to assign all trademarks and accompanying goodwill. This is fair and reasonable. You will also be asked to sign an invention assignment and confidential information agreement similar to those you have probably signed at other companies. Since you will be one of the owners of the company and will be asking other employees to sign such an agreement, this is fair. A correlative problem is the requirement that you are free to enter into these agreements and that you are not bringing any confidential information from any other previous employer.

Control of the board of directors is a matter for serious consideration. The investors will ordinarily want the right to place at least one person on the board. Since you should have selected this venture capital firm because they can provide some assistance in addition to money, you should welcome this participation. But control by one VC firm, or even several firms if you have multiple VC investors, should be resisted. The alternative is to elect several third-party outside directors. You name one or two and the VC names one or two. While they will be "your" and "their" directors, they will be less biased (if they are good).

DON'T *be severely diluted by a "ratchet" clause in the preferred shares initially issued to venture capital investors.*

A great fear of the investors is that if the early promise of the company is not realized and more capital is required, their interest will be diluted if stock must be sold for a lower price than that initially paid. This results from the set conversion price of the initially issued preferred shares. The investor will want to include a provision that states that if a share of stock is sold for a lower price, then the initial conversion ratio will be increased so that each initial share is convertible into the same number of shares as the lower-priced share. In effect, it lowers the price paid for the initial shares. But the immediate effect is to increase, possibly enormously, the number of shares that will be issued. This will greatly dilute the entrepreneurs' interest in the company. This protection for the investors is called the *ratchet* clause.

You must demand that, at the least, any shares issued to management will not trigger any antidilution rights in the preferred shares. The same should be true for any shares granted to directors or to outside consultants. It could also be demanded for any shares issued in the purchase of another company, product line, or technology. You can also fight for a ratchet clause that does not have complete antidilution, that is, the issuance in a later financing round of a lower-priced stock will only partially change the conversion rate. You can try to limit the right to the ratchet to only those initial holders of shares who invest in the lower-priced subsequent round. This is referred to as a pay-to-play provision.

37

DO *weigh preferences in negotiating with venture capitalists, even for dividends that appear remote, to obtain later leverage.*

In large corporation capital structures, the principal feature of preferred shares is the preference to dividends. No dividends may be paid to common stockholders until a dividend is paid to the preferred shareholders. Unlike a bond or a note, preferred shares are entitled to preference, but they are not guaranteed some amount, like interest. Unless the board of directors *declares* a dividend, none need be paid. There are restrictions in most state corporation laws that preclude the declaration of a dividend unless the company is solvent. In a small start-up, the thought of a dividend is remote. All available retained earnings are usually not adequate to fund growth, let alone declare a dividend. So this provision of a term sheet may usually be ignored. But occasionally the investors will try to implement a cumulative dividend provision. This means that either dividends are effectively declared each year regardless of board vote (absolutely repugnant) or if declared each year and unpaid, the amount will accumulate until later. That later is typically when the preferred has the opportunity to convert into common, such as when the company is ready to go public. If you must give in to cumulative dividends: (1) require that they be waived before conversion (the investors will want them either paid or convertible into the common); (2) at least make it payable in stock rather than cash at the option of the common shareholders. Because the payment of dividends is remote when the company starts, it is easy to give in to this provision. Remember, many of these preferences are not intended to be enjoyed in themselves but are used later as leverage to obtain other concessions from the common.

DON'T *accept a preferred stock liquidation preference in a venture capital financing that may have a more disastrous effect than dilution.*

The other standard preferred provision in large company stock is the preference in liquidation. In a start-up, you are likely to ignore this with the thought that if the company is going down, who cares. This is true. But if true, why is the investor plumping for this preference? Because it will be tied to a seemingly unrelated provision that states that if the company is sold, it will be considered a liquidation. Thus, if the company is successful, but a public offering is not feasible, and a good offer turns up from a larger company, you will soon see that the bulk of the offer will go to the investors as payment of the preferred liquidation amount, and a pittance will go to the entrepreneurs. The lesson is that you need to understand not only each independent provision of the preferred but also their interrelationship.

What is the *liquidation preference?* It is the right to take from any liquidation funds (the amount remaining after insolvency, or the price paid by a buyer) an amount equal to the aggregate price per share, paid by the preferred shareholders, times the number of shares then outstanding. And it could include dividends declared but unpaid. If you are not a preferred shareholder, you can be amused in later rounds of financing as new investors demand greater liquidation rights than previous investors. However, it is not so amusing when some disgruntled early investor is willing to kill a new investor's participation to save his preference. The most greedy provision is a *participation feature*. After the preferred get all their money back, they share equally with the common.

<table><tr><td></td><td>38</td><td></td></tr></table>

DO *expect the venture capitalist's investment in preferred shares to be convertible, but limit the adjustment provisions.*

The preferred shares the investors will take will be convertible into common shares at their election, and in at least one case, in yours. The reason for convertibility is that the investors want to retain their preferred position with respect to the common shareholder (you) during the period in which the company is private. But if the company is in a position to go public, that is, to sell shares to the public through an underwriter, the underwriter will not allow the investors to retain this advantageous position. The public will be suspect of a company with a complex stock structure, for example, a second class of shares. Nor will the public (understand that the investors in new issues are more likely to be sophisticated institutional investors, rather than the person on the street) stand still for the advantage that the venture capital investors cut for themselves when the company had no leverage.

In any event, the investors will jealously guard their conversion rights from dilution; each change in share structure will produce an adjustment in the conversion ratio. Initially each share of preferred will be convertible into one common share. But if there is a stock dividend—for example, each share of common receives one additional share—then each preferred will thereafter be convertible into two shares of common rather than one. If there is sale of shares in a later round, the investor antidilution ratchet may change the conversion rate (see **#36**). Anticonversion adjustment should also be sought for any shares issued in an employee stock purchase plan or a conversion of the preferred itself.

DON'T *allow the venture capital investors to specify the conditions for going public through the automatic conversion provision.*

The conversion provisions of the preferred shares in a venture capital financing, as explained previously, desirably, have an automatic conversion (forced conversion) if the company goes public. But what a public offering is must be specified, since there are different types of offering, and the investors may disagree on the timing of the offering (i.e., at what price and how many shares). Without going into the complexities of a public offering, the commitment of the underwriter (the institution that arranges for the sale of the stock—what you may think of as a stock broker) may be firm or only a best-efforts obligation. As you would expect, the former means that the underwriter agrees to buy the stock and resell it, and the company gets paid regardless of the appetite of the public for the issue. The latter is only an obligation to try to sell the stock—whatever sells, you get paid for. A firm commitment is to everyone's best interest, if it can be done. Most VC investors will insist that the automatic conversion trigger only on a firm underwriting.

The timing requirement is usually expressed by setting a minimum amount for the underwriting (i.e., the sale of X of company stock). There are various types of public offerings as defined by the Securities Exchange Commission (SEC). To oversimplify, a true public offering is done on an S-1 form; offerings above a certain amount *must* be done on the S-1. So, this value may be used, but it may also specify that the share price must be above a certain amount. This will be based on the return that the VC investors require (e.g., five times price paid).

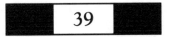

39

DO *recognize that a redemption clause in a venture capital preferred share investment may be a powerful tool, usable against management.*

A very important feature of any investment made by a venture capitalist is liquidation or the exit strategy. Unlike a share of publicly traded stock, the shares bought by the venture capitalist are illiquid. Yet the place in the investment spectrum occupied by venture capital is high risk and high reward. Therefore, it is important that once the high growth period (as defined for this type of investment) is over, the investment may be liquidated. The brass ring that the VC seeks is a public offering, because it brings the best price for the shares if sold then, or puts public shares in the hands of the investor (albeit somewhat restricted public shares) which are then liquid. If the company's fortune does not merit a public offering of stock, an acquisition is another satisfactory exit point. But what about sideways performance? This may represent the bulk of the VC portfolio. The answer is a redemption clause in the preferred share contract.

A *redemption* clause is simply an obligation of the company to repurchase the stock at a given price. In the typical agreement, it requires the company to buy back the preferred shares, usually in installments, after a certain period of time. The buyback price is the original price paid plus any declared and unpaid dividends. The clause may also require interest at a specified rate if no dividends were declared. One restriction on the company's right to buy back shares is a state law requirement that the company be solvent at the time (thereby protecting creditors from a shareholder rip-off).

DON'T *allow the redemption clause in a venture capital preferred share investment to trigger a conversion reduction.*

The redemption clause in a venture capital preferred share investment is a looming cloud. If after a few years (the requirement to buyback typically begins five years after the investment is made) the business is struggling, meaning that additional cash is required, the company must not only face the daunting task of raising new capital but must also worry about the imminency of the redemption. With each passing year the noose tightens. Now, as a practical matter, if there are no funds the redemption cannot be effected. The company is then in default, and various rights, such as increased voting power to the investors, may come into effect. This gives the VC the control of the company. Of course, it still does not create cash to pay the redemption. But if the management is sitting back on its heels (i.e., the company is stalled and management is unwilling or incapable of restarting the company), it places in the hands of the investors the means of forcing the management out.

In addition to allowing investors to take direct control, the redemption clause may provide that if any redemption installment is unpaid, the conversion price of the shares be reduced. If the reduction is implemented annually, while the company is in default, eventually management shares are totally diluted out. Thus the management may be replaced and their shares may be recouped for a new management team. This is unfair unless the management is totally responsible for the lack of success of the company, which is not always the case. The redemption clause should be strongly resisted when entering into the investment agreement.

40

DO *expect the venture capital investors in your company to obtain rights to take the company public if the opportunity arises.*

The raison d'etre of a venture capital investment is the offering of the shares to the public through a transaction referred to as *going public.* In this transaction the company sells shares to the public through an underwriter. In fact, the shares in most new issues are sold to institutional investors, meaning pension funds, mutual funds, insurance companies, and other large investors of the public's funds. These investors typically invest a small portion of their portfolios in the new issues of high-growth companies. The new issues are purchased through, and are often sold by, the underwriters who concentrate their sales activities on large buyers, while other affiliated brokers sell to the general public. The reason that venture capitalists seek sale to the public is simple—they make more money, sometimes enormously more, for the stock than the venture capital company paid. How does that affect you?

The venture investor is not about to miss an opportunity to sell stock to the public, regardless of what you may want. So, separate and apart from the preferred share rights discussed in **#37** and **#38,** you will be presented with a registration rights agreement. There are so many pitfalls in this agreement that only a few can be mentioned here. There are three typical dangerous provisions: *Demand rights*—at various times and dependent on certain conditions, the investors may demand the company to go public; *Piggyback rights*—the investors may also have the right to piggyback the sale of their shares if there is a registration in progress (a registration is the process of going public); and there may also be *S-3 rights.*

DON'T *give up all your rights with respect to registration of stock in the venture capital registration rights agreement.*

Of the three types of registration rights mentioned, the most important is the basic demand right. It is not that the judgment of the investors is likely to be less savvy then yours; on the contrary, they are much more wired into the market and the prospects for a properly timed offering. However, they typically have many companies in their portfolio, and the prospects for the other companies may conflict with your best interests. There are other reasons that may give rise to a disagreement as to whether the company should go public at a particular time. One, of course, is a difference over price. An underwriter's price range may seem too low to you. The prospects for the company over the near term may make it advisable, in your opinion, to wait. Regardless, the investors' registration rights agreement will set forth the terms by which the investors can force the issue.

One condition is the passage of at least three years. Another is that the percentage of the investors that want to go public must exceed a certain amount. (This offers the opportunity for you to "politick" among the investor groups.) Another is the requirement that the size of the offering exceed a certain amount (expressed as a percentage of the shares held by the investors); otherwise, the investors could force an offering that would be uneconomic. If the conditions are met, then the company must use its best efforts to effect the public offering. Similar conditions may apply to the S-3 offering (a series of sales over time in one registration). The piggyback applies when an offering is made; it allows the investors to join in.

CHAPTER

3

LITIGATION AND THE ALTERNATIVES

41

DO *use alternatives to litigation wherever possible.*

There are various alternatives to litigation, commonly referred to as alternative dispute resolution (ADR) methods. ADR includes the traditional form of arbitration, now used extensively in many industries. It also includes mediation, a technique that has been used informally for many years, but has been modernized with some specific structure that is becoming more or less standardized. Then there are many new combinations and variations of the traditional techniques; for example, nonbinding arbitration, minitrials (see **#45**), or contractually required negotiation (see **#44**). The general object for all of these ADR methods is the prompt and inexpensive resolution of claims. Their current popularity stems from the almost complete freeze of civil cases in the courts in order to hear the criminal cases that consume the court docket. Even if arbitration and the other ADR techniques were not quicker and less expensive, parties with disputes find that they can obtain justice only by avoiding use of the courts.

These techniques may be invoked after a dispute has arisen by entering into a new agreement that specifies a particular ADR method. Or an ADR clause may be drafted for a specific contractor as a standard clause to be used in all sales agreements, invoices, and even the employment relationship.

Before considering the use of an ADR clause or agreement, review the pros and cons. See **#42**.

DON'T *litigate.*

Ever.

42

DO *review the advantages of alternative dispute resolution (ADR) before proposing it or accepting it in an agreement.*

The principal advantage of arbitration is the speed by which the claimants can obtain relief. However, arbitration does not guarantee speedy resolution.

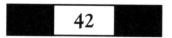

You can control speed somewhat by requiring that the arbitrator place quick resolution as the *primary* consideration. But you must also consider whether cost isn't equal in importance to speed. As in other matters, faster is synonymous with costlier.

The second usually mentioned advantage of arbitration is that it is less expensive. Again, this may not always be true, but it is still a good general rule and a reason for choosing arbitration. Arbitration is less expensive because it restricts the extensive discovery common to litigation. It also usually dispenses with the strict rules of evidence, which prolong the time and cost of trying a case—this is apparent from the difference in time it takes a case to be tried to a jury rather than to a judge. This may not always be to your advantage, from the point of view of winning the case.

Other advantages are that the arbitrator may be chosen from a list of persons who have expertise in the subject matter; there is no lengthy and expensive appeal after a trial; and the arbitration may be privately conducted, thus avoiding the disclosure of confidential information or simply private matters.

DON'T *overlook the fact that ADR has disadvantages too.*

In addition to the limitations of the commonly perceived advantages of ADR, there are some specific disadvantages. For example, many states now have effective pretrial settlement procedures that are free (the arbitrator and arbitration association charges the claimants) and operate similarly to mediation.

Courts are always bound by precedents and statutes (the rule of law—so taken for granted but a linchpin of democracy), whereas an arbitrator generally renders a decision based on broad concepts of fairness and equity. If a contract was drafted relying on a particular principle of established law, the arbitrator could, at least conceivably, ignore it.

There may be instances when you would prefer to have the issue decided by a jury of your peers rather than by a single arbitrator. You are not likely to know that in advance; except that if you are a small business, it is fair to assume that a jury will be more sympathetic to you than to General Motors.

If at the time a dispute arises it is deemed to be extremely important, and the other party believes that a full court battle is warranted (or is used to threaten settlement), that other party may deny that the dispute was intended to be arbitrated, and will sue in court to block arbitration—which is costly.

43

DO *use an arbitration clause in your contract if the situation warrants.*

As indicated in **#42,** there are circumstances where the use of arbitration is favorable to you or to both parties to a contract. To invoke arbitration in most states, the agreement to arbitrate must be in writing. The arbitration person or body is normally named, but if not, a court will appoint one if requested. Unless you state otherwise, the agreement will normally be interpreted as binding. It is better to state these matters directly: "Any dispute arising under this agreement shall be submitted to binding arbitration under the Rules of the American Arbitration Association." To learn more about the AAA rules, call for information at headquarters: 140 W. 51st Street, New York, NY 10020, or try your local phone directory.

You can also specify the place at which the arbitration is to be held. This can be very convenient as you cannot always control the location of a trial in a lawsuit. It may be very important in international contracts. It is possible that the other party to the contract may attempt to avoid the arbitration, preferring a full-blown court trial. However, you will find courts very pro arbitration if the other party sues and you tell the court that there is an arbitration clause.

The actual conduct of the arbitration can be controlled in the contract, or if you elect to use the AAA, for example, its established rules will apply.

DON'T *allow the arbitrator to split the award down the middle.*

One common complaint about arbitration is that an arbitrator, alone or as a panel, is not as decisive as a judge and therefore seeks to give a little something to both parties, or awards an amount that is totally inconsistent with the parties' evaluation of the case. There are several ways of dealing with these problems.

The parties can specify a maximum amount and a minimum amount that the arbitrator can award. This so-called *high/low* arbitration takes the minimum from the defendant's last offer and the maximum from the plaintiff's last offer. This sets a boundary in which the arbitrator must work, preventing a surprise to both sides.

There is also *baseball arbitration* in which the arbitrator is given the final settlement offers by both parties and must award one or the other—nothing in between is allowed. This effectively allows the arbitrator to decide the liability issue (who was at fault), but not the amount of damages. Therefore, the arbitrator cannot balance fault against damages. There is also night baseball arbitration in which the arbitrator does not know the amount of the damages that the parties agree to between themselves; once the arbitrator decides who was at fault, the amount is paid according to the agreement.

44

DO *use a simple technique in contracts— mandatory negotiation—for a quick and cheap possible settlement of a dispute.*

Even before turning to one of the ADR methods (see **#41**), you may *require* the parties to negotiate a solution to a dispute by a mandatory negotiation clause in a contract. This is the least costly method of settlement. Of course, it may not work, but it is so inexpensive—your time at a single meeting— that it is worth a try.

One barrier to a negotiated settlement in a dispute, particularly after the parties have hardened their positions, is to sit down and talk. You may feel that a call for such a meeting may be seen as a sign of weakness. If the agreement *requires* the meeting, however, you can point out that you are only attempting to abide by the contract terms.

You can do this in a variety of ways that meet the situation. You can exclude lawyers from such a conference or structure a process that calls for the parties to first exchange written statements of their positions. These statements can be specified to include the basis of the claim, the amount of the claim, the underlying documents if any, the persons' names who were involved, and the designated names of persons from each company who must attend.

DON'T *ignore the use of mediation as a preliminary or sole technique for alternative dispute resolution (ADR).*

Mediation is the next step toward full litigation when mandatory settlement negotiations fail. Mediation is conducted by a neutral third party who facilitates (not arbitrates or adjudicates) a solution to the disagreement. While mediation may be entirely voluntary, an agreement (post dispute) between the parties may provide for mandatory mediation before any further step, such as court action, is taken. Mediation is usually used as an alternative to the mandatory negotiation clause, rather than in addition to it, although it could be used in tandem.

The big difference between mediation and arbitration is that the former is not binding. There is no winner or loser in mediation. Therefore both parties can proceed without any fear of an adverse result. The process may involve attorneys, or it may be with the parties alone.

Unlike an arbitration or a trial, there is no taking of evidence (even informally). The real focus of mediation is to encourage each party to view the other party's position *realistically*. Surprisingly, that can be a big step toward resolution.

45

DO *investigate the use of some of the most modern ADR techniques for settling disputes.*

In addition to arbitration (see #43), you can also use esoteric ADR methods. One used in many high-stakes disputes between two large corporations is a minitrial. Another is an advisory jury.

A minitrial is not a trial at all. It is more like mediation, though there is a case presentation of sorts. Both sides, usually through their attorneys, present their case before a panel of decision-making officers from each company. A neutral party is there only to facilitate the presentation. This minitrial has the salutary effect of having each party listen to the other party's case and thereby discover the weaknesses and strengths of their own case. If you have a dispute with a large company and feel that you are dealing with a person who has a vested interest in the result (because he made the decision that led to the dispute), this technique could be useful.

An advisory jury, on the other hand, is just that. A private panel of five or six persons, selected by a method satisfactory to both parties, hears a short trial presented by the attorneys (maybe half a day for each). Then they render a (usually) nonbinding decision. It tends to open eyes and seriously promote consideration of settlement, although the winner may overestimate the favorable result.

DON'T *forget that a voluntary settlement conference may work even before a lawsuit is filed.*

Sometimes you will see that a dispute should be settled rather than formally arbitrated or litigated. This calls for a voluntary settlement conference, which differs from mediation because the judge/mediator (a settlement conference may use a retired judge or an experienced litigator from a private institution such as AAA) is concerned only with reaching a settlement, rather than attempting to encourage the parties to come up with their own resolution. A voluntary settlement conference involves some very active instigation and pressure from the judge/mediator.

The process usually involves a presentation of a short case by the attorneys, followed by a caucus of the judge and each party, separately. The judge may be very frank in expressing his or her opinion on the merits of your position. Indeed, that is the value of this method. The judge, after soliciting an offer from both parties, tries to cajole the parties into some compromise position. Or, the judge may come up with a settlement figure and obtain both side's reaction—without disclosing such reaction to the other party, of course.

The voluntary settlement conference is a nonbinding process but can be highly effective.

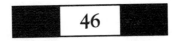

46

DO *acquaint yourself with the basics of litigation.*

A lawsuit commences when one party, called the plaintiff, files a complaint with a court and has a process server deliver a copy to the other party with a summons that proves that the complaint was received.

There are various types of courts in different states, and there is a separate federal court system. But all courts can be divided, from one perspective, into trial courts and appellate courts. Trial courts are where evidence in the form of testimony and documents is received, after which a jury or the court renders a decision. If one party is dissatisfied with the result, he may file an appeal with the higher court; the appellate court does not receive new evidence but bases its decision on the facts as established in the trial court. It is essentially a court that reviews whether the lower court applied the correct law. In practice, the appellate courts will overturn a decision based on facts, but the standard for the appealing party is very high.

The complaint can be served by a sheriff or process server. You then have a specified time, usually thirty days, to answer. Unless the matter is in small-claims court, you will almost always be advised to hire an attorney to represent you, although you may represent yourself.

Unless one party seeks a preliminary injunction (see **#47**), there may be a lull after the suit commences. Then discovery begins.

DON'T *lose sight of the value of a lawsuit during discovery.*

The most expensive part of litigation is the *discovery* phase. It can last for months or years—and it can consume all of your resources. Discovery typically involves interrogatories, depositions, and production of documents. The former are written questions that one side serves on the other and that must be answered in writing usually within thirty days. Depositions involve taking live testimony from a sworn witness, typically at a lawyer's office with a court reporter and both parties' attorneys in attendance. The purpose of these tools is to allow each party to investigate and to gather the facts surrounding the dispute. But there are many insidious uses.

Depositions of the persons directly involved in a business transaction are particularly advantageous. And deposing an expert witness (whose identity must be disclosed during the discovery process) is almost always necessary.

The problem with discovery is that there is no end. But there is a point of diminishing return; and there discovery must stop. If you now veto your lawyer's desire to continue the discovery, and you later lose the case—guess what the reason you lost will be. That is no reason not to say no, but do insist on a satisfactory explanation of the pros and cons of stopping. You know best the value of the case; apply a common sense analysis. Once discovery is completed, you will take the next step toward trial. See **#47.**

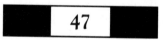

DO *try, after a lawsuit is filed, to prevent irreparable damage.*

Broadly speaking, there are two types of relief that courts typically give in a lawsuit. The first is very familiar—damages. The other is called an injunction in which the court directs one party to do some specific act, or to refrain from doing it. Examples of injunctions are court-ordered busing, forcing striking employees back to work, or demanding that one party stop infringement of a patent.

In certain types of lawsuits it may be necessary, if you are the plaintiff, to stop the offending action of the other party immediately—in other words, to obtain an injunction at once, even before the case goes to trial. Aside from other requirements, one necessary element that a plaintiff must show to obtain a preliminary injunction is that unless the court stops the defendant from doing some act, the injury to you will be irreversible. If the court decides that any damage that you sustain during the pendency of the case can be later fixed with money, the court will not enjoin the defendant. Preliminary injunctions are extraordinary, and the burden of proving that the case merits such relief is very high. If you can show merit, you can close out the case, effectively, at once. However, you may be faced with a big bond before the injunction issues, and if you do not win, the defendant can recover under the bond.

If, as in the usual case, a preliminary injunction is not requested or issued, the case proceeds toward trial.

DON'T *forgo the opportunity to settle at the preliminary settlement conference that precedes a trial.*

In most states and in the federal courts, after the parties agree (often at the urging of the court) that all discovery (see **#46**) has been concluded, there is some court-mandated process for trying to get the parties to settle. The process may be as informal as a conference called by the court a week or two before the trial date, or as elaborate as a procedure that involves court-appointed persons who try to mediate a settlement. The parties may be directly involved or only their lawyers may participate.

The purpose is to force the parties into a setting where they can negotiate. You must remember that more than 90 percent of cases filed are settled before trial. The preliminary settlement conference procedure is an aid to that end.

If the case still cannot be settled, you are going to trial. See **#48**. If you have feared this moment, you should. The costs will now mount rapidly and severely. Your own time, and also the time of your employees, will be called upon—usually to wait for endless hours (at a courthouse that is inconveniently located) to be called as witnesses—with a great loss of productivity. You are paying the price for ignoring the DON'T advice in **#41**.

48

DO *spend time to properly prepare for the trial.*

After the discovery process is complete (see **#46**), and if the settlement conference does not bear fruit (see **#47**), you must gird your loins for battle. Many of the finest trial lawyers have stated that it is not their quick wit, charming manner, clever tactic, or withering cross-examination that has led to their success, but the assiduous pretrial preparation—sweat and toil. While perhaps a rare burst of modesty on their part, there is clearly a kernel of truth in the admission.

Of course, you may think it is the lawyer who must be responsible for the pretrial preparation, but you can do your part as well. Many of your own employees may be afraid or reluctant to testify. You must instill in them the necessity for their assistance and the propriety of your cause. Jurors, like many astute observers of life, watch as closely for how the witness testifies as to what the witness says. Conviction is the thing. Witnesses must be made to feel that they are important in your quest. You must exhibit the leadership and confidence they may need.

You can also assist your counsel by providing a frank assessment of how an employee may react as a witness. Then, if the lawyer feels a particular employee may hurt the case, that witnesses testimony may be presented through another witness or a document. You can help. Be proactively helpful.

DON'T *expect the trial to be exciting.*

The typical business lawsuit trial does not keep you on the edge of your seat. Don't expect the O.J. Simpson action and excitement. Indeed, you may find that the actual trial is a bit boring, involving the introduction of many documents through a laborious and tedious process. Tempers do not flare—at least not often. Worsening the ennui is the constant frustration of how slowly matters proceed and how much that costs.

You will be dismayed as your lawyer loses some points, and temporarily joyous as the judge chides the opposing lawyer. But these are usually not indicators of the outcome. It is the constant uncertainty of that outcome that makes the experience so nerveracking.

Then when it is time for you take the witness stand, you will be overcome with the frightful thought that you will say something wrong and lose your own case—this rarely happens. You will be enraged when on cross-examination the opposing lawyer insists on asking questions that infer that you have lied, cheated, and are an unreconstructed "rat." You will be appalled when the person with whom you dealt in the transaction takes the stand and makes statements that you know are not true—but you are helpless to correct such travesty of justice.

By the end, you will be telling your friends the wisdom of **#41.**

CHAPTER

4

INTELLECTUAL PROPERTY

49

DO *protect your intellectual property—patents, trademarks, trade names, trade secrets, and copyrights.*

When starting and conducting your business, you will create certain types of intellectual property. The term *intellectual property*—sometimes referred to simply as IP—is used to define a class of property that is intangible (a mental creation), as opposed to personal property such as a car, or real property such as your house. In many businesses, this IP is more valuable than the real estate or machinery and equipment that is owned.

The type of IP created depends, to some extent, on the type of business you are operating. A manufacturing business is likely to create products that may be patentable. See **#51** for a discussion of patent rights. A retail business is more likely to focus on the creation of a presence in the community and to distinguish it through a name. A business name is referred to as a trade name. See **#67** and **#68** for a discussion of obtaining trade name protection. Both service and manufacturing businesses commonly adopt a product name, called a trademark (or a service mark). See **#59**. Additionally, many businesses can use copyrights to protect text and graphic materials— ads, catalogs, manuals, and so on. See **#74** for further discussion. The most valuable intangible assets of many information-based businesses are copyrights that protect software and databases (see **#142**). There is other IP that can be protected, such as trade secrets. See **#70**.

DON'T *become confused by the various types of intellectual property.*

Utility patents provide a limited-term monopoly for inventions of devices, compositions, processes, or machines. (There are also design patents but these are much less valuable.) Utility patents cover tangible things that are useful and new. A patent is obtained after establishing that the invention is "new" and "nonobvious." These are terms of art, that is, they mean much more than when used in ordinary conversation because the law has attached special significance to them. The process of obtaining a patent is not inexpensive. See **#50**. A patent allows you to prevent anyone from making, using, or selling the invention.

Trademarks identify the source of goods or services from a particular company. They are words or designs (logos) that can be protected if you are the first user. Trademark protection is more straightforward and less expensive than patent protection. In some businesses, a trademark is more valuable than even the strongest patent. See **#61**.

Copyrights cover a broad range of intellectual creations. We commonly think of books, songs, and movies, but copyrights are also used in many businesses to protect three-dimensional figures, jewelry, photographs, software, brochures, manuals, training videos, and so on. See **#75**.

You cannot patent names or songs. You do not protect a product by selling it under your own name; a competitor can probably copy the product identically (if not protected by patent) and sell it under a different name. There are areas of overlap, but keep these basics in mind.

50

DO *follow the right procedures to protect your invention prior to filing for a patent.*

To obtain valuable protection for your idea, you must follow a number of steps even before you apply for the patent.

Obviously, you must invent something. The best inventions seem to arise from the careful consideration of a problem that faces the inventor and others like the inventor—there is a need in the industry for a solution. Often, the appearance of a new product, such as the CD, will create the need for many other products. Or a new material may stimulate new product ideas that were not possible before.

As soon as you identify the problem and begin working on it, you must document your thoughts—breaking down the problem into its pieces, analyzing, conceptualizing, trying, drawing, redrawing, modifying, and honing. The use of a lab notebook is highly recommended. The reason for documentation is explained at **#55**.

If you are not going to build a prototype yourself, prepare a non disclosure agreement (NDA) before you visit a model shop. The practice of using NDAs is common and most shops will be willing to sign yours. For a sample, see the NDA form in the appendix.

Once you have completed these preapplication steps, you must start the protection process.

DON'T *waste money by filing for a patent without a search.*

Because the preparation of a patent application is not inexpensive, and a patent is obtainable only if you have an invention (see **#53**), many companies do a *prior art search* before filing for a patent. These searches can be conducted in the patent office by private searchers who reside there or by others (including you) who may have access to a patent database. In recent years, various databases of patent materials have been made available. Patent abstracts are searchable on-line and CD-ROM-based full-patent databases will be available soon. A prior art search can be conducted for as little as $100–$200, or for thousands of dollars. Of course, you get what you pay for. The more time spent searching, the more pertinent prior art will likely be uncovered. If an idea is simple, the search time should be limited to save money with probably little loss of effectiveness. If the search uncovers a *knockout* (a prior art reference that is almost identical to your idea), you can abandon hope for a patent.

A search also saves you money when you do file a patent application. The attorney or other patent preparer can use the prior art to draft the *claims* of the patent (the claims are the critical element of the patent—they define the scope of protection that you are entitled to) to avoid such art while still obtaining protection as broad as possible.

Once the search results are evaluated and a patent looks promising, start the process. See **#51**.

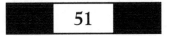

51

DO *obtain a patent because it provides strong protection for a long time.*

What can be patented? A utility patent may be obtained for a new and useful machine, method, composition, or article made by human effort (it cannot be a natural object such as a seashell). A machine may be as complex as a high-speed bottle-filling production line or a gas chromatograph instrument, or as simple as a toaster (. . . an electrical resistance heating chamber controlled by a variable timer). A machine may be used internally within your plant for producing other goods, or the machine itself may be sold.

What type of protection is provided and how long will it last? If new, useful, and nonobvious (see **#53**), no one else can make, use, or sell that machine for a period (since June 8, 1995) of 20 years from the date of filing. The right that you have is to exclude others from practicing the invention. Try not to be confused by this negative right. The patent does *not* give you a right to build your invention. This may seem odd at first, but think of it this way. If someone had a patent on the automobile, and you had a patent on a new steering system for an automobile, different from the one in the earlier automobile patent, when you build an auto with your new steering system, you will infringe the automobile patent. But the automobile patent holder cannot use your new steering system, either.

You could go on the offensive and prevent any other manufacturer from making the machine and thereby monopolize the market—as did Xerox with the dry photocopying machine. Or you may allow others to use the invention only under a license that provides for a royalty. See **#58.**

DON'T *lose your patent rights through neglect.*

To obtain a patent, the machine, product, and so on, must be *new*. See **#53.** If the machine was in existence prior to your invention, then it is not new—it is called prior art. The word art has nothing to do with fine art that hangs in a museum, but refers to the art of doing something, the practical arts. Not only are the ideas created by others prior to your creation prior art, but if you are not careful, your own ideas can be prior art.

If you sleep on your rights, your own manufacture and sale of the machine will be prior art if you have not filed for a patent within one year of the date on which you sold or offered the machine for sale. Or even if not offered for sale, if you publicly disclose it (without any confidentiality obligation from the person to whom you disclosed it), you have only one year to file. There are no exceptions—although it is sometimes murky as to what constitutes a sale or public use. For example, an offer for sale is considered a sale; how do you measure when a product has been offered for sale—what is market testing as opposed to an offer for sale?

The requirement that you must file within the one year is therefore highly important. It also makes good sense. You should not be allowed to make and sell your invention for years and then when a competitor appears, apply for a patent. This would deceive others who would have believed that the idea is free. And you would have extended the life of your exclusionary period from twenty years after the competitor appeared rather than twenty years from the date you began selling the invention.

52

DO *grasp the process that is involved in obtaining a patent.*

Once you have completed the preliminary steps to filing (see **#50**), and the benefits (see **#51**) have convinced you that filing is desirable, you are ready to file. Understand that filing is simply the tip of the iceberg. Filing requires that you prepare a detailed description of the invention, in a relatively confined format that usually includes many pages of text and one or more sheets of drawings. The application must conclude with a precise description of the invention, called *claims.* This is the heart of the application and is the most difficult part to prepare. Both Congress and the courts have been fashioning rules for construction and interpretation of claims for over two hundred years. The right choice of words is critical, even the wrong adjective can lead to disaster, and this is in addition to understanding the technology.

The application must also include an oath or declaration (under penalty of perjury) that you believe you are the first inventor. You must pay a filing fee that is reduced if you are a small entity or an individual (around $350 in 1995, but always changing). You must disclose all the prior art that you are aware of—true confessions. Then you send it on its way.

Once received by the United States Patent and Trademark Office (PTO), you are assigned a serial number and an official filing date. You are likely to wait twelve to eighteen months before you hear again from the PTO. It will have conducted its own prior art search and, almost invariably, will have rejected the application. But don't give up hope.

DON'T *give up hope if the patent office initially rejects your patent application.*

When the PTO (Patent and Trademark Office) rejects your patent application, it explains why, in a letter that is called an office action, it believes there is no invention, based on its review of the prior art. (It may also raise objections to the application papers, such as a failure to adequately describe the invention. See **#54.**) You may then respond to this threat to your invention, in writing, arguing why the office is wrong, or modifying the scope of your claims (that is why the claims are so important). "Well, maybe I did overstate the area that I claim to be covered by my invention, but will you accept *this* definition?" The office argues back. You argue again. At this point the office says: "Sorry, our position is final—no patent." There is still hope.

Maybe they didn't really mean it. When you pay your fee, you get the right to argue once or twice. If you want to continue arguing and amending the claims, you must pay another fee. The curious thing here is that you must refile the application (with the new fee), get a new serial number, and wait again. Alternatively, after that first final rejection, or on the refiled case, you may appeal to a board within the PTO. Chances here are slim; and the costs begin to mount rapidly. If you still lose at the board, you may appeal to a special court called the Federal Circuit Court of Appeal. Chances get even less slim; and money should be no (or at least nearly no) object.

53

DO *recognize that there are stringent standards for obtaining a patent.*

Patents offer a monopoly and are granted only after meeting rigorous standards. First, the invention must be new. In other words, the product, machine, composition, or process must not have existed previously. To determine this fact, the PTO makes a search of all the prior art in the patent office—issued patents as well as articles published in trade or technical journals. If a nearly identical idea is found, the PTO will refuse to issue a patent.

Second, the invention must be useful. This is rarely a problem except in the case of new chemical or biotechnology compositions for which there is no known use, or the perpetual motion machine which is the subject of endless jokes. However, the PTO can challenge the operability of the device described in your patent application and you have the burden of proving that it works.

Third, the subject matter of your invention must fall within one of the permitted classes. This problem is now largely confined to software patents. See #143.

The fourth requirement is the most difficult to satisfy *and* to understand. The concept can be clearly and briefly stated: Would the invention have been obvious to one having ordinary skill in the art at the time of the invention? But the idea is complex.

DON'T *ignore the importance of the "non-obviousness" test for patentability.*

The highest of the hurdles for obtaining a patent is the test for *non-obviousness*. Even if an invention is novel or new, it must be more. To prove that an invention is not novel, the PTO, or the defendant in a patent suit, must show that the idea is disclosed in a single prior art reference. If the idea is novel or new, the next test is applied.

To prove non-obviousness, you must look to see the state of the art in the applicable field. This is done by looking not merely at a single reference, but by imagining that the inventor had all of the prior art references before him or her at the time of making the invention. Then, the law conjures a mythical person skilled in that art, that is, aware of all this prior art. If presented with the problem, would the skilled person construct the invention using the teachings that are contained in that prior art? One way of stating this query is to ask whether the results obtained from the invention were new and unexpected. If one or many persons with ordinary skill would be surprised after working on a solution to the problem for a long time, and failing to combine the prior art teachings to obtain the invention, it may be imperceptible.

Courts and patent attorneys have struggled with the non-obviousness standard for a long time. So don't be discouraged if you find this test puzzling.

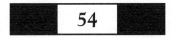

54

DO *appreciate that the government wants something in return for the patent it grants.*

Why does the government grant monopolies to inventors? Well, to begin with, the word grant sounds like a gift. But you know the government better than that. It is actually a contract. The framers of the Constitution believed that if the government would give a monopoly, it could induce inventors into disclosing their inventions, rather than keeping them secret. Then, when the patent expired, everyone could use the invention and commerce and the useful arts would benefit. In legalese, the quid pro quo—something for something. Now that sounds more like our government, doesn't it? The government also wants to induce people to invent, but it would not have to grant a patent to do that—it could pay a lump sum to the inventor based on the merit of the idea.

And what is expected in this disclosure? First, "such full, clear, concise and exact terms as to enable any person skilled in the art to which it pertains . . . to make and use the invention." If you don't provide a description that allows this hypothetical worker to build your invention after the patent expires, your patent will be invalidated. Unethical persons have been known to obtain a patent and describe only enough to satisfy this test in form, but to maintain the substance in secrecy so that others cannot use the invention after expiration. They get their comeuppance. Don't think that you can describe only a clumsy embodiment of your invention.

DON'T *try to shortchange the government when obtaining your patent.*

Not only must you provide a top-notch description of your invention when you apply for a patent, you must describe the best way to practice the invention that you know of at the time you file. This best mode requirement assures that you will not (1) describe a product, for example, that uses the invention but that is difficult to build, or expensive to build; (2) describe a method without telling that if you used one solvent in the process, rather than another, the resulting product would be purer and therefore superior.

Of most significance to the government is that you particularly point out and distinctly claim the invention. The reason for this requirement is also to promote commerce. The government, and competitors, want to know what you claim is your invention so that they do not inadvertently trespass on your territory. Maybe more important, they want to design around the invention. This is the essence of competition: to limit the monopoly that you were granted as narrowly as possible. More goods means more price competition; and more price competition means lower prices, which benefits the general welfare. That is what Adam Smith promised, and it works.

It is this particular pointing out and distinct claiming that is the bane of the amateur patent drafter. Even if you can write a reasonable description of the idea, drafting claims is an art—one not easily mastered. You might consider leaving that part to the experts.

55

DO *not believe old wives' tales regarding post office patents.*

It was once thought, at least when I grew up, that toads caused warts. The second silliest thing I have heard, often repeated by otherwise savvy inventors, is that you can protect your invention by describing it on paper, putting it into a sealed envelope, sending it to yourself in the mail, and keeping it sealed thereafter. Why anyone would bother filing a patent, as described at **#52,** when protection is available for a 32-cent stamp is a mystery no one can explain to me. It is a myth. It does not provide any credible evidence of the date of invention—although this has at least some rational basis. It is just that the evidence is not very convincing to the United States Patent Office or to the courts.

Somewhat more valuable, but also often mistaken, is the patent office disclosure document program. If you send a description of your invention to the USPTO under this program, with a small fee, it will establish your date of conception and ownership. It does *not* however give you any patent rights, more time to file, or allow you to use patent pending.

Another old wives' tale is that you obtain some protection if you place "patent pending" on your product. No such thing. You have no protection until the day your patent issues. You cannot demand damages for infringement that takes place prior to that date. All that "patent pending" may do is what it is intended to do—place some competitor on notice that you are seeking protection. You may not place the pending notice until you actually file—there is a fine if you do and get caught.

DON'T *be sloppy in keeping records of your invention.*

There are a number of reasons for keeping good records of your invention, not all of them of legal importance. One reason is so you know what you have tried earlier, staying organized, and so on. Legally, it could be of value if you had discussed the idea with someone who is now claiming it is their idea. My advice is, don't discuss the idea with anyone who will not sign a confidential disclosure agreement before you file your patent application.

In this country (and in no other) when two or more inventors claim the same invention, the PTO declares a proceeding called an *interference*—a trial to determine who was first to invent, not first to file (as in other countries). For large companies who are often simultaneously pursuing a solution to a new widespread and serious problem (AIDS, for example), inventorship can very well be a close contest. But for most inventions the idea has been blown out of proportion. However, records can occasionally be used to show the USPTO that the reference it is relying on to deny your patent was presented later than your invention. An interference sometimes can be used to straighten out who are the true inventors when there are joint inventors.

So, keep good records. Date them. Have them witnessed. But most of all, keep your idea secret and file early.

56

DO *use your patent to stop infringers or to license others.*

Since the patent gives you the exclusive right to prohibit others from using your invention, it may be exploited in several ways. Assume that you are a manufacturer and that the patent covers the product you make. You may elect to stop anyone else from making an identical product, using the same method of production, or compounding the same composition—if such activities infringed the patent. Infringement is discussed in **#57**. Or you may decide to license others to use the invention and pay you a royalty. Licensing is discussed at **#58.** How do you decide?

This is a business decision with strong legal overtones. It is *not* obvious that you should keep all rights to yourself because capturing the manufacturing profits from 100-percent market share will maximize your profit. Maybe. But if the demand cannot be met, the market size may be smaller. Overdemand is the surest way to attract the most unscrupulous competitors. If you are supplying a patented component to another manufacturer, that manufacturer may demand a second source for purchase before it will approve your component. If the product is revolutionary, you may find that purchasers are skeptical of the technology. You may need to license the patent to a large company that provides credibility—an imprimatur for the technology. You may find that a standards body requires that you license others before the patented technology is incorporated into the standard specification. There are other reasons to license.

DON'T *think that a patent infringement suit is out of reach financially.*

Patent infringement litigation is notoriously expensive. It is not unheard of to spend over a million dollars for attorney fees alone. There are additional costs for experts, elaborate exhibits, and more. It is common wisdom that ten years ago a patent was only as good as a balance sheet. But things have changed.

There are two solutions to cut costs that are regularly used and some more esoteric ones that can be investigated. First, more patent lawyers are accepting contingent fee cases. The reason is that the number of patents being held valid today has increased significantly, for several reasons. The principal criterion is whether there are substantial damages that may be collected—past or future (through licensing the entire industry after the suit is won). Expect to surrender up to 50 percent of the recovery for a pure contingency fee. Because the cost of a suit is so high, the law firm itself may be hard-pressed to finance the entire suit and may require at least a partial payment of its fees. It is definitely worth investigating this possibility.

Another possibility is offensive patent insurance. Defensive insurance has been provided in many policies for a long time; offensive insurance is relatively new. Talk to your insurance broker or patent attorney. Finally, consider forming an investment pool to finance the litigation and split the proceeds with your investors. This technique has become more popular in recent years.

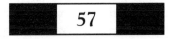

DO *understand the basic concept of patent infringement.*

When someone takes your patent rights, it is called patent infringement. To prevent such infringement, you must sue the infringer in a federal court. The suit is enormously expensive. The alleged infringer will not only deny infringement, but will also attack the validity of your patent. How infringement is determined is a complicated matter. Basically, when you obtained your patent you carefully defined the invention in the claims. See **#52.** Infringement occurs when someone other than the inventor makes, uses, or sells the invention in those claims.

Literal infringement occurs when the words in the claim can be read on the accused device—word for word. If one element is missing, there is no literal infringement. To take a simplistic example, suppose you have a patent that covers a four-legged stool. If someone made a three-legged stool, because one element (the fourth leg) is missing, there is no infringement. If the accused stool had four legs, of course, there would be infringement. If the stool had five legs, it would also infringe, because it would have four + one legs. If the patent claims define an opening as round, and the accused device has an oval opening, it does not infringe. If the claim used only the word *opening,* it would cover both the round and the oval holes. It is because of this persnickety manner of comparison, among other reasons, that patents have multiple claims.

What if there is no literal infringement? All is not lost.

DON'T *give up on patent infringement, even if there is no literal infringement.*

As explained previously, if a patent claim does not read on the accused device, there is no literal infringement. This may seem unfair—so small a difference has such a large effect. It has struck courts that way, too. They have responded by fashioning a rule where there is no literal infringement. It is called the doctrine of equivalents. In concept, it is logical and straightforward. In application, it is highly inscrutable and frustrating.

Remember the example of an opening previously discussed. If the claim indicates a round opening, and the accused device has an oblong opening, the court will ask if the two are equivalent—do they provide the same function, in the same way, to obtain the same result. If the purpose of the opening is to expel a fluid through it, the court may find the two openings equivalent. Thus, the inadvertent use of the word round that precluded literal infringement may be avoided. However, the application of the doctrine is much more complex, involving a consideration of the prior art, a close reading of the specification of the patent, consideration of all the statements that were made by the patent office and the applicant during the period in which the patent was being obtained, and more. Courts attempt to balance the desire to accord wide scope to meritorious inventions, while still providing some certainty to competitors as to what they may not do. You only need to understand that if there is no literal infringement, the success of your infringement case is in much greater doubt.

DO *exploit your invention by licensing it to others.*

Your patent gives you the right to exclude others from making, using, or selling your invention. You are the landlord of the property described and defined in your patent and may allow others to use your property on terms and conditions suitable to you. You may grant such rights in a wide variety of ways. You may define the territorial scope of the license. For example, if you wish to franchise a business that processes material in a particular way, and that method of processing is protected by a patent, you may define territories that would otherwise be prohibited by the antitrust laws (not normally anything to worry about in the small business but a potential later problem). You may also limit the time that the licensee may practice (patent lingo for using) the invention, up to the end of the life of the patent.

You may license one party to manufacture, and a number of other companies to sell the product after buying from that party, but precluding them from manufacturing. This may allow you to select an excellent manufacturer to make your product, but place the sales and marketing into other more capable hands. You may license a company to make or sell only a particular type of product for a particular market, commonly called a *field of use* license. So you could allow one manufacturer to make a bearing for the automotive market, another for the machine tool market, and another for the turbine market. You may wish to do this because each of the companies that you license are dominant in their particular market, but couldn't sell cash at a discount in the other markets.

DON'T *grant an exclusive patent license without some guaranteed royalty; and don't believe that there is some magic standard royalty rate for patents.*

An exclusive license may be granted to use your patent (i.e., there will only be one licensee, or if nonexclusive, many licensees). Of course, a licensee would prefer exclusivity, but you must consider that the licensee may not properly exploit your invention. In other words, since your compensation will likely be a royalty based on the volume of sales by the licensee, your success is dependent upon the licensee's. The rule here is that you should never grant a patent exclusive license without a minimum annual royalty guarantee. The best negotiation strategy is to request a sales forecast from the licensee for the patented product and then to determine the minimum at perhaps 50 percent of that forecast. You may increase or decrease this minimum over time.

It is not possible to give a ballpark royalty rate for a patent license, although nearly everyone believes they know what is a standard royalty. It is often true that a particular industry has developed a standard, but even that is subject to numerous exceptions. There are a variety of ways of looking at this. Obviously, net profit on sales is a benchmark. If the patent will allow a price that generates a high gross margin, the excess profit over the commodity product profit is directly attributable to the patent protection. Should the patentee capture that entire amount? Probably not, but it is a good starting point from the patentee's point of view. Or consider that a patent is a replacement for a successful research project—what is the value of that research, spread over time?

	59	

DO *protect your trademark or service mark.*

The fundamental thing to understand about trademarks is that the process of obtaining this protection is completely different from obtaining patent or copyright protection. A trademark is automatically created as soon as you use the word, phrase, or symbol on or in connection with the goods or services you sell. You do not need to apply for a trademark to any government agency. Not now, or ever.

That said, there are several other aspects of obtaining protection that you should know. First, although the trademark is created through use, it is also possible to protect your right to a word, phrase, or symbol by filing an intent to use (ITU) application with the United States Patent and Trademark Office (PTO). Essentially, you can reserve the right to register the mark for one year by paying a fee to the PTO. During the year, if you begin using the mark, you can convert the ITU registration to an application for registration on the federal register.

Second, there are significant benefits if you register the mark. See **#63.** You can register the mark in a state or with the federal government (PTO). Whether you should, or can, file in a state or with the PTO depends on a variety of factors. See **#65.**

But even before commencing use, do a trademark search.

DON'T *invest money in a trademark that belongs to someone else.*

Because the ownership of a trademark commences with use, if someone is using the same or a similar word, phrase, or symbol prior to your use, you cannot obtain rights to such word, phrase, or symbol. In fact, you may be infringing *their* trademark. See **#62.** You protect yourself by a clearance search to determine if your proposed trademark is available for use. It is recommended that you come up with several words, phrases, or symbols, or a combination of a word and a symbol that appeals to you. (The strength of your trademark is determined by its uniqueness. See **#61.**) Some you will know are in use by others. (You *know* that McDonald's is used for hamburgers.) You can also do a preliminary check through a database that may be accessible on-line or at your local library if you live in a major metropolitan city. These searches are inexpensive—free (at your library) or less than $100 if you go through a low-cost search firm. They usually cover only federal trademark registrations and search only for an identical or *very* similar mark. There is, therefore, a risk that you may *not* be cleared.

Then (particularly if you intend to invest big money in advertising or plan other uses of the mark) conduct a full search through one of the major researchers, such as Thompson & Thompson (800-692-8833). It is more extensive and therefore more expensive. It searches for federal, state, and common-law (unregistered) marks and looks for marks that are confusingly similar. This type of search can run from several hundred to several thousand dollars (international). Then you must decide if the mark is clear. See **#60.**

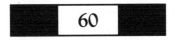

DO *select your trademark (after clearance) and then file for registration.*

After you have completed your clearance search (see **#59**), it is recommended that you use the services of an experienced attorney to give an opinion as to whether your use will infringe someone else's trademark and whether you can obtain protection on your mark. If hiring an attorney is beyond your means, you will have to make those decisions, based on the principles set forth in **#62.** If a mark used by another company is too similar, you may want to check that such company is still using the mark—companies go out of business, discontinue products, and so forth. If your investigation of the other mark shows that it is still in use, but you may be using the mark for different goods or you may be using entirely different channels to move your products to market, you may still be in the clear. If not, you have no other alternative than to choose another mark and go through the search process again.

Once you are satisfied that your mark is clear, I recommend that you file an application for registration. If your business is entirely local, a rare occurrence in today's society, you may file for a state trademark registration. See **#75.** But if you are selling goods or services across state lines (interstate commerce), you must file for a federal registration. It is somewhat more expensive but also more valuable. You may file the application yourself or you may use an attorney. See **#63.** For more information on filing an application see F. Foster and R. Shook, *Patents, Copyrights, and Trademarks*, p. 128 (1993).

DON'T *pick a weak trademark.*

There are good trademarks and bad trademarks—legally speaking. By and large, most trademarks fall in between.

A good trademark is a word, phrase, or symbol that has absolutely no meaning nor does it identify any person or place. The best examples are Xerox and Exxon. They are so-called coined words—words that did not exist until they were made up for use as a trademark. From the outset they served the singular trademark function—to identify the products of a single supplier. It is also true that because these words were devoid of content, their users had to spend significant sums to associate the mark with their product.

A bad mark may not be a mark at all. *Diet cola* describes a drink and cannot identify the drink of any one manufacturer. It is descriptive. If companies could obtain the exclusive right to a descriptive term, the language would be depleted, and other suppliers would not be able to describe their goods. It will not help to use a foreign language to describe the goods (café latté). Nor will it help to misspell the words (dyet kola).

There are many words that are suggestive of the product or its function that may be protectable, but only weakly. For more advice on choosing a mark, see **#61.**

DO *choose your trademark with a view to its legal strength.*

There is a common tendency for small-business people to choose a name for their business or a word to describe their service or product that is suggestive, if not downright descriptive. This is a mistake. As noted in **#60,** *no* protection is afforded to a descriptive word or phrase.

A *suggestive mark* is one that describes some desirable characteristic of a service (Dependable Trucking Service) or product (Best Candies). Because other providers cannot be deprived of the use of these words to describe their products or services, these marks will be given very narrow protection. Narrow means that others will be able to use very similar sounding words with impunity. So you have not achieved any material level of distinctiveness and will be surrounded by copycats. Of course, there are various degrees of suggestiveness.

Coined marks are the strongest, as discussed above. But arbitrary or fanciful marks can be nearly as strong: Apple, for computers; Jaguar, for an automobile (or is this suggestive?). The line between suggestive and arbitrary is blurry. Reasonable people disagree on the strength of marks, but the further you recede from common words, the stronger the mark will be.

There are other ways of creating distinctiveness.

DON'T *rely solely on words for selecting a strong trademark.*

Avoiding weak marks is not easy. The language is finite and as commerce expands, there are fewer and fewer words available for exclusive ownership.

One alternative to words or phrases is the use of a design, symbol, logo, or other graphic. Particularly in combination with a word that is reasonably strong, the combination may be quite distinctive. Like the use of words, the more arbitrary or coined the design, the stronger the protection. In other words, the use of a jaguar picture in conjunction with the mark Jaguar is not as strong as, for example, the circular design used by AT&T for its services.

An infringer who is attempting to obtain a free ride on your mark is harder put to come up with a word *and* a design that is close to yours. You should have an easy time convincing a judge or jury that the infringer was taking a cheap shot. And that is the effect you want.

One problem with designs is that they are solely visual. They will not add distinctiveness in sound, meaning, or effect, which is part of the test for infringement (see **#62**).

62

DO *test whether your intended trademark may infringe on another.*

The primary purpose of the clearance is to determine if the mark you chose will infringe the trademark of another company. The test for trademark infringement is whether a reasonable consumer would likely be confused by the two trademarks. In other words, will a consumer think that the product he or she is purchasing comes from a source they know, by virtue of their recognition of the trademark? There are two primary and a number of minor factors to consider when deciding this question. See **#65.**

First, are the goods or services similar? This is a relative matter about which people can honestly disagree. Would you think that a manufacturer of automobile mufflers may be the source of women's clothing? How about perfume and women's clothing? It is not just whether the process of manufacturing is similar, but whether the businesses that sell these goods are typically related. Of course, there are marks that are used on a broad line of goods, usually through licensing or sponsorship, which clouds the issue.

The second test is whether the marks are confusingly similar. This calls for a comparison based on sight, sound, and meaning. All three of these bases for similarity must be made. See **#61.** It is obvious that this test is highly subjective and other factors are required for an answer.

DON'T *overlook the other factors in determining whether a trademark infringes on another.*

In addition to the similarity of goods, the channel through which the goods pass also affects the result. Are the consumers the same? Are the goods advertised in the same media (i.e., magazines, billboards, TV, etc.)? Are they sold in the same type of stores (i.e., department stores, airport tourist gift shops, fast food outlets, etc.)?

How expensive are the goods? Is the product typically an impulse purchase? Candy bar purchasers are more likely to be confused than an automobile buyer. Is the mark strong or weak? See **#60.** If the two marks have been in use for a period of time, can the trademark owner show actual confusion? Why not? If the two marks allegedly cause confusion, then some actual purchasers will, in fact, have been confused.

Be particularly careful about celebrated marks. McDonald's. IBM. Kodak. Xerox. Gucci. These marks are so famous that they are accorded a wide berth in trademark protection. Even if the goods are quite dissimilar, and admittedly there is no probable customer confusion, they may be protected against dilution. In other words, your use may deprecate the reputation of the owner, or at the least cause a lessening of distinctiveness. Strong marks should be approached warily.

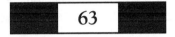

DO *take advantage of the benefits of a federal trademark registration.*

There are several reasons for filing a federal trademark application, not the least of which is that it will permit you to pursue an infringer in a federal court (an unbiased forum) where intellectual property is generally more understood.

Let's first clarify one point that appears to cause a lot of confusion. The symbol ® denotes a federally registered trademark. It may *not* be used before a registration is issued; there is a penalty for false marking that can be serious. Before registration you should use the symbol ™ as a superscript to your choice of mark to denote your use of the word as a trademark and your claim of ownership. (You may use SM for a service mark, though TM will do also.)

There are several reasons for using the ® symbol. First, and most important, it gives notice. It will be hard for an infringer to claim that they were unaware of the registration and use of a mark when the ® is used diligently. Second, in an actual infringement case, there are better opportunities for receiving actual damages if the ® is used.

Federal registration should always be pursued if possible. See **#65.** Once obtained, it provides *national,* exclusive protection for your mark. Once a mark is registered, it constitutes constructive notice (similar to recording a deed to real estate) to all others who may wish to use the mark that you own it. You must continue to maintain the mark.

DON'T *fail to maintain your trademark registration.*

The advantages that stem from your federal registration can be renewed indefinitely. The original registration lasts ten years (twenty years if registered before November 1989) and must be renewed at that time through a renewal application filed with the PTO.

After five years, you must file an affidavit with the PTO, swearing to your continued use of the mark. If you don't, the registration is canceled. You can also increase the strength of your mark by simultaneously filing an affidavit (the two are commonly referred to as the "Section 8 and 15 Affidavit") that provides so-called incontestability. In fact the mark is contestable, but you do get the added advantage that if you have used the mark for five continuous years and file the affidavit, the mark cannot be challenged on the grounds that it is not distinctive.

Even if you file the 8/15 affidavit, you will still lose your exclusive rights to the mark if you do not use it. If you have a federal registration and have filed the affidavit, but fail to use the mark for two years, you will be presumed to have abandoned it. The reason for non-use can be explained, but the result is a burden.

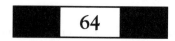

DO *not lose rights to your trademark through poor use.*

As indicated in **#63,** you should use your mark with ® after federal registration. But you also must use it correctly.

In **#61,** it was pointed out that the words, phrases, or symbols that you choose for your mark will define the strength—initially. But even if a mark is a coined word, and therefore the strongest type of mark, it can become generic as described in **#60.** A mark is always an adjective; it must be followed by the name or noun that describes the product—for example, Xerox copies, Kleenex tissues, and so forth. In your copy you should be careful not to use the mark as the name of the object—and you should warn those who prepare your advertising materials against such use. Initially, it appears advantageous to have everyone use your trademark when they want to purchase the goods. But then you will find that consumers are using the same word when they are purchasing your competitor's product ("Make me a Xerox"—using the Canon copier!). That is a sign that the word is becoming generic and you will have to struggle hard to keep it distinctive.

Always use the mark with an initial capital letter, or capitalize the entire word or phrase. If you use a symbol with a word, use the symbol alone occasionally in your literature or packaging to show that it is an independent indicator of origin. You can then claim rights to the symbol alone and file a separate registration later.

DON'T *let others use your trademark without proper contractual restrictions.*

If your business operates through retailers or dealers who sell your product or services exclusively (i.e., they are not handling the products of many other suppliers), they may wish to use a part of your trademark or trade name in their name or in the sale of the products or services in their territory.

You may allow them to do this, but be careful. First, you should expressly allow such use in your dealer contract. It should specifically state that the dealer acknowledges your exclusive right to the mark (and name). You should have obtained a federal registration or you should apply for one. See **#65.** The contract should expressly provide that in the event the contract is terminated for any reason, the dealer will immediately discontinue use of the mark *and* any confusingly similar mark. If it is a service business, you must control the manner in which the dealer delivers the services. You must preclude the dealer from using the mark on any goods or services other than yours.

There are no worse disputes than those arising from a broken dealer relationship. You will materially strengthen your position if you can stop use of the mark on termination. So, rather than look the other way or vacillate, set clear restrictions of use in your contract.

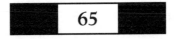

DO *file for a federal trademark registration.*

There are two ways to acquire a federal trademark registration, depending on whether you have already begun to use the mark or have only selected it and intend to start your use soon. For the latter, see **#66.**

If you have used the mark in interstate commerce, you may file an application for registration with the PTO. The form is quite easy to fill out and may be obtained from the PTO. You will need three samples of the mark as used to send to the PTO. These may be labels, packages, tags, or any appearance of the mark *on* the goods. Advertising materials, catalogs, manuals, and letterheads are not acceptable because they are not used on or in close connection with the goods when sold. If the mark is part of the goods—for example, an embossed word in a cast iron staircase—photos will be acceptable as a specimen. The PTO will not accept any object of other than tiny size as a specimen. For services, advertising materials, such as brochures, flyers, catalogs, or even advertisements in a newspaper, are acceptable.

Trademarks are registered by class. But you do not need to choose the class; the PTO will do it for you. Just make sure they understand the goods and that the class adequately covers the goods you sell.

DON'T *fail to follow through with your federal trademark application.*

You must send a drawing of your mark with your application. There are fussy little details about the drawing you will have to learn from the materials available from the PTO. If your mark is a word, and any font is acceptable, then you may simply type the word in all capital letters. Otherwise, you will need a drawing that is in ink and conforms to other PTO requirements. It is important that the specimens, showing the use of the mark, conform with the drawing. You cannot have a drawing that shows the mark in fancy script, while the specimens show the mark in block letters; however, the opposite is true.

Once your mark is filed, you will receive first a receipt indicating that the PTO has in fact received your application. Then you will receive an office action (a letter) indicating if there are any procedural or technical errors in your application and whether the examiner, after a search, has found any confusingly similar mark. You may respond to the action in writing in the appropriate time period, correcting any difficulties. If there is a rejection based on another mark, it is advised that you see an attorney who is experienced in trademark matters.

Once the mark is accepted by the PTO for registration, it is published in a PTO weekly journal for *opposition.* Any party that feels that your mark is not proper for registration can file an opposition proceeding. At this point, an attorney's help is highly recommended.

DO *consider filing an intent to use (ITU) application for a federal trademark.*

Until about five years ago, unless you had actual use of your mark in interstate commerce, you could not register your mark with the federal government. This practice was out of step with the manner in which other countries treated trademark protection. Now you can file an ITU application and effectively reserve the mark for up to three years if you can show good cause why you have not put the mark into use earlier.

The requirements are simple. The form for actual use and intended use is the same. Of course, there are no specimens to be filed, since the mark is not being used. The fee is the same. To file an ITU, you must have a bona fide intent to use the mark in commerce within six months from the date of your application.

If the PTO finds that your ITU mark is allowed for registration, you will be notified. Thereafter, you have six months to file a statement of actual use; if you don't, you will be required to pay a fee to extend the six months for another six months (this may be done until the total time for extension is three years). For the first extension, you need no explanation of why you still have not begun to use the mark. Thereafter, you will need to put a reason for the continued delay. A short statement regarding a delay in production, product development, preparation of advertising, and so on will usually suffice. However, before you receive a registration you will have to allege actual use.

DON'T *waste money filing an ITU federal trademark application, if unnecessary.*

Before your ITU application can mature into a registration, you must file a statement of actual use of the mark in interstate commerce. If such use occurs before the PTO notifies you that the mark will be published for opposition, you can amend the application to allege such actual use. You must await the expiration of the publication period before you can file the statement. You must also file the three specimens with the statement of use.

The real advantage of the ITU, of course, is that the filing date establishes a constructive date of first use (meaning that although not in actual use, it will be deemed to be in use for the purpose of determining who was the first user). There are several things to weigh, therefore, before you file an ITU application. If your estimate of time to actual use is delayed, you may require several extensions that can cost up to $600, in addition to the $245 (current) application fee. How important is it to claim this early use? Or, to put it another way, is it likely that a competitor will begin use of a similar mark during the period before you begin actual use? And if so, will you have invested a significant amount of money in advertising or other materials that will be lost with a change of mark?

67

DO *protect your trade name—but that is not as simple as you think.*

A trade name is the name of a business. Most people think that if they form a corporation with their chosen name they are the owner of that name and can use it exclusively. Nothing could be further from the truth. Let us start this confusing area with a basic distinction. There is the state approval of your corporate name when you form a corporation. Some agency, such as a corporation commissioner or secretary of state, issues such approval. It confers no rights other than to commit that if another person attempts to form a corporation with the identical name, it will not allow such name to be used for the new corporation. Can that person continue to operate as a sole proprietor as it had prior to your adoption of the corporate name? You bet they can. They were the prior user. You have only one right after you have captured the corporate name—no one else can later form a corporation with that name. It means very little.

A trade name is protected not by state name statutes but by the common-law doctrine of unfair competition. Unfair competition is a fuzzy world with a collection of rights, half rights, and odd wrongs. It is best crystallized in the areas of trade secrets and common-law trademarks and trade names. But that does not say a lot. Because it is so vague, most businesses rely on registration for trademark protection for the advantages it offers. You can rely on your trademark for protection against another's use of a confusingly similar trade *name*. See **#62.**

DON'T *rely on corporate name clearance from a state corporation registrar.*

Suppose that you apply in California to create a corporation whose name is CNN. The secretary of state, who has the responsibility to clear (approve) corporate names, checks its register. If CNN is not a California corporation, *and* is not licensed to do business in California (which is probably not the case), the secretary of state cannot refuse your incorporation under that name.

Now you begin to use your new corporate name. If you are operating a local seafood restaurant, you may not draw the ire of Mr. Ted Turner, and you may continue use of the name. But suppose you are a news-gathering service for Hollywood gossip. CNN, owner of a federal trademark registration for the mark CNN, will sue you. You will point out that the secretary of state has approved your use of the name. But you will lose because you will find it nearly impossible to advertise your services without using your name as an indication of source of the service. That is, a service mark use. Even if you didn't use your corporate name in conjunction with the offering of your services, CNN would prevail on its common-law rights against unfair competition—where there is no difference recognized between trade names and trademarks.

Rights to fictitious names are similarly fictitious. See **#68.**

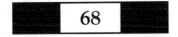

68

DO *choose your business name as if it were a trademark.*

As you saw in **#67,** merely obtaining a corporate name from your state agency will not protect you from a prior user of a confusingly similar name or trademark. This concept will be clearer if you consider that there are two functions of a trademark—your protection against use by another and protection of the public against erroneously buying goods from one company, when they wanted goods from another. Consumers do not distinguish between a trade name and a trademark. The law will protect them against any business that attempts to palm off inferior goods as those of another (usually of higher quality—and price) by using a similar word as a source indicator.

Before you file to incorporate your business under a name, check it out for noninfringement as if you were choosing a word for use on the goods you are going to sell. See **#60.** If you choose a word or symbol for use as your name or as your trademark, and find that it is clear for the goods you want to use it on, you may still find that you cannot form a corporation under that name. If the holder of the name is in an entirely different field, and the name is not used publicly, however, you still have a way out. File your corporation under any name—ABCDEFGH, Inc.—then file a fictitious business name registration under the name you actually want to use.

DON'T *rely on the filing of a fictitious name as clearance for a name.*

A fictitious name (not a true name) is used by a business for identification. In a sole proprietorship, it is a name other than your own. In a partnership, it is a name other than the names of all the partners in the firm. In a corporation, it is a name other than the name under which the corporation was registered when it was formed (or later changed). In short, it is not the legal name of the entity operating the business.

Most states have some provision for registering or filing a fictitious name (usually with some notice to the public that no one ever reads or pays the least attention to). No states appear to maintain a record of such names. The legal purpose of requiring recording or filing a fictitious name is to expose the underlying owner so that other persons can identify such person to file a lawsuit. It does *not* function to protect the exclusive right to a name.

So clearance of your name by allowing you to record, register, or file your fictitious name is meaningless if you are using a name or trademark that is in prior use by another business. That business can prevent you from infringing its common law right by asserting unfair competition. Conduct a search as if you were going to use the name as a trademark or a service mark—and act accordingly. See **#59** and **#60.**

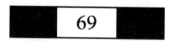

DO *not believe that you have an absolute right to use your surname as your business name or a mark for your products.*

There is a common misconception that you have an absolute right to use your surname in any business venture in which you are engaged. This is wrong. The use of personal names is a qualified right, and the circumstances must be investigated before you can determine the extent of those rights. To begin with, the first use in all trademark and trade name contests is the most important factor in deciding who has the right. In the area of personal names, the "use" is a use in business. The fact that you (or your family) have been using your name to identify yourself longer than the other person is irrelevant. Have you been using the name to identify your business, products, or services—and for what length of time—is the appropriate inquiry.

Furthermore, the key to claiming rights is whether the use of the name has created a secondary meaning. Once you show that the consuming public associates the name with your business, products, or services, and that you are the senior user, there is still the matter of fashioning the relief that you are entitled to. The courts take several approaches. One is to allow the junior user to use the name but only as a corporate or legal name and not in connection with any advertising, packaging, or on the product, business, or service. This is not much help to the second user. The more common approach is to allow the latecomer to use the name but only with a disclaimer. (For example, "Pinnochio Industries and Jeppeto products are not affiliated in any manner with the puppet Pinnochio or its maker.") This is usually not a very satisfactory solution for the senior user. No one really wins these disputes.

DON'T *choose descriptive or geographic words as trademarks; but if you do, recognize that you can still claim ownership through secondary meaning.*

The concept of secondary meaning is at once abstruse and simple. Here is the background that should clear it up. Trademark law prohibits a business from exclusive appropriation of a common word that describes a product, service, or business. You cannot call your clothes cleaning business "Cleaners" and stop any other cleaning establishment from using that word as part of its name or as a description of its service. The same rule applies for a geographic description. You cannot call your brand of artichokes "Castroville," because there are many growers in that area who should be able to identify their artichokes as grown in Castroville.

But what if *your* use of a descriptive word or a geographic location becomes so prominently known that consumers do in fact think of *your* product or service when they encounter that word? For example, Roquefort cheese. When that happens, the law recognizes that the original or first meaning of the word has acquired a second meaning and that the company that has created that occurrence should be protected against other later users. To obtain protection, you must prove that this secondary meaning exists. You do this by showing long and continuous use, by showing that your use has been exclusive, by showing that you have advertised heavily and attempted to create this association, and by showing that you have been successful and that the volume of your business is significant. If the later user has willfully copied your mark, you may argue that the copying itself is an admission of the association. But it isn't easy.

70

DO *protect your trade secrets.*

What is a trade secret? It is information that (1) is valuable (in an economic or business sense); (2) is not generally known to or easily ascertainable by others who could benefit from it; and (3) has been diligently kept secret (see **#71**). Typical trade secrets include processes (the Zildjian brothers make the best musical cymbals in the world—the secret metal casting technique is maintained as a closely guarded secret); computer programs (the source code may never be released and is kept under lock and key); compilation of data (market research data that is gathered at great expense and is not disseminated in reports or news articles, etc., and is not readily ascertainable, i.e., the raw data is not easy to gather—and making such a determination creates a difficult factual question); customer lists, but see **#72**; machines (assuming that you built the device or that it was built to your specification under an arrangement of secrecy); and like matters. A method for doing something—know-how—is a trade secret if it meets the three requirements listed above.

While perhaps most of what you do at work has value, it cannot readily be measured. Since a trade secret must have measurable value, it may be difficult to prove such value in court unless you can demonstrate a competitive advantage (for example, lower production cost, stemming from use of secret process). Trade secrets need not be high technology. The best trade secrets originate from trial and error attempts to create a method that is used internally in performing a service or building a product. Ask yourself: "How difficult would it be for my competitor to achieve this same level of information?" If the answer is "damn hard," protect it. Remember, to go to court to prove a misappropriation is a very expensive task!

DON'T *think that just any information you gather is a trade secret.*

The concept of value is directly related to availability. If information is generally known, your knowledge is simply not secret. No matter how hard you may try, the cat is out of the bag. And not *everyone* has to know. If those in the industry know, but not the rest of the world, the secret is gone. Of course, if the secret is published, regardless of how obscure the publication, there is no secret.

The critical element is whether the amount of public information known about the subject is so minor that the possession of the whole by you creates an appreciable advantage over your competitors. So scarcity is the key to value. As always.

It is not only whether the material is known, but whether it is readily ascertainable. So, a competitor is free to purchase a product on the open market and reverse engineer it. For most products, therefore, the very act of selling it discloses the secret. Some products, like computer chips or software, can be sold without disclosing the design—to the ordinary person. But if a company can peel away the layers of a chip or decompile and reconstruct the software (providing no other protection exists, see **#142**) it is free to do so with impunity. Indeed, there are companies that are engaged solely in the business of reverse engineering. If you purchase the results of their efforts, you must still be careful that you are using people who are squeaky clean to build your own replica.

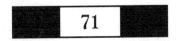

DO *maintain your trade secrets as secrets.*

You must make reasonable efforts to keep information in confidence. You cannot leave materials lying around and try to prevent the stealing of your trade secrets by an employee. Conversely, you need not lock the secret up in a vault every night with a combination known only to you and your priest or rabbi. Here are some guidelines.

Require that each employee sign a nondisclosure agreement. Most employees, especially those who create the products or services that the company sells, such as engineers, technicians, and service developers, should also be required to sign an invention assignment agreement. A confidential disclosure agreement form is included in the appendix.

Restrict visitors to certain areas of the plant. Place signs on doors leading to such areas. Instruct employees not to allow visitors, even if accompanied, into such areas. Make access to such areas unavailable to even your own employees who are not working there. In fact, make all information available on only a need-to-know basis.

Mark all documents CONFIDENTIAL, boldly. Add "For Internal Use Only." Then, carefully monitor those documents. Do have a secure area of the plant or a locked cabinet in which these documents are kept.

DON'T *allow ex-employees to take trade secrets.*

The single largest class of disputes over trade secret theft is between employers and ex-employees. This is natural since a company's secrets are created and used by its employees. No one has better access than such an employee, and no one knows the value of the secrets more than the employee. There are three ways by which trade secrets are acquired by another: (1) breaking and entering; (2) obtaining the secret as a result of a special relationship of trust; or (3) receiving it by mistake. The employee usually obtains company secrets by the second method.

It is therefore important that you inform and constantly reinforce with employees their duty to maintain information in confidence. Too many companies wait until it is too late. "I trusted him." There is nothing inconsistent between trust and prudent business practices. Most employees in key positions will understand the competitive advantage of a trade secret. They will therefore understand that secrets should be expressly protected from competitors. It is the employees who can honestly state that they didn't know and weren't told that the material was confidential who cause problems. They are being naive, vindictive, or simply dishonest.

When employees leave, they should be reminded that they have signed a nondisclosure agreement, and they should be notified that the company will enforce it. Other steps can be taken in the more severe situations.

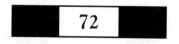

72

DO *prevent misappropriation of your trade secrets.*

Misappropriation is a term used in polite circles for theft. Perhaps it is used for intangible property simply because it is somewhat more difficult to be certain that you have been relieved of some of your assets. If an employee steals a company truck, you can easily ascertain that it is gone and who has it. If the formula for a chemical composition is stolen, it may be a little harder to catch the thief red-handed.

Some cases cry for justice. A supplier who has learned your composition through required access to your entire process and then later becomes a competitor using your composition must be stopped. And a competitor who had been unable to replicate your manufacturing process until it hired a knowledgeable former employee of yours is very likely a thief.

But what will you win if you do take the blackguard to court? Your best recovery is probably that the court will enjoin the thief from using or disclosing the property. But for how long? Only as long as it would have taken him to develop the information alone. In fact, a trade secret action is effective only if you can go into court and obtain a preliminary injunction, that is, one that is obtainable in a month or two (see **#47**)—before the culprit can actually harm your business. Your customers will ordinarily welcome competitors and will give them some business to keep you honest and on your toes. So quick relief may be the only relief.

DON'T *rely too heavily on protection of your customer list—but protect what you can.*

Customer lists are trade secrets. But not good ones. As stated in **#70** and **#71,** there are requirements to protect what you consider proprietary information: The information must not be well known; it must have independent economic value; and you must be able to show that you attempted to keep the material confidential.

If a competitor or ex-employee can simply go to trade directories and compile a list of purchasers of your company's product, it is readily ascertained and not likely a secret. If the compilation process is not too time-consuming it is even less likely a trade secret. And if the selection process is relatively unsophisticated, it probably won't qualify as a trade secret. It is very difficult to prevent an ex-salesperson from calling on your customers. The salesperson may have called on some of the customers before they joined you. (Have you ever forbidden a newly hired salesperson, who had industry experience, to call on one of his or her old customers?) If the needs of a customer are unique, and the salesperson learned these needs from calling on the customer, you stand a better chance. If the ex-employee is in accounting or in production, you have a better case. How else would that employee know if he or she did not use information that was accessed improperly?

Even if you prove a trade secret did exist, you may be entitled only to prohibit solicitation, not to prevent the salesperson's announcement of his or her change of company to the customers.

DO *develop additional protection for your products in the marketplace by creating a trade dress.*

Over the last twenty years, a new form of protection similar to trademark protection has developed. Some consider it simply an extension of trademarks, but because it is still developing, it is easier to discuss it separately. Trade dress started as a form of protection for packaging of products. While a trademark may be a word, symbol, or design, it is difficult to think of a mark as a shape. However, there is no question that many consumers can identify the source of a product by recognizing its packaging. The Coke bottle is a fine example. Even without the words Coca-Cola molded into the glass, the shape is clearly distinctive. The same is true for many other bottles and containers. The analogy to the word mark is obvious. But courts also recognized that the primary function of the container is to hold the contents; so, like a weak, descriptive mark (see **#61**) whose primary function is to describe the goods or the place of origin of the goods, a container would merit protection only if it could be shown that as a mark it had also acquired a secondary meaning, that is, indicating the source of the goods to the consumer. See **#69** for additional discussion of secondary meaning.

Then the concept was carried further. Even a store decor could acquire a secondary meaning—sort of the container for the dispensing of services and products. Several years ago the Supreme Court condoned this expansion when it held not only that a fast-food building and its decor and colors could be protected but also that the distinctiveness that consumers recognized could be inherent in the package as well as acquired through secondary meaning.

DON'T *overlook the protection for a new package or product design under the concept of trade dress—an expansion of the trademark laws.*

Trade dress is now firmly recognized as a form of protection for either a package that has acquired distinctiveness or a package that was inherently distinctive upon adoption. At the same time, the concept was also spreading to the product itself. That is, could the shape of the product itself be recognizable by consumers as stemming from a single source?

It was here that the concept ran into a bramble bush of difficulty. For example, the shape of a product, if functional, could be protected by a utility patent (see **#49**). When the patent expired, the right to make that shape was supposed to enter the public domain, free for all competitors to use. But a trademark or trade dress lasts forever, or at least as long as the public recognizes the word or feature as a source of origin indicator. Here was a clash. Not surprisingly, the court limited product trade dress to nonfunctional features, including any feature that allowed the product to be made more cheaply or with higher quality. Still, there was a conflict with design patents and copyrights on visual arts. So the courts expanded the functionality protection for free commerce by adopting the oxymoronic expression *aesthetic functionality*. In other words, if the feature was adopted primarily as an aesthetic enhancement to the product, rather than an indication of source, it was functional. The lesson to be learned is that if you hire an industrial designer to create a unique shape for a product—a shape that others do not absolutely need in order to compete—and you can show that the shape has been recognized by the consuming public as an indication of your product, you can protect that shape.

<hr>

74

DO *obtain copyright protection for the works you create—it is inexpensive, long lasting, and easy to obtain.*

A copyright comes into existence when the *work* (a term used to refer to the thing) is fixed in a tangible medium—in other words, printed on paper, recorded on computer memory, captured on videotape, or in some manner "stored" so that others may have access to it. It is not necessary to apply to any government agency to create or preserve the copyright. Since March 1989 (when the United States joined the worldwide Berne convention) it is no longer necessary to place a copyright notice on the work. However, both registration and applying a notice are very valuable, as explained below. A copyright, when the author is a natural person, lasts for fifty years plus the life of an author. If the creation is made while employed, copyright belongs to the employer (see **#75**) and lasts for a total of seventy-five or one hundred years.

Unlike a patent, a copyrighted work need not be unique, novel, or inventive. It is only necessary that the work be independently created and embody a very minimal amount of creativity. Copyrights may be sold (assigned) or licensed.

You will be pleased to know that registering your copyright is the best bargain you will ever receive from the federal government. The filing fee is $20 currently. Nor do you need to employ an attorney to obtain the registration; the copyright office (a part of the Library of Congress) provides forms that are a lot less complicated to fill out than your tax return (and much more fun). You can reach the office through Washington, D.C., information.

DON'T *fail to register your copyright for maximum protection and to use a copyright notice even though not technically required.*

The key reason for applying for a copyright registration is that you may not bring suit on the copyright unless it is registered (or registration has been applied for). However, this may be ten years after the work was created. In the application you state that the year of creation dates back ten years. The problem with waiting is that when you sue, unless you registered within five years of creation, you may not collect statutory damages and attorney fees if you win. This is serious; copyright litigation, like all litigation (see **#46**) is monstrously expensive. In many cases the damages are not large even though the competitive injury is great. Since the cost of obtaining the copyright is nominal, there is no excuse for not registering. Don't be lazy.

The importance of the notice is twofold. If you sue, you may collect damages for all infringing copies sold or distributed within the prior three years, if and only if your work was published with a copyright notice or the infringer had actual notice. Actual notice often does not occur until you become aware of the infringement and send the infringer a cease and desist letter. By then, many copies may have been sold—you cannot collect for these. However, the copyright notice on your work is a substitute for actual notice. Second, all works published before 1989 were required to have a notice on every copy (with some forgiveness for omission from a small number, etc.). "Published" is a tricky concept. Don't assume that an older work was not published before 1989 and, therefore, the notice is now not required. Don't copy the nonnotice-bearing work of others, either, without a search. Use of the notice also shows that you have not abandoned the copyright.

DO *appreciate the scope of the types of works that may be copyrighted.*

The eight categories of works covered by the copyright laws are set out directly in a statute. Some are of primary interest to the entertainment industry—motion pictures, dramatic works, musical works, and sound recordings. But in this age of the digital revolution, it becomes more difficult to speak of the entertainment industry since many companies create and sell sound, image, and graphics products and services. The Internet (see #137) is greatly changing the manner of conducting business. Information published is more critical to success. That information can be protected by copyright. Even older technologies such as training films, slide presentations, and videotaped stories can and should be protected.

Pictorial, graphic, and sculptural works form a broad category of materials that are copyrighted by toy manufacturers, photographers, jewelers, graphic designers, and many others. In addition to registering products that may be copyrightable, you should also copyright all of your advertising and packaging materials. Some of the marketing materials may be classified as literary works, rather than pictorial or graphic works. Don't fret about choosing the wrong form; the copyright office is very helpful and will tell you the proper classification. Don't worry about copyrighting the same image in different contexts (for example, the same product picture on a package, brochure, manual, etc.) as long as there is a difference in each work; and the difference need only be minimal.

DON'T *hire a freelance programmer, photographer, architect, and so on, without a contract that covers ownership of any copyrighted work.*

Because of the influence of the entertainment industry, the copyright law has a unique provision with respect to works made by a person hired to create the work, commonly referred to as the "work-for-hire" doctrine. If you employ, for example, a computer programmer, any copyrighted program created by that employee on the job is owned by you entirely from the moment that the copyright comes into being. There is no need for an assignment as with an invention. When you file for a copyright registration, you will identify the author as the company, not the person who actually created the work. The life of the copyright will then be seventy-five years from the date of publication or one hundred years from the date of creation, whichever is shorter.

If, as in the case of a freelance programmer (or photographer, writer, etc.), the person is not hired but is a temporary or contract employee (see **#104**), the work-for-hire concept is somewhat vague. It is now clear from a recent Supreme Court case that an independent contractor is not covered by the work-for-hire doctrine. The only safe course to use with a freelance person is to have a written contract. Not only does the work-for-hire doctrine require a writing, it applies only to certain types of works. The agreement should provide that the work is being made for hire, but if the doctrine does not apply, then the freelancer's rights are assigned to you. The reason for using the work-for-hire provision as the first choice is the possible longer life of the copyright—of no consequence probably for software.

76

DO *understand exclusive rights obtained with your copyright.*

The copyright act is explicit in the exclusive rights that are granted to the copyright owner. These include the exclusive right to reproduce copies, distribute copies (or phono records), create derivative works, perform the work publicly (if it is performable), and display the work publicly. A derivative work is most easily understood as a translation, but it encompasses a wide variety of other works based on an original work, such as abridgements, annotations, new editions, and condensations. While a compilation is similar and is also one of the exclusive rights of the author, it is technically an aggregation of previous works, copyrighted or in the public domain, to which some coordination, arrangement, or selection is applied. Of course, if you are preparing a compilation and one or more works are copyrighted, you must obtain permission from the copyright owner.

A unique right is given by the copyright act, almost unknown in any other branch of the law. If a copyright owner grants any rights to another, even an exclusive right, the owner (or his or her heirs) may terminate the agreement. This right lasts for five years beginning in the thirty-fifth year. No matter what language is used in the agreement, the right cannot be extinguished. Nor can a copyright be seized by the IRS or a bankrupt trustee (unless the copyright was given as collateral for a loan). Copyrights may be licensed just like any other intellectual property, and the license often breaks up the various rights mentioned above with only one right to a particular party; for example, the right to perform, but not to reproduce copies.

DON'T *rely on fair use in copying portions of the copyrighted work of another unless you have considered the four factors used by the courts.*

All the rights of a copyright owner discussed previously are subject to one broad exception: fair use. Everyone understands that taking a small snippet of material from a copyrighted work is permissible, but the question is always—how much? There is no quantitative answer to that question. Nor is it clear when any material may be used at all. The act provides four factors to be considered by a court in deciding if a use is fair. The courts have held that the most important factor is what effect the use will have on the market for the owner's work, or the value of the owner's work. The second most important factor is whether the use is for commercial purposes. The courts are reasonably lenient when the use is by a nonprofit establishment, but in the area of publishing technical articles for a select group of readers, it has been held that copying an entire article and making it available to researchers is not fair use.

The nature of the work is also taken into account. Works that are particularly useful for education or are used in a political campaign are subject to more fair use. Finally, the amount of the material taken is considered, but there is no magic percentage that is permissible. And incidentally, there is an old wives tale that copyright infringement may be avoided if only X percent is used. That is flatly false. Infringement occurs when one has access to the work and the infringing work is substantially similar to the protected expression. What constitutes substantial similarity is a fact question in each case. Formulas are not used.

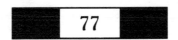

77

DO *protect your copyright, even by bringing suit if necessary.*

Your copyright is an asset of your business. It is valuable and provides you with a competitive advantage. But it may be necessary for you to bring suit to protect that advantage. The first step is to analyze the competitive situation and determine if a suit would produce the desired result. In other words, just because a competitor has copied some part of a copyrighted work that you own, a suit is warranted only if the relief that the court would give would reestablish your competitive advantage. That seems obvious, but egos oftentimes get in the way of that rational decision. If the copyrighted work is a product of yours, whether a book, research report, doll, game, piece of jewelry, or software program, it is much more likely that a suit would restore your competitive advantage. If it is an advertisement, slogan, product manual, package, instruction sheet, or brochure, it may never pay to sue. The reason for copyrighting the latter is that ordinary competitors will usually avoid your copyright, thereby causing them to expend the funds to create their own work. That is, in itself, a worthwhile purpose.

Once you make up your mind that the infringement must be stopped for economic reasons, you are advised to send a cease and desist letter. Calling your ownership of a copyright to the attention of the infringer may achieve the result of causing the infringer to stop. Many infringements are innocent mistakes. Drawing the attention of upper management to the situation may cure it. If not, you may choose to go further.

DON'T *sue on your copyright unless you can prove ownership of a valid copyright, and access and substantial similarity of the accused work.*

When you sue, you must prove two facts: You own a valid registered copyright, and the party sued has copied your work. The former is proved by showing that you applied for and received a copyright registration. The certificate that you received is proof of that ownership and validity. However, the infringer may try to attack the validity by showing that the work is so simple or trivial that it does not warrant protection. Few copyright cases involve the issue of copyrightability. The reason is that the standard is so low. Any nontrivial original creation qualifies. So long as you did not copy from another work (whether or not copyrighted), you will prevail. If you are the author, and are so identified in the certificate, ownership is established. This, too, is usually not an issue unless the other party claims they were involved in the creation.

Proving something was copied is the gist of most copyright cases. This is a two-step process. First you must prove access, that is, the infringer bought, saw, reviewed, heard, or at least had the opportunity to access the work. Then there is the major question—is there substantial similarity between the two works? The test is whether an ordinary observer would believe that the infringer copied from the original copyrighted work. Experts are often used to dissect the two works and show the similarities and differences. Since the results of this dissection could depend on which side hired the expert, this is only an aid and the jury is eventually responsible for coming to its conclusion based on its own observation of similarity or difference.

CHAPTER

5

COMMERCIAL
TRANSACTIONS

DO *distinguish between the powers and the rights of a person acting on behalf of a business to bind the entity.*

To fully understand the dangers inherent in partnerships and LLCs, it is necessary to be able to distinguish rights from powers. This is often confused by even very savvy businesspeople.

Consider the problem from the perspective of a third party who is about to do business (i.e., enter into a contract) with a corporation, partnership, or an LLC. How can that third party know that the person who is about to sign the contract has the power to do so? This has nothing to do with corporation, partnership, or LLC laws; it is the *law of agency* that controls. If a person is carrying on business on behalf of an entity in a usual way, the business will be bound, unless the third party knew that person did not have the authority to bind the business. The entity cannot *later* state that the person who signed lacked the authority to do so. The reason for the rule is twofold: The entity could have prevented the confusion in the first place, and carrying on business would be difficult without the rule.

As noted in **#19,** in an LLC (just as in a corporation or a partnership) the power of a member or manager to bind the LLC may be limited by agreement, but it cannot bind outsiders for the reasons stated above. If there are many members in an LLC, it would be dangerous to elect a member-managed structure.

DON'T *accept the authority of a person representing a business without investigation.*

While it is true that a third party is protected by agency law in relying on the apparent authority of a person to bind an entity, you should exercise care to protect yourself.

In general, the power to bind a corporation can be assumed if the person signs as an officer, because it is well known that the shareholders delegate power to the board of directors who then appoint officers with broad powers. It remains true that an officer may have limited powers by board decision, but the officer title is safe to rely on, unless the transaction is fundamental—sale of the corporation, for example. When unsure, you can ask for a certified resolution of the board (banks typically require such documentation when opening a new corporate bank account) that states the scope of authority of the officer.

For a partnership, it is usually sufficient to ask for the signature of a partner. Again, if the transaction is fundamental, you would be well advised to ask for the signatures of *all* the partners.

In an LLC, you will need to know if the LLC is member- or manager-managed. If the former, you may rely on the signature of a member. If the latter, you may rely on the signature of the manager; but not on the signature of a member, anymore than you could rely on the signature of a stockholder to bind General Motors.

79

DO *understand bankruptcy basics as a defensive measure in doing business.*

Bankruptcy is a daunting subject. The bankruptcy laws, which are federal rather than state laws, are complex. Worse, the rules are known to a relatively small coterie of lawyers who specialize in the field. Still worse, there is a clubiness to the lawyers who practice in this field because of the frequent appointment of these lawyers as referees, receivers, and other quasi-officers of the court. And if all that isn't bad enough, bankruptcy involves some abstruse accounting practices and rules that few understand.

If you want to read what a nightmare bankruptcy may become, try *Bankruptcy: A Feast for Lawyers,* (M. Evans & Co., Inc., New York). It will convince you to stay as far away from bankruptcy court and lawyers as possible.

Nevertheless, there it is—an unavoidable feature of the business landscape. So some familiarity is necessary. Let's start with the observation that personal and business bankruptcy are covered by the same general laws, but we are concerned here only with business-type bankruptcy. Bankruptcy is either voluntary or involuntary. In other words, if you are in financial difficulty, you may file a petition with the bankruptcy court for protection against creditors. The court will immediately stay any actions or threats against you, for collection of a late payment, for example, giving you time to assess the situation while remaining in business. This breathing spell is a chief feature of bankruptcy.

DON'T *become involved in an involuntary bankruptcy if you can avoid it.*

You may be forced into bankruptcy by your creditors. It takes three creditors, who are each owed an unsecured amount that is fixed (i.e., not contingent), in excess of $5,000. If you have less than twelve creditors, involuntary bankruptcy may be instituted by one or two persons. These creditors do not include employees to whom you owe wages. These creditors must also allege that you are generally not able pay your debts. Not a single or several instances of nonpayment, but as a matter of course. Or, if you have made an assignment for the benefit of creditors, this is a sufficient ground for involuntary bankruptcy. (An *assignment for the benefit of creditors* is a state-law remedy for a business in financial difficulty; it essentially allows you to reach an agreement with all your creditors to pay your debts, in full or in part, over a scheduled period, in return for their agreement to forego court collection of the debt. It is always less costly, but it is not often useful because of the lack of ability to reach a compromise among aggressive creditors.)

Once you are in bankruptcy, either voluntarily or involuntarily, your assets are effectively transferred from you to a bankrupt estate. It includes all your interests in property, such as all real and personal property as well as contract rights, rents, profit, and almost everything else that you can think of. Moreover, any future profit is part of the estate. Most important, you cannot avoid this result. If you enter into a contract that provides that if you enter bankruptcy the property must be returned, that provision is voidable.

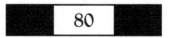

80

DO *respect the enormous power of a bankrupt trustee to avoid fraudulent transactions.*

One of the powers of the bankrupt trustee to treat all of the creditors equally is to avoid any transfer that may give preference to one creditor over another. Nominally, this power extends backward one year. A fraudulent transfer occurs if there is either fraudulent intent or a combination of (1) less than fair value for the transfer and (2) insolvency at the time of transfer, only a small amount left after the transfer, or after the transfer the debtor intended to incur debts beyond the ability to pay. A fraudulent transfer includes an interference with a creditor's right to an unhindered delay. There are also provisions in the law to go even further beyond the one year limit if certain events occur. Additionally, the Uniform Fraudulent Transfer Act that has been enacted in many states may also be used to assist a defrauded creditor.

Aside from a fraudulent transfer, a trustee may also avoid any transfer that was a preference, regardless of whether it was fraudulent. Such transfers, however, are only avoidable if within ninety days of the petition. There are several requirements to avoid. The debtor must have been insolvent at the time of the preferential transfer. The debt discharged must have preexisted, that is, the transfer could not be for goods or services that were performed at the time of the transfer. Third, the creditor must have been better off than he or she would have been if he or she had participated in a Chapter 7 distribution (i.e., it must have really been a preference).

DON'T *fail to consider some other bankrupt trustee rights.*

There are a number of exceptions to the preference rule that recognize legitimate transactions which enable lenders to continue to keep the debtor afloat while not jeopardizing their loan as a preference for some past consideration, for example, an earlier loan that the lender is attempting to bail out. Another approved transaction that is unavoidable is the right to setoff. The setoff must involve mutual claims that arose before the petition was filed, and the creditor's claim is not otherwise disallowed for other reasons.

Still another power that the trustee has is the right to reject, assume, or assign an executory contract. An *executory contract* under contract law means a material obligation remains to be performed by one party. But an even narrower view is applied under the bankruptcy law. Nevertheless, the power can be disturbing. Suppose you are midway through a blanket contract for goods and the buyer goes bankrupt. That does not mean that the buyer is unable to pay all of its debts; you may be willing to deliver, particularly if the goods are tailored to the bankrupt's needs. But the trustee rejects the contract, not because the bankrupt does not need the goods, but because it can purchase the same goods elsewhere at a lower cost. There is nothing you can do.

Nor do you have much more protection with a forfeiture clause that declares that the contract is terminated if one party enters bankruptcy. These are generally unenforceable.

DO *participate in the distribution of the bankrupt estate if you are a creditor.*

As a creditor of the bankrupt, you will be notified to file any claim that you may have against the bankrupt. A *claim* is any right to payment from the debtor. It does not matter whether the claim is secured (such as a mortgage), unsecured (an *unsecured claim* is one that is on open credit, i.e., there was no security given, such as an interest in the goods that could be recorded with a UCC-1 financing statement), contingent, unliquidated, or not yet due. In other words, the concept of a claim is extremely broad. In deciding whether to file, file. In a Chapter 7 (straight bankruptcy or liquidation), you have ninety days from the date of the creditors' first meeting. In a reorganization under Chapter 11, the court sets a date.

After your claim is filed it must be allowed by the trustee. There are eight grounds for disallowing a claim. But most are brought on the grounds that the claim is unenforceable; the debtor outside of bankruptcy had a defense. These defenses are usually the same defenses that a person has to a suit based on a contract. But there are some limitations to the defenses that are ordinarily recognized in a contract action. For example, an employee claim for wrongful termination may not be for more than one year's salary or wages plus prebankruptcy salary and expenses. Similarly, there are limitations on the amount of rent and property taxes a landlord may recover (the limit is the amount of the bankrupt property owner's equity).

DON'T *be deceived into believing that all creditors in a bankrupt proceeding are on an equal footing.*

After all the claims are allowed or disallowed and the estate is ready for distribution, there is a pecking order by which claims are paid. First come all secured claims to the extent that the collateral value exceeds the amount of the claim. If it is less, the claim is split; the amount covered by the collateral is treated as a secured claim, the remainder is treated as an ordinary unsecured claim. In addition to having priority, a secured-claim creditor may be given immunity from the automatic stay and may proceed to enforce the lien, or may wait until the collateral is liquidated by the trustee and obtain payment directly out of the proceeds of the sale of the collateral.

After the secured claims are paid, the unsecured creditors line up in the following order, generally. First, all administrative expenses of the bankruptcy proceeding (including attorney and accountant fees) are paid. Second are claims that arose after the petition in bankruptcy was filed, if incurred in the ordinary course of the business. Third are wages, salaries, sick pay, and so on, but only up to $2,000 per person and these must be incurred within ninety days of the petition (or cessation of the business, if earlier). Fourth are employee benefit plans. Fifth relates only to farmers. Sixth are deposits (for example, a rent deposit) made by individuals up to $900. Seventh are unsecured tax claims (otherwise, government claims are treated the same as any other creditor). In Chapter 11 proceedings, the order may be different. See **#82**.

82

DO *use Chapter 11 of the bankruptcy laws to save your viable business.*

You may commence voluntary bankruptcy proceedings to seek to rehabilitate your business. Generally speaking, courts are favorable to the Chapter 11 reorganization over the Chapter 7 (straight bankruptcy) liquidation. It is not even necessary that you be insolvent or that you are unable to pay your debts as they mature. At any time in a Chapter 11 case, you may convert to Chapter 7 (and your creditors have a right to force the conversion under certain conditions—such as a bad-faith filing or if the Chapter 11 case was involuntary).

In straight bankruptcy, there is a trustee appointed almost immediately after the proceedings begin. Chapter 11 is different in that you become a "debtor in possession" and you have all the powers of a trustee. However, the court may appoint a trustee to take your place in the event of fraud, dishonesty, incompetence, or gross mismanagement. All, including you (the debtor), your management, and the board of directors are completely replaced.

However, when the debtor stays in possession, it is the committee of creditors that exercises control over the debtor and the whole process. This feature of a Chapter 11 case has been criticized because in smaller cases the committee may be insufficiently interested to properly monitor the debtor's activities. The committee generally is formed of the seven largest creditors who are willing to serve. But the court may make changes upon request.

DON'T *give up your right in bankruptcy to operate the business and to propose your own plan.*

In a Chapter 11 bankruptcy, the crucial early question is whether the debtor (you) should continue operations. The debtor will be allowed to do so unless the committee (usually) petitions the court to terminate operations. The court may then do so, or convert the case to Chapter 7, or dismiss the case entirely. If you continue to operate the business, there are usually disputes between you and the committee regarding the actions mentioned above that are within the power of the trustee—selling unproductive assets, using a secured party's collateral, borrowing money to finance operations, and the denial or acceptance of uncompleted contracts.

The heart of Chapter 11 is the reorganization plan. You have an edge here: for 120 days you have the exclusive right to file a plan. Creditors can shorten this period only by having a trustee appointed in your place. But this latter power is usually sufficient to keep you realistic. In certain cases, the creditors and the debtor work out a plan before the petition is filed. If it is fair and equitable, as the statute requires, this plan will be accepted by the court and the whole proceeding may be very brief. The plan itself may be virtually any business arrangement that may be conceived of except for several protections (see **#83**) that are specified in the bankruptcy law itself.

As a *creditor,* you do not have to file a claim in a Chapter 11 proceeding since the debtor's scheduling of the claim is sufficient (of course, if omitted or in error, you may file a claim).

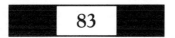

83

DO *use the Chapter 11 bankruptcy reorganization plan to give a fresh start to your business.*

As indicated at **#82**, the plan in a Chapter 11 bankruptcy proceeding is the critical element and you have the opportunity to submit the first plan. What is in a plan? There are few mandatory provisions, and the creditors and you can work out almost anything you like. The mandatories include a division of all claims into classes and a statement of which classes are "impaired" and how the plan deals with such impaired creditors; equal treatment for all the creditors within one class; a plan of implementation, that is, sale of assets, accepting or rejecting contracts, merger with another company, and so on; recognition of the priority claims; and certain limits on the postdischarge voting rights of security holders.

The classification of creditors is extremely important in attaining confirmation (approval by the court) because each class votes separately to accept the plan, with a majority controlling. If a debt is to be discharged in full, that class is unimpaired. Thus, a plan that can narrow a creditor into a single class and pay that creditor off in full can prevent a challenge of the confirmation. Small claims are usually classified together and discharged for cash on confirmation. Theoretically, unmatured and matured claims, contingent and liquidated claims, and no interest and high interest rate claims can be classified together. However, claims with different priorities (see **#81**) must be separate.

DON'T *develop a reorganization plan in your Chapter 11 bankruptcy proceeding that won't be accepted by the classes.*

As noted previously, classifying the creditors to obtain acceptance is a key to confirmation. The process of acceptance of each class is too complicated to be explained in full now, but here are a few important points. First, you must submit adequate information for use by the creditors and this must be approved by the court. Then the vote must be by a majority, but also two-thirds of the amount of the claims of that class must accept. So you can see that structuring the classes may be the difference between success and failure.

If one class will not accept, short of preparing a new plan, can anything be done? Yes. Congress appreciated that a class could frustrate a reasonable plan for selfish reasons. Thus, we have the *cram down* confirmation. This requires passing three tests. First, is there acceptance? If not, is that class unimpaired? If so, does the plan discriminate unfairly and is it fair and equitable? The latter, of course, is a veritable hornet's nest. It apparently embodies a rule that precedes the present bankruptcy code that to be fair and equitable means the senior creditors must receive priority over any junior creditor. Of course, if a senior creditor class accepts a plan that provides for some consideration to go to junior creditors, even though the senior debt is not completely satisfied, the fair and equitable test for those senior creditors does not arise (and note that only a majority of those creditors need vote for acceptance). There is much room for wheeling and dealing in a Chapter 11 plan to attain your rehabilitation.

DO *adopt a simple purchase order form for your business that suits your needs.*

Too often a small starting business obtains a blank order form from some stationery house to use as its purchase order form, or it copies from its last employer. The former is too simple because it rarely specifies the terms on which you are agreeing to purchase. The latter is usually too complex—having been adopted to fulfill the myriad variety of purchasing done by a large company, but not meeting the specific needs of your business. Why is this even important? Because if you do not control the terms of your purchase order, the seller's terms will prevail and they may not be pleasant. As explained at **#130,** a contract must have definite terms for it to be binding on both parties, and a purchase order, once accepted, is no more than a simple contract. There is some mistaken notion by most small-business people that a contract must be a multipage document that has at least two "whereas" clauses and one "witnesseth." Of course that is not true. When you send or call in an order for a new machine or a sandwich, it is an offer to purchase and if the seller responds by delivery or a call accepting your order, you are in a contract. What are the terms? That is what the purchase order form is all about.

You will undoubtedly focus on the front side of the purchase order for price, quantity, credit terms, and delivery. But what about late delivery? Or breach of warranty? Or nonconforming goods? Or a change in quantity or other terms? That is why you have a reverse side.

DON'T *pass up the opportunity to control the purchase transaction.*

Consider a typical purchase transaction. Your purchasing agent (maybe you) sees a widget in a catalog that has a description and a price that meets your requirements. You call and check availability. Satisfied, you decide to send a purchase order. If you send it to the seller with an attached acknowledgment copy, and the seller signs and returns it, you have a contract on your terms. Suppose you do not have an acknowledgment copy. The seller delivers without any acknowledgment but with its standard invoice. If you have terms on the reverse side of your purchase order, the purchase has been made on your terms. If you are dealing with a large organization, it may send its own acknowledgment (with terms that are favorable to it, of course). If you do not respond, and you rarely will unless the transaction is very large, the seller's acknowledgment terms prevail. This is the transaction that will set the terms, and you have lost control. You can jawbone the large supplier, but your lawyer will tell you that if push comes to shove, the terms are against you. How do you avoid such a predicament?

A good purchase order form has some basic protection. You can cancel if the order is late. You can threaten the seller with the clear language of the form. You do not need to rely on whether delivery is material and therefore a breach of the agreement. You can also add a clause that allows you, within limits, to change the quantity of the order. You can protect yourself in the event that the goods infringe a third party's patent by requiring indemnification. There are other advantages that you can gain. See #85.

85

DO *include terms in your purchase order that will assist you in any future dispute with a supplier.*

Before addressing the type of terms that you should include in your purchase order form, you must first assure that the terms will prevail over the terms of the seller. See #87. You do this by including an introductory paragraph that specifies that any acceptance of the purchase order is limited to the terms and conditions of the purchase order and that any additional or different terms in the seller's acknowledgment or invoice are excluded. This prevents the seller from sending an acknowledgment that has different terms, which, more than likely, will not be read by you and will, to the extent that they modify or add to the purchase order terms, control the transaction. In other words, you must not only have the last word, but you must include in your last word that you will ignore any attempt by the seller to have the last word. Then you must state that if the seller ships without any prior acknowledgment, the act of shipping shall constitute an acceptance; and that if the goods arrive with a shipping bill that modifies or adds terms, your acceptance of the goods does not constitute acknowledgment of the seller's additional or modified terms.

Now you can select the proper terms to control the purchase transaction. Some terms that you should consider are warranty, delivery, shipping, changes, inspection, patent indemnity, indemnification, proprietary information, buyer's property, termination, assignment, and so on.

DON'T *let warranty and delivery terms in your purchasing transactions be controlled by the seller.*

Once you have control over the terms of a purchasing transaction, choose the terms that are most beneficial to your particular business. Let's say you have several sources for a certain product that is critical to your production and you do not wish to carry any more inventory than necessary. Include a delivery term that states clearly that if a shipment is late, by even one day (time is of the essence), you may cancel the order or defer the delivery verbally. You may wish to state that if delivery is late, the seller will be obligated to deliver by expedited method without additional cost to you. Remember that there is no magic language to obtain the legal effect, so express what you need in the best English you are capable of writing. Clarity is everything.

You likely made your purchase decision based on a catalog or data sheet that spelled out the specification and performance capability of the product. You may have received by fax drawings of a component that were critical in your decision to choose this vendor. If so, capture the promises of that material in your purchase order by stating that all specifications, drawings, and other data submitted by the seller are expressly incorporated into the purchase order and that the seller expressly warrants that the goods will conform to the data. There are a number of warranties that the law supplies without any requirement for an express statement in the purchase order. Often the seller will attempt to modify these warranties (to the extent allowed under state law). By reciting them in the purchase order you can preserve them, intact.

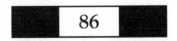

DO *reserve the right to change terms in your purchase order and to terminate in the event of breach of the seller.*

A not uncommon occurrence when you are purchasing goods is a change of plans after the order is sent. Technically, if the seller has not acknowledged your order, nor delivered, nor commenced production if the goods were custom, you can change your order at will since no contract has been formed. But the seller may very strenuously argue that if the goods already have been sent, even though you have not received them yet, there is a contract and you must pay for them. This potential hassle may be avoided if your purchase order recites that you have the right to cancel or change some of the delivery terms at will. However, you cannot reserve the right to cancel the entire order. If you do, there is no contract. If you do want the goods you are out of luck, because the purchase order terms prevent you from enforcing the order to obtain the goods. So the right to change must be limited to changes of less than an entire cancellation, for example, a change in the number of the units ordered, the time or place of delivery, or similar terms.

Of course, you may, and should, reserve the right to terminate the order in its entirety if the seller fails to perform in the manner required in the purchase order (i.e., breaches). You may claim the right to terminate upon financial insolvency of the seller or bankruptcy (but see **#80**). Be sure to reserve all your other legal rights, in addition to termination, or you may be held to have elected termination as your sole remedy for the breach; in other words, you still want the right to sue and collect damages, if any, in addition to termination.

DON'T *accidentally give away proprietary rights in ordering goods and services from vendors.*

Your purchase order should protect any proprietary and confidential information given to a seller or supplier of services, particularly if you are developing new products. Say something like: "All specifications, drawings, data, or prototypes delivered by Buyer to Seller are the property of Buyer and Seller agrees not to disclose such information to any other person nor to use such information for any purpose other than the performance of this order." This should not be considered an alternative to stamping or otherwise marking your drawings with a notice of confidentiality. In a theft of trade secrets case the more evidence that the seller was aware of your claim to proprietary rights, the stronger the case.

In this area of proprietary rights, you may also wish to consider the use of a patent indemnity clause. As mentioned in **#49,** a patent owner may sue anyone who makes, *uses,* or sells the patented product. There may be strategic reasons for the patent owner to sue you, alone or with the seller, to stop the infringement. You are not the real object of the suit, but to become embroiled at all will be very expensive. You can avoid this entanglement by providing for patent indemnity in the purchase order. The language may be brief: "Seller agrees to indemnify and save Buyer harmless from, and to defend at its own expense (and to reimburse any legal expenses incurred by Buyer), any claims asserted against Buyer for the goods sold by Seller to Buyer under this order based on infringement of any patent or violation of any other proprietary rights." The key is to include the obligation of the seller to pay your legal costs.

87

DO *understand the varied circumstances used in different industries in the formation of a sales contract.*

In **#84, #85,** and **#86,** we discussed the sales transaction from the point of view of the buyer, that is, a purchasing transaction. As the seller, you have your own opportunity to control the transaction. The difficulty here is attempting to draw generalizations that will be useful to you because the practices in different industries are varied. The manner in which the sales transaction is entered into and consequently the documents used vary widely. You must survey these first so that you may place yourself in the right context.

In large purchases, there will be a negotiated sales contract. There is nothing special here from the point of view of protecting your position except that many of the terms will be drawn specific to the particular transaction. But much will be common to all sales transactions, too. The contract will be used because the seriousness of the money involved will demand a closer look at the standard terms and conditions contained in the parties' purchase orders and sales forms. These contracts can run fifty and one hundred pages with a boatload of exhibits incorporated into the agreement. Also common in large transactions, and in many industries for even medium-sized purchases, are the RFQ (request for quotation) or RFB (request for bid) sent out by the purchaser and responded to by the seller with a quote or bid, usually in writing. The purchaser sets a date for response that is, to maintain fairness and legitimacy, strictly enforced. Bids are opened and the submitter with the best terms and conditions wins a contract. At this time either the contract is negotiated or a purchase order is executed.

DON'T *allow the manner in which the sales contract is formed deter you from controlling the transaction terms.*

In addition to the negotiated contract and the RFQ/bid processes of entering into a sales contract, a simpler method commonly used is the issuance of a purchase order by the buyer and the return of an acknowledgment by the seller. Of course, millions of sales transactions take place daily based on purchase orders that are filled without any acknowledgment of the order. If the purchase order is larger, or especially if the order is for a large quantity to be delivered over a prolonged period of time, the parties may want to make it clear that the order, while not immediately fulfilled, remains a binding obligation for future delivery. This allows the seller to plan production and the buyer to be assured of the delivery of components when and as required. The complication here is that either party may supply the acknowledgment form—with terms that favor the preparer. The buyer may include an acknowledgment form as a part of the purchase order—a multipart form. Or the seller may use its own form making reference to the purchase order. In either event, when the acknowledgment is signed it forms a sales contract on the terms there recited. (If a purchase order is sent and the seller responds with delivery, rather than an acknowledgment, the contract is immediately executed.)

In other businesses, the salesperson may carry a sales order form when he or she visits the buyer—common in the sale to retail establishments. The form provides all the terms and conditions other than product identification, quantity, price, and delivery. These are filled out at the time of the sales call. The buyer signs the form and the sales contract is made on the terms there specified. Terms for all these types of transactions are discussed in **#88.**

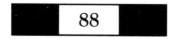

88

DO *attempt to maintain control of the sales transaction terms by using the right acceptance language in your sales form.*

As noted in **#84,** the control over the buy-sell transaction is a game of one-upmanship. If either side uses a form with terms and conditions, and the other party submits no form at all, obviously the party with the terms will prevail. (If you are wondering what terms apply if the entire transaction is verbal, there is a detailed set of rules generally referred to as the UCC, meaning Uniform Commercial Code, that apply. Certain terms are implied by this law if they are missing in the verbal description of the contract. Other rules apply to determine which terms of which party control.) If both parties have used forms (say, the buyer submits a purchase order and the seller submits an acknowledgment) there is a battle of forms. In **#85,** the acceptance terms the buyer should use for control were described. What can the seller do?

The best that you can do as the seller is to include a clause in your form (sales order, acknowledgment, or bid) that states that buyer's acceptance is expressly conditioned on the assent of the buyer to the terms in your form. If your form is signed by the buyer with this term intact, then your terms will control. If the buyer does not sign your form, no contract is formed by the exchange of forms at that point in the process. If you include an additional term stating that acceptance of delivery constitutes an acceptance of your terms, then acceptance of delivery will form a contract based on the conduct of the parties on your terms. This is the best you can do as the seller.

DON'T *assume that the prospective buyer understands the conditions of the prices stated— spell them out in your sales order form.*

While we ordinarily assume that there will be no issue with respect to price in a sales transaction, this is not always the case. A common problem is the point at which the price applies. FOB means Free On Board, that is, the seller will load the goods on the common carrier vehicle, and any further freight charges, duties, excise taxes, and so on, will be borne by the buyer. In other words it is a way of specifying who pays the freight (i.e., whether it is included in the price quoted). But the most serious pricing problem likely to arise is the delivery over an extended period. This is particularly true where the economy is highly inflationary. A clever buyer could lock in today's price by submitting a purchase order for delivery over the next twelve or even twenty-four months.

The seller must be protected in the scheduled delivery transaction by limiting the period of the delivery to a term that is within the foreseeable range of stable material prices. If not, the seller should add a cost escalator based on some index that can be easily obtained. A common instance when this type of provision is included is where the product includes a material component such as gold, which is both volatile and a large-cost component. Adjusting prices to the change in cost of gold at the time of delivery is simply sensible. And always, the seller who quotes prices should make them subject to change until the purchase order is accepted or perhaps agree to hold the prices firm for a set period of time (as short as possible) from the date of the quote.

89

DO *put into your sales order or other sales form provisions against changes and termination by the buyer, as well as delivery terms.*

The seller should consider the effects of a change in the terms of the order by the buyer. Should *any* change be allowed? Some changes under certain circumstances? You must look at your business and the manner in which your industry operates to decide what is an acceptable change clause. Perhaps the easiest way to handle the problem is to make any change subject to the permission of the seller. Then you can evaluate the change under the existing circumstances. One likely response to a request to change by the buyer, after a contract has been formed, is to reconsider the price. Similarly, you may want to consider a provision against termination without penalty. The problem is making the penalty large enough at the outset to warrant pursuit after the breach. Courts always react harshly to penalty clauses.

Delivery is another area of concern that can be treated in the sales form. Perhaps most important is to make clear that promised delivery dates are estimates and are not guarantees. You should attempt to maintain the right to deliver in installments and to tie this to the payment obligation so that the buyer may not withhold payment until all deliveries are complete. You should also add a provision that allows you to allocate production between existing orders in the event that production cannot keep up with demand or is interrupted by a failure of a supplier. The sales order form should include a paragraph stating that you retain the right to withhold delivery in the event that the buyer is in arrears in the payment for deliveries. This right relies on the right to make installment deliveries.

DON'T *overlook warranties—express and implied—in your sales documents.*

Warranting your goods is not a matter of choice. Regardless of what you say or do not say, the law fastens a warranty on the seller of goods. There are express warranties (those you specifically state) and implied warranties. The latter may be implied in fact, that is, the circumstances surrounding the negotiation and transaction show that the seller promised and the buyer expected, although not verbally or in writing, a certain performance. Or it may be implied in law (i.e., regardless of the conduct of the buyer and seller, the legislature has decided that the sales transaction should require at least some minimum level of performance).

It is common for the seller to make an express warranty for a limited period of time as to defects in material and workmanship and to performance within the specification. The time period is almost entirely dependent on the custom in the industry, although a manufacturer may exceed industry standards as a sales promotion or a statement of confidence in its reliability. There are two implied warranties of significance in law: the implied warranty of merchantability and the implied warranty of fitness for a particular purpose. (See **#90** for a discussion of the scope of disclaimer that the seller may assert to limit these implied warranties.) The former means that the goods must meet the reasonable expectations of buyers of this particular type of product. The latter says that if the buyer tells you the intended purpose and you say that the product will suit that need, it must.

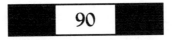

DO *limit your warranty exposure by proper terms in your sales order forms.*

As discussed in **#89,** you will be saddled with warranties when you sell goods, whether you expressly assume such warranties or the law implies them. Can you limit the scope of your warranty? First, you must be able to distinguish between sales to consumers and sales to other businesses. The law treats disclaimers differently on the presumption that a business buyer is more capable of negotiating a warranty, if it is important, than a consumer. For consumers, Congress enacted the Moss-Magnuson Act that limits the rights of manufacturers to limit their warranties, in part. You must expressly state if the warranty offered to a consumer is limited (if unstated, the warranty is full). If you have a full warranty, you cannot disclaim any implied warranty. However, in a limited warranty, you may make various disclaimers.

In the business-to-business context, the implied warranties derive from the Uniform Commercial Code (UCC). They may be disclaimed providing they are in writing, conspicuous, and specifically make reference to the warranties of merchantability and fitness for a particular purpose. This should be done regardless of what express warranty you may wish to make.

You should also limit your business warranties to proper use, installation, and repair of the goods. This places the obligation on the buyer to take good care of the goods and to prove such good care if there is an attempt to make a warranty claim. Consider how you may wish to evaluate a warranty claim and what you may wish to specify as the buyer's remedy—repair of goods, new goods?

DON'T *indemnify against patent infringement except where it is advantageous.*

Sellers normally warrant or indemnify the buyer against any liability for patent infringement. It should not be the buyer's obligation to determine if the product infringes, unless the buyer actually specifies the design of the product. You do not want to entrust defense against patent infringement to a single buyer who the patent owner may have chosen to sue to obtain a quick capitulation. You must therefore warrant against liability for infringement and agree to assume defense of the suit. Make the buyer notify you if the buyer has been charged with infringement by the patent owner.

The seller should also limit its patent indemnity to exclude certain uses of the product. For example, a chemical manufacturer may make and sell a compound that is noninfringing. The buyer may take that compound and combine it with another so that the final compound infringes a patent owned by a third party. The seller should not be liable for this infringement, and this should be expressly set forth. However, the patent law not only prevents direct infringement, but also proscribes contributory infringement. If a manufacturer sells a product that it knows is specially made for use in an infringing product, it will be a contributory infringement unless the product is a staple article of commerce, meaning that it is useful for other applications that are not infringing. It is recommended that these possible infringement problems be specifically disclaimed in the sales order form, acknowledgment, bid, or negotiated contract.

CHAPTER

6

INTERNATIONAL
TRANSACTIONS

DO *closely examine international contracts for unfamiliar terms and conditions.*

Assuming that your international contract will be interpreted and, if necessary, enforced in the United States, the principles of contract law are equally applicable. But if the contract will be construed in accordance with U.S. law, there are particular terms and conditions that are specific to the process of doing business abroad that can be confounding.

For one, the importance of sales and delivery terms dealing with freight in domestic sales transactions discussed in **#88** looms much larger here. In addition to FOB (free on board; see **#88**), there are a number of terms, such as FAS (free alongside—meaning delivered to the dock of an ocean-going port), that must be clarified. Your banker or the Department of Commerce should be able to give help here. Because the trip is longer and presumably more dangerous, insurance coverage during transit is more important. Again, expert guidance is necessary.

You must specify the currency to be used for payment in the contract; United States currency is definitely preferred. Other currencies are more unstable and will require conversion costs. Moreover, you are probably much less aware of the stability of the other currency; the foreign party, who typically does more international business than you do, will have a significant advantage by specifying its own currency. If you must accept payment in another currency, specify the rate of exchange. Pricing should also specifically state if there is duty included in the price or not.

DON'T *allow your dispute to be resolved in some foreign country.*

In **#43** it was suggested that arbitration may be a satisfactory manner for resolving a commercial dispute. In the international arena, it is not merely satisfactory, it is highly recommended. Many foreign companies will find the American Arbitration Association (AAA) rules and procedures satisfactory for reaching a resolution. If not, try the International Chamber of Commerce rules. There are others. The point is to avoid the necessity of trying to enforce a contract in a foreign jurisdiction where justice may be delivered in a much different manner, if at all. You cannot simply sue a foreign company here. You must succeed in getting a United States district court to exercise jurisdiction over a foreign entity, and more important, to render a judgment that can be satisfied in the United States on assets of the company here.

Name the forum in which the issues are to be resolved as some city in the United States. (You may find that a foreign entity will agree only to a large East or West Coast city for convenience and because commercial centers are presumed to be knowledgeable about business disputes.) It will be cheaper for you regardless of which arbitration entity you choose. Furthermore, attorney's fees are less expensive in the United States than in most European countries. You must specify which country's laws will apply to the dispute. Just because the matter is tried in one country does not mean that a court (or arbitration panel) will apply its own law. It may apply the law of any country that the parties specify. Since you and your attorney will be more knowledgeable and comfortable with your own law, specify it.

92

DO *price your shipment depending on the point at which you must deliver the goods in an international shipment.*

When goods are sold FOB for domestic shipment, it means that the seller must pack the goods for shipment in a satisfactory manner and have the shipment ready to be picked up by the buyer, or more likely the buyer's agent (the freight company that the buyer has specified). The comparable arrangement in an international transaction is *ex works*. (Works is the ancient term for factory and it is still used in some countries and in international shipping.) If the product shipment is large, the term may be *free carrier*, meaning that the seller must pack, ready, and load the goods on the buyer's truck, railcar, or so on. As noted in **#91**, FAS is also a favorite term in international shipping, meaning that the seller will deliver the goods ready to ship at the export port specified by the buyer. The seller will charge the buyer the cost of hauling (usually by common carrier) the goods from the factory to the port.

The latter is important from the point of view of the responsibility and the necessity of insurance coverage. If you ship FOB internationally it has an entirely different meaning than when used domestically. It means that you arrange for the goods to be placed on board the ship. You must pay the freight and loading costs (wharfage) and will have to make arrangements with a freight forwarder. There are essentially two types of forwarders, ocean shippers and air shippers, although many do both ocean shipping and air shipping. Their responsibility is to see that the proper documents are prepared and to handle the shipment from factory to vessel.

DON'T *be afraid of the term* pro forma invoice *used in international transactions—it is simply a quotation, though an exact one.*

In addition to specifying the point of delivery of an international shipment, there is the matter of cost. If you quote the terms as discussed previously, the buyer will bear the freight costs (i.e., the freight costs are collect). But you may be asked to quote C + F or CIF. The former means that you will pay for the freight and this amount will be included in your invoice. The latter simply adds insurance to your responsibility and this too will be added to your invoice. If you do a lot of international business, you may purchase a *blanket* insurance policy which relieves you from the tedium of applying for quotes and securing the insurance for each transaction.

Most foreign transactions are done by a quotation. In the international arena this quotation is referred to as a *pro forma* (in the form of) invoice. By putting the terms in this format the buyer will presumably know exactly what the price will be *and* all of the terms that are included in (or excluded from) that price. In a domestic quotation, many terms are taken for granted, although it is advisable to have a standard quotation form specifying all of your terms and conditions (Ts & Cs). In an international transaction, because the customs of the countries may vary widely, more care must be exercised in specifying the terms and conditions. Another important aspect of the pro forma invoice as to its specificity and exactness is that if you have a letter of credit (LC) covering the transaction (see **#93**), the pro forma invoice terms and the LC terms must be identical.

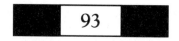

DO *use the letter of credit in an international sales transaction; it is not mystical—it is in fact very pragmatic.*

A letter of credit (LC) is one of the most basic documents used in international transactions. There is a certain aura about it. Yet it is really very simple and perfectly logical. If you have a new domestic customer, do you extend credit without any questions asked? Of course not. But there are many reliable ways of checking the credit of a new customer here in the United States: check Dun & Bradstreet, call references, contact the customer's bank, demand security for payment. If you do decide to extend the credit, you may still be stiffed. But you have the last recourse—the availability of a judicial system to which you may resort for payment.

Now assume that the customer is a foreign company, perhaps in a country that you didn't even know existed. Imagine the difficulty—and cost—entailed in establishing that the customer is creditworthy. Assuming that with the aid of the Commerce Department or other government agency that is encouraging domestic companies to export, you satisfy yourself that the customer is large and prosperous. You ship, and you get stiffed. Now try to collect with the assistance of a court system that may be run by the brother-in-law of the customer's president. Security won't help. But try to ask for cash in advance. The customer, particularly if your company is small, will be dubious as to whether *you* will ship the goods ordered. The LC resolves this stalemate by using a stakeholder of sorts, but it is not quite an escrow.

DON'T *worry about the letter of credit used in your foreign sale; worry about the terms of the transaction long before—they are what is critical.*

You tell your customer to go to its bank and to obtain a letter of credit in your favor. You give the customer the name of your bank. The customer's bank promises to pay to your bank *if* you will deliver the goods as promised. The customer's bank must first assure itself that its customer can make good if you deliver. It will do so if the customer's credit is good, or if not, it will debit funds that the customer has on hand with the bank. In the transaction (as described thus far) your bank simply handles the paperwork. If the LC is irrevocable, meaning that the issuer cannot cancel it or alter its terms in any way, you and your customer have placed your trust in the banks. (If the customer's bank is unknown, your bank may require another known bank to guarantee the LC.)

Why then are letters of credit viewed so cautiously? Because there is hardly any other document in commerce that must be adhered to, in even the most minute detail, as strictly as the LC. The reason is that the banks are paid a relatively small amount to effect the transaction. Consequently, they absolutely refuse to become embroiled in any dispute between the participants to the transaction. They do this by scrupulously avoiding any interpretation or construction of the terms the parties agreed upon. They demand that the parties put into the LC each and every detail that the parties agreed on. In **#92**, the pro forma invoice was discussed as the basis for carefully defining the terms of the sale. Now these terms can be memorialized in the LC. Everyone is bound—the customer, the banks, and you.

94

DO *appreciate that the letter of credit used in international sales transactions must be adhered to as stringently as any document you will ever sign.*

In **#93** it was pointed out that the terms and conditions in a letter of credit (LC) used in an international sales transaction are critical. The price and quantity are no more critical than in any other transaction; but other terms are. The description of the goods must be perfectly accurate. If you specify one model number, and change it in the normal course of business after the LC is issued, and invoice the correct product with the new number, the LC will fail. No excuses or explanations will suffice. It's gone. You may be able to get the customer to change the LC, but there is no legal obligation to do so. An unscrupulous customer can use that mistake as leverage in demanding a lower price. You have lost what you bargained for—a guarantee of payment.

Furthermore, the documents that accompany the shipment (packing slip and bill of lading) and those that are sent to the customer (commercial invoice—meaning your standard invoice, as distinct from the pro forma invoice) and the certificate of origin must perfectly conform to the LC terms and the be in perfect order. These papers must be presented within a strict timetable set forth in the LC (the customer wants to arrange for customs clearance to avoid any storage charges). The shipment date is not approximate as in most domestic transactions, it is exact. If you miss it, the LC expires. The LC generally has an expiration date a week or two after the shipment date, and even if the customer forgives late shipment, it cannot be later than the expiration date. If insurance is required, it is carefully specified.

DON'T *allow the terms in an international letter of credit (LC) to confuse you.*

There are some unfamiliar terms in the letter of credit used in international sales transactions that you should learn if you are going to do this often. You can rely on your freight forwarder as a source for an explanation of unfamiliar terms.

The LC was originated by the customer's bank, called the *opening* or *issuing* bank. Your bank, which does nothing other than to advise you when payment is received, is the *advising* bank. The agreement to pay when the documents are delivered is between the two banks and is for your benefit, so you are called the *beneficiary*. You obtain payment by writing a check to yourself drawn on the *paying* bank (which usually will also be the *advising* bank). In legal parlance a check is a type of *draft*. If a draft is to be paid immediately when the documents are delivered, it is paid on first sight. It is then a *sight draft*.

Who pays the banks? You pay yours and the customers pay theirs.

When the documents are delivered, your bank is not technically obligated to pay you until it is paid. But if it deals regularly with the issuing bank, it may be willing to *confirm* the LC. This means that your bank will pay immediately upon presentation of a copy of the documents (that you delivered to the customer) to your bank. Even if the issuing bank later becomes insolvent, you are guaranteed payment *if* your bank confirms.

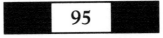

DO *have a rudimentary understanding about tariff rates—and what GATT and NAFTA mean in a nonpolitical sense.*

If you have ever traveled internationally, you have a very definite opinion of customs. Furthermore, if you are reading this, you are either (a) seriously interested in doing business abroad, or (b) badly in need of a good social club. Assuming the former, here are some basics for understanding the thicket of rules that controls the movement of goods into and out of this country.

Tariffs. What is this GATT thing all about? Tariffs were once set primarily by separate treaties with each nation. Because some politicians thought we ought to have better relations with one country than another, some countries received more favored tariff rates. Since World War II, international trade has increased tremendously, primarily because the major industrial countries began lowering tariffs to most countries to the level of the previously most favored nations. *GATT* (General Agreement on Tariffs and Trade) is the agreement that underlies the basis for the reciprocity of these agreements. It has resulted in a general tariff that is low. But there is another tariff classification system called *special* that may be even lower. One that has made lots of news over the last five years is *NAFTA* (North American Free Trade Agreement), which is a tariff schedule for Mexico and Canada that will eventually eliminate tariffs for these countries completely. There is also a special tariffs classification for the lesser-developed countries, a political decision. There are some other regions of the world that get special treatment. These duties are very important to you if you are importing goods.

DON'T *be deterred from carrying samples to other countries; use a customs broker for the most efficient clearance through customs.*

How do you clear goods through customs? If you are an exporter and expect to have goods returned to the United States for repair, you will be interested in the American Goods Returned (AGR) rules that allow goods to be returned from a foreign country to the United States duty-free. (Unfortunately, this provision also applies to goods made here, shipped to a foreign country, and bought here by another person—so-called *gray market* goods.) If gray market goods are trademarked, customs may be alerted by the manufacturer and will stop the importation. If you would like to import samples, or you are going on a foreign trip and would like to carry samples, you can use a *carnet* (sort of a passport for goods) or a temporary import bond (TIB).

But what of regular purchases from overseas? Clearance depends on value. If less than a certain amount (a little over $1,000 today), clearance is informal and the bureau is very helpful. It is still easiest to hire a customs broker (a private company that is approved by the customs bureau) simply because it will be more efficient than you. But you can do it alone. If the value is over this $1,000 amount, then a broker must be used. The duty charged is only approximate, giving customs up to one year to adjust the final duty payable. For this reason a bond must be posted; that is one of your advantages in using a broker. But the biggest advantage is that they know the rules, which can be very complicated in large transactions. (If you are wondering about those courier packages that come through customs in a flash, it is because there is another exception for packages under $200 in value.)

DO *consider protecting your invention in foreign countries; but it is expensive and should not be undertaken automatically.*

Your first impression of protecting your invention in a foreign country is that it is unnecessary. That may be the case for many small businesses. However, many products have equal potential in other countries and if you can arrange a foreign sales representative, protection of the invention may be quite important. But at the outset, you should understand that foreign patent protection is extremely expensive.

To grasp the necessity of discussing foreign patent protection, you need to understand that patent protection, in all countries, applies only within the borders of the country issuing the patent. If a company in Germany manufactures your invention and you have no patent protection there, you cannot do anything about it. The company can sell it there but cannot sell it here. You can prevent importation of a product that infringes a U.S. patent.

If you want to protect the invention in Germany you must file a patent application in Germany. The same rule applies to every separate country in which you want protection. But there is some good news. When you file in the U.S., you may file an application under the Patent Cooperation Treaty (PCT). This is not an application for a patent as such, but rather an interim procedure for claiming the benefit of your U.S. filing date in all the countries you designate in the PCT application for a period of up to thirty months. You can obtain a nonbinding examination. The cost is $3,000 to $4,000 (depending on the number of countries) and $1,000 for the exam.

DON'T *pursue trademark rights in foreign countries unless you are actively doing business in that particular country.*

The matter of trademark rights is even more complex than patents. There is no international multilateral treaty in this area. There is considerable activity in trying to establish such common ground, but this is not as likely to make progress as fast as the patent efforts.

If you are exporting to a particular country, then it may be worthwhile to investigate the cost and filing requirements for that country. You simply cannot afford to file in every country in which you do business. Most of the foreign countries use a first-to-file system; that is, it is not important who was the first to use, in that country or elsewhere, but who was the first to file for the trademark in that country.

The result of this system is that you may own and use trademark rights in all the major countries of the world, but some exploitative person in some third-world country may own your trademark there. You must then negotiate for the right to use your own trademark in that country. That is simply a fact of life. The problem, of course, surfaces when you have appointed a distributor in Zigglestein who complains that a competitor is claiming to be a representative of your company—that is, your brand name. The competitor is actually representing a relative's broken-down, out-of-date product. What can you do? Apply for your trademark as soon as you can, but at least apply before you appoint a distributor.

CHAPTER

7

EMPLOYMENT

DO *watch the number of your employees to determine the applicable laws.*

You and one other, with sales of $500,000 or more in interstate commerce:

Federal Labor Standards Act (FLSA) and Equal Pay Act

Federal and State Income Tax withholding and Social Security (FICA) withholding

Child labor laws

Immigration Reform and Control Act (I-9 form)

OSHA

ERISA (see **#114**)

Check your state for other laws.

DON'T *forget that as you get larger more laws regarding employment apply.*

With 15 or more add:

Americans with Disabilities Act (ADA)

Title VII Equal Employment Opportunity Act

With 20 or more add:

Age Discrimination in Employment Act (ADEA)

COBRA (must continue health care coverage)

With 25 or more add:

Drug/Alcohol Rehabilitation Act

HMO Mandate (if you offer health benefits)

With 50 or more add:

Federal Family and Medical Leave Act

With 100 or more add:

EEOC Employee Information Reports (EEO-1 forms)
Plant Closure Law (WARN Act)

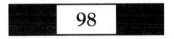

DO *test your employees for drug use if such use would be reasonably related to safety considerations in your business.*

The applicable law here is dependent on the statutes in your state, your state constitution, and cases involving drug testing by private employers. The only cases that have been decided under the United States Constitution (and therefore applicable to persons in every state) involve regulations that apply to railroad employees and to customs agents. The obvious need for safety and the necessity for testing in these cases may make them poor prognosticators of what the Constitution says about private businesses. The constitutional limitations on drug testing stem from the right of a private citizen to be free from an unreasonable search and seizure. To force a person to deliver a blood or urine sample is a search and seizure. Thus, the right to test employees and applicants for a job must be reasonable. The courts have been quite willing to recognize the legitimate interest of an employer to do testing if there can be shown at least some need, particularly from a safety point of view.

There are other restrictions on the employer's right to test. One is the employee's right to privacy. However, this applies more to surveillance or locker/desk searches without warning and without any prior notice. There are other dangers in an aggressive policy, such as defamation actions, false imprisonment, and infliction of emotional distress. But a policy that is designed properly can minimize the risks from these types of actions. The key is to create a good policy.

DON'T *be afraid of employee drug testing—just follow a sound policy.*

The first step is to prevent the employee or job applicant from claiming a right to privacy. If a job applicant is informed about drug testing immediately upon applying for a job, his or her application becomes a waiver of the right to privacy. Such informed consent has been approved by courts. The policy must clearly state that drug use is cause for immediate dismissal. The use of random drug screening or testing without any suspicion is marginally legal but strengthened if done in a truly random way (e.g., by computer selection). It is preferable to base drug testing on a suspicion of use determined by a supervisor with some amount of training in reasonable cause.

Second, the use of drug screen test results should be carefully guarded and used only for making a decision on continued employment. To allow such sensitive and confidential information to be publicly disseminated would be an invasion of an employee's right to informational privacy. Like all testing of applicants and employees, there is no reason to allow anyone but those with a need to know to be informed of the results. There must be a strict injunction against repeating the information. Third, the testing should be as nonintrusive as possible. A hair follicle test is less intrusive than a urine test. A urine test is less intrusive than a blood test. If a witness urine test is administered, a female employee should monitor the test if the employee is female. Testing should be in private. It will be advisable to use a drug testing firm that is familiar with the applicable laws to assure compliance. But you will ultimately be responsible for the tester's results, so careful selection should complement your policy.

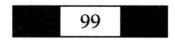

DO *be sure to comply with the requirements for hiring aliens—it is easy.*

Unlike many of the other employment policies regarding fair treatment of employees that are vague or difficult, the law regarding hiring aliens is a refreshing change. The Immigration and Control Act of 1986 prohibits two acts of employers.

First, it is against the law to hire an alien if you know that the person is an unauthorized alien. To assist you in determining what type of knowledge is culpable, the law establishes a verification system.

The verification system becomes the second act that must be followed. The verification system requires three steps: (a) obtain documents that (i) establish the individual's identity and (ii) authorize employment in the United States; (b) complete the Form I-9; and (c) retain the I-9 form for three years or one year after the employee terminates, whichever is later.

There are some types of documents that satisfy both the identity and authority requirements and some that satisfy only one or the other. In the former category is a passport, a green card with a photo, and a certificate of U.S. citizenship. The identity requirement can be met (if one of the above is not available) by a driver's license or identification card. The authorization requirement can be met with a Social Security card or a birth certificate from within the United States. So, a driver's license and a Social Security card together will suffice, just like a passport alone.

DON'T *trip over the discrimination laws in complying with the alien hiring laws.*

The penalties for violating the alien employment laws are not trivial. If you knowingly hire or retain an employee after finding that the person is an alien, you may be fined from $250 to $10,000. If you are a repeat offender the conduct becomes a criminal offense. There is even a penalty for failing to comply with the verification requirements—$100 to $1,000 per incident.

On the other hand, you may not discriminate against aliens in hiring. The immigration laws prohibit such conduct, but discrimination also is prohibited by Title VII of the Civil Rights Act if discrimination is based on national origin. Merely requiring that the person demonstrate that he is a legal alien does not alone, of course, establish discrimination. However, if you require more documentation than outlined above or you question the validity of such documents that appear reasonable on their face, you are in violation of the law. So, again the test is fuzzy, as in the entire area of discrimination. The by-word is to be cautious but not overly suspicious of documents. Of course there are fake ID cards of all types in many areas of the country. It is prudent to photocopy all documents shown to you and to retain them with the I-9 forms.

Not widely known is that if you have two applicants with equal skill, you may select the citizen (vis-à-vis the alien) for that reason alone without any discrimination law violation.

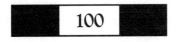

DO *maintain your right to terminate employees.*

If you do not have an employment contract with an employee, his employment is termed *at-will* employment. This simply means that either you or the employee is free to terminate the relationship at any time, with or without cause. There is no formal requirement for giving notice. By and large, this is the most preferable relationship for the employer. But you must carefully guard this right.

If you enter into an employment contract intentionally, both parties are bound to the employment relationship for the term stated in the contract. Therefore, if you terminate the employee you will be liable for the entire amount that remains to be paid under the contract. However, you may obtain some relief if you are sued (and lose) by the rule that a party must mitigate its own damages whenever possible. So if the employee finds another position during the remaining term of the contract, you will have to pay only the difference between what the employee earned at the new position and the amount owed under the contract. On the other hand, if the employee voluntarily quits, *there is no legal recourse.* No court will force the ordinary employee to continue employment. As a practical matter, the best technique for retaining a valuable employee is to make part of the compensation conditioned on continued employment. This commonly involves stock options, but it is also possible to use deferred compensation to induce the employee to stay.

DON'T *stumble into an oral agreement that commits you not to terminate an employee except for cause.*

The typical problem that an employer gets into when terminating employment is that the at-will relationship has inadvertently become a contract for a fixed period. In other words, the at-will nature of the relationship has been lost. How? Usually by careless verbal statements. A contract need not be created in writing. It may be an express oral agreement, or an implied agreement. There are two occurrences in the employment relationship in which the oral or implied agreement may arise: upon hiring, or in convincing an employee that has resigned to stay. In the former, a hiring manager, in his or her zeal to recruit, may make statements to a prospective employee that become an oral agreement. Even an innocuous statement that the employer has a no-layoff policy may be binding, depending upon circumstances and future conduct of the parties. The employee is verbally assured that the company will not ever fire him or her if good job performance continues. What is good performance will later be settled in court if the employee is fired.

The solution is to warn all managers that they are not to make any promises of employment. More important, your employee handbook should expressly state that all employment is at will unless there is an agreement in writing. And you should further state that none of the policies set forth in the handbook, nor the handbook itself, create a binding agreement. It is a good idea to have the employee sign a receipt for receiving the booklet and for acknowledging the at-will nature of the relationship. You must retain your right to modify the provisions of employment at your discretion. Say it.

101

DO *keep employee records confidential.*

The law relating to employee records is based on the state in which you reside. But some general principles can be derived from cases and statutes in the larger states where these matters are more likely to arise.

An employee has a complete right to inspect his or her employment records. That includes any documents that are collected during the hiring process and future documents such as performance reviews, since they are used in making retention decisions. You must be careful when you put any documents in an employee personnel record. There are some documents, such as warning notices, that *must* be put into employee files if you intend to rely on them. These notices should be signed and dated by the employee.

The right to access, however, does not extend to a rejected applicant.

No one other than the employee has a right to review these employer records unless ordered by a court. And the courts have been very firm in rejecting the attempts of others to access these files. Even where an employee suing the employer is attempting to get access to prove that the employer treated other employees differently, the courts have sided with the privacy protection of the other employees over the interests of the litigant.

DON'T *automatically provide written performance evaluations of employees.*

It is traditional that employees receive an annual written evaluation, which is placed into the personnel records. Honest performance evaluations done by trained managers are valuable for running a business. But that is a separate issue from retaining indefinitely the evaluations in the employee personnel record. A good evaluation will focus not only on the employee's performance over the past year, but also set goals for the employee, note any area where improvement is desired, and include the need for training. But is it necessary to keep these evaluations indefinitely?

The reason for rethinking this traditional approach is that in today's litigation-happy society, if an employee is terminated there is a possibility of suit. Only too often the employee's file will show sterling evaluations for a long period and then a sudden termination. This is an invitation to litigate. As noted, if an employee's conduct or performance is unacceptable, a *fair warning* or other note should be discussed with the employee, signed by him or her, and kept in the file. It strains the credulity of the jury that a good employee for many years is suddenly unacceptable. But it happens, although it is difficult to explain. If you don't keep the old records, you may have nothing to explain. The whole problem stems from the failure of supervisors to highlight weaknesses in writing. But this is a much larger problem that may be insoluble. A makeshift solution may be limited record retention.

102

DO *consider employee testing if you believe that it will assist you in employee selection, but be sure the test is valid.*

Prior to the 1970s, there was a trend in the use of general aptitude testing as a selection tool for new employees. While the utility of these tests has been controversial for many years, large companies used the tests extensively. In the early 1970s, however, a case was decided by the Supreme Court that cast a long shadow on the legality of these tests. The case involved a fairly blatant misuse of tests to discriminate against blacks. After a great deal of case law helped to shape the contours of when these types of tests may be used, the law is now reasonably settled.

Without extensively analyzing the underlying legal theory in Title VII race discrimination cases or suits involving other protected classes, you should at least understand that these cases may involve either disparate treatment or disparate impact to establish discrimination. Treatment is as you might expect: Was there some conduct toward the person that was based on his or her race? It involves specific action toward a particular person. Impact is more subtle: Was that race underrepresented or negatively impacted as a group compared to the available population? If so, the presumption then is that there was a racially based motive behind the identified policies. It is the latter standard that is used to challenge testing. While there are many aspects of test validity, the preeminent question is whether the test is job related. It is the same concept that is used in the ADA (See **#123**).

DON'T *use a preemployment test from commercial test vendors unless it is validated, then use it carefully.*

Your assurance that a test will pass muster under the discrimination laws is whether it meets the Uniform Guidelines on Employee Selection Procedures. This guideline was adopted in 1978 by several branches of the federal government. It establishes the rules for *validating* the test. This simply means that the test in fact tests what it purports to test. There are various validation techniques, and there is a lack of professional unity as to which, if any, technique should be deemed satisfactory.

Odds are great that you will never as a small business have a test prepared specifically for your business. There are many companies offering these tests in the marketplace. You should evaluate them for your purposes if you believe that they will aid you in employee selection. But your key legal determination should be based on whether the test has been validated in accordance with the UGESP. This is a necessary, though not sufficient, basis for concluding that you will not violate the law if you use the validated test. Quite simply, the test may be *used* in a way that accomplishes discrimination. It is desirable to implement testing only in accordance with a strict procedure that guarantees that the test will not be misused.

In all events, for assuring that the test is giving you meaningful results as well as a legal result, be sure the test is job related. That is the key here.

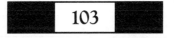

103

DO *recognize the religious rights of your employees and avoid a charge of discrimination.*

Title VII, which we have seen before in contexts such as race, sex, and other forms of discrimination, also prohibits religious discrimination. Two problems arise when this issue is approached: What is religion and what is a discriminatory act in the context of religion? As you can well imagine, the resolution of what is religion is but a crude attempt to define the impossible. Current law, going far beyond the traditional religions, of course, appears to land on "a sincere belief" in God or some parallel to God. Current law also appears to require that the belief be shared by some group, although that group does not necessarily have to be an organized church, temple, mosque, and so forth. Atheism definitely qualifies. But at the far extreme (perhaps of common sense), an employee who claimed that it was part of his religious belief to eat Kozy Kitten cat food on the job had to be rebuffed before the EEOC, a United States District Court, and a United States Court of Appeal before the employer prevailed.

The discrimination element comes into play when measuring whether a particular employer practice results in discrimination. This can occur in hiring, promotion, wages, and work assignments, to name a few. But there are many more cases that involve the reasonable accommodation requirement in these situations. One area where outright discrimination has become a workplace issue is religious harassment. The advice here is absolutely clear. Don't let employees harass other employees for their religious views.

DON'T *overlook your obligation to accommodate an employee's religious views.*

When Congress passed Title VII, it expressly provided that an employer should be required to give "reasonable accommodation" to an employee's religious views. The Supreme Court, however, has narrowly construed the obligation of the employer to accommodate. It has stated that there is an undue hardship limitation on the accommodation obligation. This limitation includes the right to deny accommodation if the cost is anything more than minimal. It appears that the rationale for this severe limitation is primarily the interests of other employees—not the employer. Another aspect that frequently appears in larger organizations is the interests of unions and their rules.

The problem that the court was wrestling with in coming to its stringent application of the reasonable accommodation standard is the potential religious discrimination against the other employees. For if one employee is entitled to require that her employer spend additional sums to accommodate her religious views, are not the other employees being deprived of equal benefits from the employer and therefore discriminated against? It is the quandary of the zero sum game—if one obtains more, the others must take less. If there also is a loss of efficiency in accommodating work schedules, for example, then there is still additional reason to relieve the employer from any other than a small accommodation.

DO *use independent contractors, but comply with state and federal rules.*

Independent contractors (ICs) are often preferable to employees for a variety of reasons. If the worker is properly classified as an independent contractor (see **#105**), you are not responsible for witholding taxes on wages; although you must file a Form 1099 to report the payment of wages after the end of the year. You do not have to pay the employer's half of social security (FICA) taxes; the worker is responsible for paying self-employment tax. You will not have to pay workers' compensation insurance premiums. There are no federal unemployment taxes (FUTA) due. See **#112** for the rules regarding these payments.

More importantly, independent contractors are not ordinarily paid for vacations or sick leave. ICs are not generally covered by group health insurance, nor do they participate in any pension or 401(k) program.

Overtime laws do not apply to ICs. Anti-discrimination laws that are directed specifically to employment also do not apply to independent contractors. Various employment regulations apply only to businesses above a certain size as measured by the number of employees; workers who are classified as ICs are not counted in such a tally.

In addition to the inapplicability of many laws, there is the lessened administrative burden.

DON'T *misclassify an employee as an independent contractor.*

If you misclassify a worker as an IC, rather than as an employee, you will have serious problems from a number of government agencies. Tax authorities are not the least of them. You will be required to pay all payroll taxes (FICA, FUTA, Medicare, and state unemployment) for both the employee and your company for a period of three years. The taxes that should have been withheld are estimated between 1.5 percent and 20 percent and are also due for the preceding three years. You owe interest on these amounts based on the rate of inflation. There are potential penalties based in part on whether you filed a Form 1099 (it is advised that you do) and on whether the classification as an IC was an intentional attempt to evade the law.

These are only the federal tax troubles—you will also have state tax problems. There are potential assessments for failure to pay state disability insurance premiums and state unemployment insurance. States typically have severe penalties in addition to assessments and back taxes. Some even have criminal penalties.

There are potential liabilities for minimum wages and overtime (assuming that the worker would be classed as nonexempt) if the worker was misclassified. Workers' compensation premiums will be due. And finally, you run the risk that if workers are reclassified, you may not have the required number of employees to meet the nondiscrimination rules for pension plans.

105

DO *understand that there is no single test for whether a worker is an employee or an independent contractor (IC) for all occasions.*

Unfortunately, the classification of a worker as an employee or an independent contractor is not simple. There are at least three or four different tests used by state and federal agencies and by the courts.

In a state, there may be some consistency between agencies and courts in that state, but not always. For example, in California the issue may arise in an unemployment claim. The state Employment Development Department and the courts use a Common Law (see **#107**) test for whether the worker is an employee or an independent contractor. Yet in a Workers' Compensation case, a combination of the Common Law, "6 Factor," and "Economic Realities" test is used. The "6 Factor" test and the Economic Realities tests are too similar to the Common Law test to bear further discussion here. The controlling factor on the decision as to what test is applicable may be the statute in your state that governs the situation. Your lawyer, or a call to the applicable agency in your state, should help you identify the correct test to use.

The good news is that the federal laws are equally applicable to you regardless of where you reside. Unfortunately, the most important is the "IRS 20 Factor" test (see **#106**). The sheer number of factors to be considered is enough to dissuade you from completing an analysis. Furthermore, there is a great deal of commonality between these various tests.

DON'T *ignore the applicability of the safe harbor to IRS disputes regarding independent contractors (ICs).*

A special provision was enacted by Congress in 1978, called Section 530, to avoid the possibility of a dispute with the IRS over whether a worker is an employee or an IC. It provides what is called a safe harbor, meaning that if you meet the criteria of this section, you are safe from attack by the IRS, even if you do not pass the "IRS 20 Factor" test. See **#106.**

To qualify, you must have a reasonable basis for classifying the worker as an IC, based on (a) earlier court cases that involved the same or similar facts; (b) a favorable IRS ruling (these are published positions taken by the IRS in response to a specific factual situation submitted by letter to the IRS requesting a determination which the IRS decides to publish to provide guidance to taxpayers); (c) a past favorable audit determination for a similar position; or (d) proof that an industry practice treating the worker as an IC was in widespread existence in 1978. You will need the assistance of an accountant that is skilled in this area in order to take advantage of the safe harbor.

In addition to meeting one of the above four criteria, you must have filed a 1099 and treated all workers in the same position in the same manner. Incidentally, the safe harbor is *not* available for engineers, designers, computer programmers, system analysts, or other skilled workers in similar lines of work.

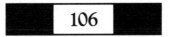

106

DO *apply the first 10 of the "IRS 20 Factor" test to determine if a worker is an employee or an IC.*

To analyze the factors in depth, obtain a copy of IRS Rev. Rule 87–41 from your accountant. Here is a quick overview. For further discussion see **#107.**

1. Control—do you give instructions on how to do the work?
2. Training—do you teach or has the worker the skills?
3. Integration—are the services of the worker peripheral or essential to delivery of the goods or services?

4. Delegation—are the services to be personally performed or can the IC subcontract them?
5. Subordinate control—does the worker hire and fire his own employees or subs and supervise them; is the worker supervised by your employees or does he supervise your employees?
6. Project—is this a project that when completed will end the relationship?
7. Hours—who sets them, you or him?
8. Full time—can the worker spend the time he feels is needed or are you demanding full time?
9. Workplace—can the worker choose to work elsewhere; is he there every day?
10. Sequence—who controls what is done first, second, and so forth?

DON'T *forget the last 10 of the "IRS 20 Factor" test.*

11. Reports—is the worker responsible for the result or must he report progress?
12. Payment—is payment to be made in a fixed amount or is it variable (i.e., hourly, weekly, etc.)?
13. Expenses—do you reimburse for expenses or does the worker pay his own?
14. Tools—does the worker provide his own or do you?
15. Investment—has the worker made an independent investment in equipment, facility, and so forth?
16. P & L—does the worker risk loss and stand to make a profit from the work performed?
17. Multiple clients—does the worker work for other companies at the time he works for you?
18. Services available to public—does the worker advertise or otherwise solicit clients?
19. Firing—can you fire the worker or are you bound by contract to make payment if the job is finished?
20. Quitting—can the worker quit or is the worker bound by contract to complete the job?

It is difficult to say what factors are most important because it varies with the situation. Some of these are variations of the same factor. There is also the possibility that the IRS may soon abandon the 20 Factor test.

DO *familiarize yourself with the Common Law factors used to classify a worker as an employee or an independent contractor (IC).*

The single most important factor in determining whether a worker is an employee or an IC is control. Do you have the authority (regardless of whether you use it) to prescribe how the worker performs the work? If you specify the number of hours the worker must spend each day or week, or if you instruct the worker to spend full time on the project, you are exercising control. If you require interim reports or direct the sequence of the tasks, you are in control. If you demand that the work be performed at a particular place, you are in control.

The second most important factor is whether you can fire the worker or he can quit, without cause, with no further liability. An IC usually has a contract for the job. If you fire the IC without a justifiable reason, you will be responsible for damages. If he walks off without finishing, he could be liable.

Is the worker engaged in a distinct occupation or separate business? How many years has the worker been in business? Does the worker carry health, workers' compensation, and liability insurance? Does the worker have a license, his own tools, a base of customers, business cards, and stationery? These are the sorts of questions to be considered in deciding the outcome of the employee versus IC decision.

DON'T *overlook other Common Law test factors in determining a worker's classification as an employee or an independent contractor (IC)*

The method of payment is also important. Do you pay on a periodic basis, as to an employee, or on completion of the job—a lump sum? If the worker could lose money because he underbid the job, he is most likely an IC. Is the worker responsible for his own expenses? You can show IC status by paying a lump sum that implicitly includes expenses.

Is the worker simultaneously working for other companies? If so, he is likely an IC. Does he advertise consistently or list himself for hire with the public at large? If so, it weighs in favor of an IC classification. Is the engagement for a project or indefinitely? The latter looks like an employment relationship.

If the worker has invested money in the business buying tools and equipment used in rendering the services, he is probably an IC. If the worker has other persons working for him as an employee or a sub-contractor, he has his own business and is not likely an employee.

Aside from the Common Law test, see **#106,** the IRS test.

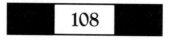

108

DO *deal with job shops for workers where you do not want an employee relationship.*

Reasons for not wanting an employee relationship are stated in **#104.** The dangers of attempting to create an independent contractor relationship and failing are also set forth there. One way of avoiding the dangers is to contract with a job shop (sometimes called a Principal) in a three-way relationship referred to as employee leasing.

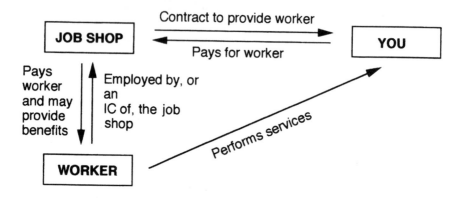

DON'T *ignore the advice of how to treat workers as ICs even in a three-party deal.*

If the worker is an employee of a job shop, there is little or no chance that any agency or court will find an employment relationship. But if the worker is an IC of the job shop, it is possible that the *combined* actions of the job shop and you may create a basis for finding an employment relationship.

So the factors in the various tests (see **#105, #106, #107**) cannot be entirely ignored.

It is advisable to have a contract with the job shop specifying who has the responsibility for filing tax forms, who is providing workers' compensation, who is responsible for OSHA compliance, and so forth. And include warranty and indemnity by the job shop against a finding of any court or agency that you are the employer of the worker.

Some job shops provide other benefits that you may be unable to offer to employees because you are so small that the administrative burden is overwhelming. A job shop may have a credit union, a pension plan, or a less expensive health package than you may be able to obtain. Just relieving you of the burden of payroll duties may be sufficiently attractive to warrant your consideration of this method.

109

DO *use temporary workers to manage your workload fluctuations with the added benefit of lower overall costs.*

In addition to direct use of independent contractors or the job shops described in **#108,** you may also need to vary the size of your workforce to meet seasonal or unanticipated work requirements. With the assistance of temporary agencies and flex work plans, some employers are finding a reduction in cost and regulatory burden through the ongoing use of a temporary hire policy. Employers may use the maximum number of weeks before a worker becomes an "employee" to avoid regulatory burdens. But there is a trend toward workers seeking these types of jobs, and this may result in revision of many of the old rules.

One clear advantage of these policies is the avoidance of the minimum trigger provisions of many state and federal laws. See **#97.** Most of these laws distinguish between temporary and permanent personnel. Typically, a line is drawn at less than thirty hours per week, but you cannot rely on this.

It is also typical that temporary employees do not receive ordinary company benefits, such as group health insurance, vacations, sick leave, and so forth. Whether these temporary workers are classified as employees under your state law will determine whether they are covered by rules for workers' compensation and unemployment.

DON'T *overreact to a wage garnishment—in either direction*

When a person obtains a judgment against another in court (and in some cases before the judgment is issued), and the party who lost has not paid, the judgment creditor may seek collection in various ways. One method is to garnish a worker's wages. To garnish is to require the employer to deduct a portion of that worker's wages or salary at the order of a court.

Wage garnishment occurs frequently these days in conjunction with child support orders and back tax collection by the IRS or state. For child support, there is a federal statute permitting such garnishment (to prevent a person subject to such an order from simply moving out of the state and avoiding state enforcement efforts). The taxing authorities use garnishments with a vengeance. If as employer you are served with a garnishment order, you must comply, no excuses. If your employee threatens to quit if you deduct wages, you still have no excuse. If an employee approaches you to receive part of his or her pay in some other way (e.g., use of an automobile in lieu of wages that could be garnished), do not do it.

More important, you have no right to terminate an employee if his or her wages are garnished. Indeed, it is illegal to do so. There is a limit to the amount that may be garnished. Under federal law, the maximum is 25 percent of the employee's after-tax withholding pay or $125 per week, whichever is less; however, the amount may be more for child support and tax garnishments.

110

DO *comply with the provisions of the Consolidated Omnibus Budget Reconciliation Act (COBRA) for employees covered by group health.*

If you offer group health insurance to your employees, you become obligated to continue to make available this insurance in the event that the employee terminates employment or is otherwise made eligible. But only if you have 20 or more employees. The under-20 employee exception is applied to the calendar year preceding the event. The counting of full-time, part-time, temporary, and contract employees is complicated; if you are close to the line and decide to deny the benefits of COBRA to an ex-employee, you must discuss how to count the 20 with at least your insurance broker or carrier, if not your lawyer. And you cannot take advantage of the under-20 exception by creating multiple companies.

COBRA applies to the employee, spouse, or dependent child of the employee ("covered person"). The covered person must have been a plan participant on the day before the termination or other "qualifying" event. Qualified event includes death, termination for other than "gross misconduct," reduction in hours, divorce or legal separation, a dependent child's loss of coverage because of age under the plan, or the employee's entitlement to Medicare. While theft is certainly "gross misconduct," it is not certain what other acts of an employee that result in involuntary termination will exclude such employee from COBRA coverage.

DON'T *find that you have to pay the tax for failure to comply with COBRA provisions relating to group health plans.*

A breach of the COBRA obligations is not treated lightly. A tax is due to the IRS if you fail to comply, even unintentionally. (Obtain a letter from your broker or carrier that you are not required to comply, if that is the case; it will help establish your good faith mistake.) The tax is $100 per day that you are in violation, up to $500,000, or 10 percent of your group health plan premiums for the last year, whichever is less. If you make a mistake in denying coverage, you must place the qualified person in the same position as if he or she had chosen the coverage of his or her choice before the violation ends. The implications could be serious if the qualified person incurs substantial medical bills that are not paid by any alternative plan. And an employee may bring a civil suit for damages under ERISA. (See #114 for a discussion of ERISA).

When you hire a new employee (assuming you have more than twenty employees and have a group plan covering your employees), you must give notice of COBRA rights to the new employee (and spouse). The Department of Labor issued a model notice in 1986 and it is available by calling them. Your insurance broker or carrier also will provide this notice as plan administrator subject to the same penalties for failure. This provision points out that, generally, you should and can rely on your insurance provider to help you keep within the law.

DO *offer COBRA to qualified persons only as long as required.*

In **#110,** it was pointed out that in most cases where you offer group health benefits and have more than twenty employees, you must offer a qualified person (see the definition in **#110**) continued coverage. If the qualifying event is termination or the divorce of a spouse, then the person has sixty days to make a decision on whether to continue coverage, and then another forty-five days to make the retroactive premium payments. Thereafter, if premiums are not paid, coverage can be canceled. If the person covered reaches the age where he or she is entitled to Medicare, or the person takes other employment and receives coverage from the new employer, coverage can be canceled. Or, if the covered person is a divorced or widowed spouse, coverage ends if the spouse remarries. If the employer discontinues offering a group health plan to its current employees, it can terminate coverage for the qualified person as well.

The length of the term to which the qualified person is entitled to coverage depends on the circumstances. It is at least eighteen months (subject to the limitations above). The longest is thirty-six months for death, divorce or legal separation, or loss of dependent status. In other words, protection is longest where required for the spouse or children. If there is a disability (as defined in the Social Security Act), coverage is for twenty-nine months. If any of these "extenders" occur during the first eighteen-month standard period, the extension is still available. There are special rules that also apply to situations involving the Family Medical Leave Act (FMLA). See **#126–129.**

DON'T *offer group health plans without making employees aware that this is compensation with pretax dollars.*

There was a time when medical costs were reasonably related to other necessities of life. This ended by the 1980s. Premiums sky-rocketed and employers that previously viewed group health plans as a minor benefit were awakened, rudely. Employers have reacted to the higher costs in various ways, including simply not offering group health. More often they have been looking to engage independent contractors rather than employees. This has given rise to its own set of problems, see **#104.** It is likely that employers absorbed the higher premiums reflected in this cost by lower wage increases.

You should understand that there is no law that requires you to offer group health—that is what the 1993–94 brouhaha with the Clintons was all about. Employers have in fact tried to cope with high costs in other ways, such as with HMO plans, a prevention theory, or Managed Care plans, where strict scrutiny of a medical procedure was necessary before payment was authorized. Meanwhile the federal government offered more tax relief by allowing an employer to set up a "flex plan" that may be funded up to $5,000 and used by the employee for either child care or group health payments (such as the copayment or deductible required in most policies). Since this amount is pretax, it is an excellent compensation tool. The downside is that the plan must provide that if the employee does not use the flex dollars during the year, the money is gone. The point here is that you should let your employees know what the group health benefit means in after-tax dollars.

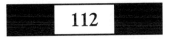

DO *not fail to withhold and pay federal payroll taxes.*

If you take any advice in this book as gospel that must be followed to the letter—this is it. The IRS can be awfully mean if you fail to pay taxes withheld from your employees. And you are *personally* liable if you are an officer of the company!

Once you have received your federal taxpayer identification number (and this must be done within a short time after hiring an employee), see your accountant as you are in "the system." This number is used when filing your business federal income tax returns and for many other purposes.

Your accountant should provide you with the necessary information on how to withhold payroll taxes from employees, and when these taxes must be paid to the government. If you like to know these things for yourself, the IRS has various circulars that explain your obligations. Simply stated, an employee upon hiring must designate the number of exemptions claimed, and you can calculate the withholding based on this form from IRS Circular C. Payment for Social Security taxes (FICA) is also due with payment of the withheld amounts. The withheld amounts are payable, depending on the aggregate amount due, semimonthly, monthly, or quarterly. A quarterly federal tax return is due on the last day after the close of the quarter. Don't miss it.

DON'T *fail, either, to pay the Federal Unemployment Tax (FUTA).*

The only issue in determining your obligation for FUTA is whether the tax is due for a particular employee. The rules are not complicated.

If you have even one employee, part- or full-time, temporary or permanent, at least one day per week during each of twenty calendar weeks (whether or not consecutive) during this or the last calendar year, you are liable for the payment of FUTA. Or if you paid more than $1,500 in aggregate wages during any quarter of this or the prior calendar year. That's a pretty low standard—almost any employee will create the obligation.

FUTA must be paid at the same time as the withholding payments discussed above. The two payments are made with Form 8109-B. Circular C provides more information on FUTA. An unemployment tax return also must be filed before January 31 following the close of a calendar year, with the payment of any amount still owing.

Not only is the above information abbreviated, it relates only to federal obligations. Since the laws in each state differ on state income tax withholding, unemployment insurance taxes, and perhaps other related obligations for employees, it is impossible to cover all such material here. Most of this information will be at the fingertips of any bookkeeper or accountant you hire. Don't learn details; rely on a *good* advisor.

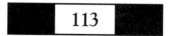

113

DO *create benefits for your employees, including vacation and holidays.*

I have a simple rule when hiring lower-level employees—if they are highly concerned over the benefit package, they are not going to be happy in your small company. You may wish to do something special for such employees, but it will create ill will within the organization and they probably will still not be happy. The fact of life is that larger organizations offer superior benefit packages; smaller organizations offer a family feeling and an opportunity to impact results. Persons who value security, require a high level of support, need leading edge equipment, and like to come to work to a breath-takingly beautiful facility will not be happy with you. They may deny it. But trust me. They won't be happy. I also believe, based on my limited experience with one large company, that it works the other way too.

Nonetheless, every employee expects a minimal package of benefits, including vacations and holidays. You should either join an organization that polls its members about the benefits they offer and publishes an annual report to its members, or talk with other owners in your area—preferably in a similar business. You must at least meet minimum standards. And you can turn this on its head; you can make your benefits outstanding, counting on capturing the best people available and that their superior qualifications and performance will create the revenue and gross profit that allows the payment of these extraordinary benefits. It is a business strategy issue. The law regarding vacations and holidays is usually dominated by state laws, but here are a few pointers.

DON'T *run afoul of several laws relating to vacations and holidays.*

Before addressing the laws on vacations or holidays, it is well to understand that with respect to all of the laws on fringe benefits of employees, there are class-discrimination rules that must be observed. Discrimination pervades the whole of the law, and especially the worker-company environment. As you consider any benefit program, or the continuation of an existing program, you must ask whether your policy favors a particular class of employee, or discriminates against a class. If so, you need to consult the remaining points under this subject or discuss the issue with your lawyer.

The policy that you adopt and publish becomes your obligation, supplemented perhaps by employee-favorable laws in your state. California allows vacations to be capped as to accrued amount (but forbids a "use it or lose it" policy), allows a period to be set before vacation begins to accrue, and allows accelerating accrual (higher rate toward end of year than beginning). These rules must be followed upon termination—where the issue usually arises. Contrary to the belief of many, there is no obligation for an employer to give employees time off on a federal or state holiday. You could literally not allow any holidays—you could also not find anyone that will work for you!

One real issue in vacation benefits relates to so-called funded benefits, but that subject is beyond the scope of our discussion here.

DO *attempt to develop a rough understanding of ERISA.*

There are many things in life that most thinking people have no desire to know about. Some of these, we must. None stands out more than ERISA, the Employee Retirement Income Security Act of 1974. It is dense, unwieldy, and covers matters you would never know existed. And, yes, somewhere is a lawyer, government employee, or insurance administrator that understands the whole of it. That person is probably the dullest person in America. But we must know *something* about it.

ERISA applies to employee benefit plans. Most people think, logically relating the words "Retirement Income" in the title of the Act, that it covers pension plans. Indeed it does. And . . . profit sharing plans, thrift plans, all group health plans, unemployment plans, vacation policies, and . . . here are some that will strike you as curiously relating to retirement . . . apprenticeship and training programs, prepaid legal services, daycare centers, and . . . are you ready? . . . scholarship funds. There is one common link in all of these benefits: a sum of money that the employer sets aside (or designates) for benefits that the government feels must be protected. Forget the title. We are dealing here with the government's distrust of its citizens—at least that class of citizens composed of employers. You may agree or chafe about this conclusion of your government, but it is the law. And you must deal with it if you wish to do business in these United States.

DON'T *scorn ERISA—it is with you till the end of your days.*

ERISA is broadly aimed at keeping employees aware of their rights and benefits. The required disclosures are used by federal agencies to supervise the funds established in any benefit plan. It requires that the funds are invested safely and prudently. It prevents the employer from using the funds at the risk of the employees. If there is any impropriety it gives rights to employees to recover any losses.

On the other side of the ledger, the information required to achieve these objectives is an enormous burden on employers. The reporting requirements are relieved somewhat for some smaller businesses, by allowing reports to be filed every three years and on short forms. Of course, the burden does not fall directly on the employer in all instances. For example, for the obligation to give each participant in the plan a sheaf of papers (that no one ever reads), you may rely on the plan administrator who prepares these documents and passes the costs on to you in higher plan administration fees.

And yet don't misunderstand that ERISA requires that benefits of any nature be offered. We must look at ERISA applications to pension plans because *these plans offer tax savings opportunities that cannot be passed up by the small business.* They are an employee benefit and can be used to motivate employees like any form of compensation. But they are also your chance to plan for your own retirement with pretax dollars. See **#115.**

115

DO *differentiate between the two basic types of retirement plans.*

The two types of plans are the defined benefit and the defined contribution. The defined benefit plan is the standard, accepted idea of a pension plan. After retirement, the employee receives a fixed amount of income for life or a defined period. The amount is related to the rate of earnings and years of service of the employee. ERISA largely came into existence because several of the funds established to pay these defined benefits were unable to do so. Congress also enacted the Pension Benefit Guaranty Corporation (PBGC) to collect a premium ($19 per employee plus an amount based on potential liability of the PBGC) that in effect insures the solvency of all defined benefit funds. It guarantees any covered person's payments up to approximately $2,500 per month. Under PBGC regulation, an employer can voluntarily terminate a defined benefit plan only in accordance with the regulations. This usually requires a lump sum payment assuring that the promised benefits up to that date will be met. There are special termination regulations for insolvent companies. (There also are separate regulations that refer to multi-employer plans, which are not addressed here.)

A defined contribution plan is much simpler to administer and to understand. Instead of a single aggregate fund, a defined contribution plan sets up an individual account for each participant. The participant has some say-so over the investment choices. From the employer's view, it is safer because the amount contributed is controllable.

DON'T *confuse the types of retirement plans, because they are quite different.*

The defined contribution plan is compared with the defined benefit plan where the success of each yearly investment determines the amount the employer may have to contribute in the subsequent year. This is determined by the PBGC. It can be a cash flow nightmare for a small business. Furthermore, if the PBGC must make good on the employer's promise upon termination, it may charge a premium of up to 30 percent of the net worth of the company. The PBGC plays no part in the defined contribution plan and this is the only plan you should consider.

Before discussing the types of defined contribution plans further, see **#117.** Several requirements of both types of plans must be met to be "qualified." Congress did not want to allow the owner-employees of small organizations to develop plans for their benefit only—so there are limitations on participation, coverage, and discrimination. For a small business, at least 40 percent of employees must be covered. The regulations define a Highly Compensated Employee (HCE), a status based on salaries in your company even if these are no more than the pay of a midlevel manager in a large organization. The plan must cover at least 70 percent of non-HCEs, or 70 percent of the non-HCEs must be greater than 70 percent of the HCEs. (I told you this was mind-numbing!) For example, if you have twenty employees, at least eight (40 percent) must participate in the plan. If as HCEs you and your key people are five of the twenty, then the plan must cover at least eleven (70 percent) of the fifteen non-HCEs; or if all five HCEs participate, then at least fourteen (70 percent) non-HCEs must participate. In addition, there are contribution restrictions as discussed at **#116.**

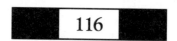

DO *apply the tests for what is a "qualified" retirement plan, with the aid of a professional.*

Continuing the discussion of the minimum requirements for qualifying a retirement plan for your small business at **#115,** the contribution discrimination standards require that the same percentage must be contributed for non-HCEs as for HCEs. There also are maximum amounts that may be contributed to either type of plan. The maximum *benefit* payable per year is $90,000 or 100 percent of the average of the three consecutive years of highest salary. For a defined contribution plan, the yearly contribution maximum is $30,000 (plus cost of living since 1987) or 25 percent of compensation. Note that the first maximum is measured by the benefit, while the other is measured by the annual salary. Understand that application of these requirements (for example, what is annual compensation, who is a non-HCE, etc.) lead to more complexity. Here, your ally is your insurance broker, financial consultant, or the like; they are familiar with the rules and will apply them to your specific circumstance.

For defined benefit plans, there also are minimum requirements for when employees must be covered after starting work and when their participation in the plan must be vested (meaning that they have an absolute right to possession). But because defined benefit plans are really not suitable for small organizations, these complexities will not be addressed.

Also remember that the form of business entity you choose will affect choice of plans.

DON'T *fail to consider the retirement benefit rules when selecting the form of business entity (see #1).*

Generally speaking, the most favorable form of business entity to maximize fringe benefits is the C corporation (the standard type of corporate entity). That is, if a benefit is available under the tax law, your access to it will be the greatest if you form a corporation and become an employee of that corporation. That can only be explained by the fact that large businesses in this country are corporations, and Congress responds to the needs, or one might say desires, of these economic giants. However, in Congress' favor, the differences in treatment between C corporations and S Corps (see #5 and #6) (or partnerships and sole proprietorships) have been narrowed in recent years. The major remaining advantages of C corporations in the area of retirement benefits are threefold: the owner-employee may borrow from the fund; may elect a lump sum payment (not available to a sole proprietor); and if forced into the red by a contribution (allowable if other requirements are met), may treat the deficit as a net operating loss with tax-loss carry forward.

You should also appreciate the importance of separation of salary and dividends in a corporation. The maximum contributions to a plan are based on "salary," not on "payment." To the extent you can justify the payment as reasonable compensation, you can put away more tax-free dollars. Years ago salaries were taxed at more favorable rates than other income, so what was reasonable was a big issue. The question is still with us, but it is less important.

DO *use one of the defined contribution plans for retirement benefits.*

As related at **#115**, there are several types of defined contribution retirement plans. The most popular is the 401(k), named after the Internal Revenue Code section. The 401(k) is more of a pretax savings account, similar to an IRA (Individual Retirement Account). The employee may contribute a certain amount each year. The employer may participate, but does not have to. Many larger employers match a portion of the funds that the employee saves. The cost of administration of a 401(k) is minor; this is an employee benefit that buys good will at a low cost.

The defined contribution plan that is more similar to the defined benefit plan is the profit-sharing plan. The term is misleading—the company does not have to make a profit to contribute. And unlike the old days, the employer rarely pays cash; it pays the money into individual accounts toward retirement (cash is not available to the employee until later). The desirability of the profit-sharing plan from the point of view of the employer is the flexibility: it contributes only what it can afford at the time, the amount may vary from year to year.

The annual limits to the amount contributed to a defined contribution plan are with respect to overall payroll—no more than 15 percent of total payroll—and no more than $30,000 to any one employee. But do not forget that there are other limitations applicable to all qualified retirement plans, as discussed in **#115.**

DON'T *look at an ESOP as only a retirement plan.*

While the ESOP (Employee Stock Option Plan) allows an employer to contribute funds into individual employee accounts each year, similar to a profit-sharing plan, it is much more powerful—and more vulnerable. The vulnerability stems from the fact that the funds contributed are used primarily, though not exclusively, to purchase stock of the employer. So the investment is at the risk of the success of a single company. On the other hand, some of the power comes from the same source (i.e., you can *impact* the success of your investment).

But ESOPs are used for many more purposes than retirement plans. In the nonfamily owned business, they can be used to liquefy your private stock.

Over a period of years you effectively sell the company to your employees. They may pay more for the company than if you tried to sell it to a third party. You also have the satisfaction of having your "child" in the hands of foster parents that you choose. But the real advantage again is the favorable tax treatment of the money received by the owner-seller, the 1042 rollover. This subject is covered in the Succession Planning section of this book. See **#152.**

ESOPs also may be used as a financing tool to capitalize a company. The concept requires more explanation than can be offered here. The downside of ESOPs is complexity. An army of professionals is required. And that means that there is the inevitable skim off the top. As in all investing, never forget the transaction (middleman) cost.

118

DO *understand the basics of sexual harassment law.*

There are both federal and state laws that prohibit sexual harassment. Unless there is a state agency responsible for a state law that is more severe than the federal law, the likely source of problems will arise under the Equal Employment Opportunity Commission (EEOC). The EEOC has defined sexual harassment broadly as unwelcome sexual conduct that is a condition of employment. But the interpretation of this statement has taken on a more concrete form. As to what is unwelcome, see **#120.**

There are two types of sexual harassment that the law recognizes. The first is quite explicit and is relatively easy to recognize and deal with. It involves the withholding of employee benefits (for example a promotion or good performance review) unless the employee cooperates sexually. The other is the "hostile environment" offense, where the employee is subjected to an environment that prevents the employee from reaching his or her potential. Generally speaking, a charge based on a hostile working environment is more subtle than the explicit demand to engage in sexual activity. However, if the environment becomes so offensive that a reasonable person would be forced to quit, then it is assumed that the employee has been involuntarily discharged and the charge is treated more like a sex-for-pay case. In certain cases, the hostile environment may turn on the issue of whether a coworker's conduct has the effect of interfering with the employee's work performance. This appears to be another way of measuring the level of hostility in the environment.

DON'T *think that sexual harassment is different from other discrimination problems.*

What defines a "hostile work environment"? There are a number of factors that are deemed telling. How frequently does the conduct occur? If it was a single instance, the complaining person may simply be too sensitive. If it is repetitive, the atmosphere is already tainted. The severity of the action is highly relevant. Is the conduct physically threatening or humilitating? Is there proscribed touching? Or is the complained-of conduct verbal? If so, how descriptively offensive are the verbal statements? And how are the statements made? In a bantering, nontaunting way, or in an abusive and condescending manner? It is not possible to point to a word or phrase or even a single action and say that such conduct has been found by the EEOC or the courts to be prohibited because the context is extremely important.

When the harassed person is a female, the standard for establishing whether the environment is hostile is whether it would be considered so by the "reasonable woman." In other words, the fact that men were not bothered by the environment is irrelevant.

Does it interfere with the employee's work performance? Is the employee temporarily upset and unable to perform his or her work? Will the employee avoid an encounter with the coworker that is the perpetrator? What was the reaction of other persons at the time—were those of the same sex offended? Determining if an environment is "hostile" is very difficult to describe in the abstract. It is more recognizable in reality.

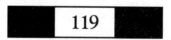

119

DO *recognize that sexual harassment is not always easy to determine and erring on the side of cautiousness is advised.*

If an employee is approached by a coworker for a date, and refuses, the requesting employee may not continue to pursue the unwilling coworker. If the unwilling employee makes it clear that he or she is uninterested in any further discussions of personal matters, continued requests could constitute harassment. The situation would be judged much more severely, of course, if the employee that requested the date were a supervisor and it was clear that the intended date was expected to lead to sex. It is not necessary, to establish a case of sex-for-pay, that the supervisor explicitly conditioned the favor on the performance of sex. Simply discussing one at the same time as the other is enough, at least if it happens repeatedly, to establish the link between sex and employment.

Perhaps more surprisingly, it is not enough to defeat a claim to show that the offended employee voluntarily engaged in sexual activity. If there is an unwelcome advance, followed by initial resistance, there is no defense if the employee eventually succumbs. This is particularly the case where the sexual activity is made the basis for continued employment. The rule was fashioned to account for the power imbalance.

On the other hand, in a hostile environment case, it may be shown that the employee's provocative dress or speech may have contributed to unwelcome approaches. And contrarily, if the employer requires the employee to wear suggestive or sexy clothing, it is harassment.

DON'T *give up hope that sexual harassment is impossible to deal with because it is so vague.*

How do you cope with something that is amorphous—changing with developing law—and at least subjective in some measure? As with all such problems, do not wring your hands in despair and spend sleepless nights in worry. And do not ignore the phenomenon thinking that it will go away. You need to develop a policy that will prevent the occurrence, but not one that is so restrictive that you will be held to a higher standard than the law imposes—unless that is your intent.

It is the sign of our times that if there is a problem that may result in legal liability, it will generate a coterie of consultants that offer to assist you with a solution. In general, avoid people who have simply read a book or two and have become self-styled experts. Particularly in matters such as these, common sense is all that is required. If you or your top managers are insensitive to sexual harassment, a course or two will not undo your obtuseness. Chances are great that there are one or two people in a small organization that are not sensible about being sensitive. You need to frankly discuss the matter with such people and make it clear that this conduct will be considered in your evaluation of their overall managerial performance. A man cannot be a "good manager"—except that he is a skirt-chaser. Refraining from such conduct is *part of* the manager's job. If he can't deal with that, he is *not* a good manager. Period. In any event, you must have a policy that effectively deals with sexual harassment: seek out, strongly disapprove, discipline, sensitize.

DO *listen to whether there was in fact an unwelcome advance—don't prejudge; take action if there was.*

The Supreme Court has stated that the essence of a sexual harassment case is whether there is an unwelcome advance. On the one hand, if there is physical sexual aggression, there is clearly an unwelcome advance. On the other, there may be cases where there simply was no credible evidence that the accused made any approaches to the complainant. In many situations, however, the issue of what is an advance looms large.

The Supreme Court also has made clear that the fact that the complainant engaged in sex-related conduct does not mean that the advance was not unwelcome. In other words, if there was sex-related conduct, it does not have to be by force. But there must be a showing that there was some manifestation by the complainant that he or she did not welcome the words or conduct. Thus, if the complainant makes statements to others, particularly supervisory personnel, that he or she is offended by the approach and wants it stopped, the "unwelcomeness" is shown. What about the complainant's conduct preceding the approach? It is relevant in determining whether the complainant's protest is credible. The appropriate advice to be given to an employee who complains is to "just say no." Once the person says no, then any further advance is "unwanted." You must step in.

The situation of a broken relationship presents problems. If one of the participants insists on continuing the relationship, there is a higher burden on the complainant to show rejection.

DON'T *think that only improper advances constitute sexual harassment.*

The hostile environment (see #118) cases involve sexual implications, but not necessarily unwelcome advances. The EEOC guidelines clearly state that in addition to unwelcome advances the law proscribes "other verbal and physical conduct." Here the active participation of the complainant is highly relevant. The test of unwelcomeness still applies. If the complainant participates in the verbal and physical conduct, he or she cannot be heard to complain that such conduct was not welcome. But the issue is a little more complex. An employee may go along for awhile, tolerate the environment, avoid being a prude, and still draw the line at some *particular* conduct. But the line must be clearly drawn. The "No" must be a little more forceful than if the unwelcome conduct was fresh and new. Pranksters have a hard time proving a case of unwelcome verbal and physical conduct. But that does not mean that they lose all their rights to protection against sexual harassment.

The courts have been fairly strict on harrasment if there is no sex discrimination. That is, suppose that a supervisor makes sexual advances to both sexes. Or uses sexually oriented vulgarities about both sexes. Can such distasteful conduct be corrected under the sexual harrasment laws? No. But a mixed bag? Maybe. If the conduct, while having no sexual overtones, is directed at only one sex, there is harassment. In other words, abusive language or acts that degrade a person are not in themselves proscribed; if applied only to one sex, it becomes sexual harassment. Sexual debasement is illegal only if it is more than being crude. And that is a shame.

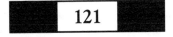

121

DO *realize that condoning sexual harassment may be implied.*

In ordinary agency law (see #78), the principal (company) is not liable for the acts of its agent unless the principal is made aware of the agent's actions or the actions are those ordinarily required in carrying out the duties of the assigned responsibility. So if you have a supervisor acting within the scope of his or her authority, sexual harassment is imputed to the company (i.e., it is assumed that the company knew and condoned the acts of the supervisor). But what if the person who is harassing the victim is not a supervisor?

Generally, for an employer to be liable for the acts of an employee who is not vested with the authority of a manager, there must be notice to the company. For example, if a coworker is harassing another employee, the company is not liable if it has no knowledge. But once the harassed employee calls the matter to the attention of a manager, there is company knowledge and responsibility. That is one reason that it is so important to make managers aware of the company's responsibilities when an employee is being harassed. A proper policy will require the manager to alert the proper managerial personnel to the potential problem. Manager awareness is therefore critical. After notice, the company must take action as necessary to stop the conduct. Simply pointing out that the actions of the coemployee were against company policy is not enough.

A policy is the most important protection that you have.

DON'T *delay; establish a sensible policy against sexual harassment—and enforce it.*

There is no easier way to find yourself in legal difficulty with a sexual harassment charge than to have failed to act in the face of earlier occurrences. If you receive a complaint, it is axiomatic that it must be investigated. But you must do more. You must discipline the person effectively. This may be an escalating policy in which you first give a verbal warning. But you cannot continue to simply give warnings. Even counseling may not be enough. The EEOC requires "... appropriate corrective action." And the action must be increasingly severe until the harassment stops.

So your guidelines are clear. First, adopt a policy that forbids sexual harassment. Do not try to describe every type of conduct because you will simply provide the perpetrator a loophole or you will provide the accuser with a basis for complaining that the policy was not proper. Second, be sure that the policy is communicated to all of the employees in a meaningful way. No, you do not need to hire a consultant. But you cannot trivialize the subject. Third, and most important, establish a grievance procedure that is easy to use and is effective. That is, one that investigates the accuser's charges with a degree of diligence, provides a written warning, then escalates to a disciplinary measure, such as time off without compensation, and then, if necessary, results in termination. And obtain employee participation in the grievance process if possible. Peer judgment is usually fair, in both appearance and in substance.

122

DO *not live in fear of the Americans with Disabilities Act (ADA).*

Perhaps no law has drawn more protest from small business than the ADA. And perhaps no law has a more justifiable goal. The problem arises when a bureaucracy implements a sound objective. You may laud the goal and despise the law. Or you may feel that government cannot solve the types of problems encountered by any society seeking to achieve noble ends. More than likely, you may just want the government to more quickly curb the obvious abuses of the law. The great expense in solving trivial problems and the inanity of trying to cover mental disabilities when defined so broadly by psychological and psychiatric workers as to include drugs and alcohol is the pitfall of the ADA. I predict that the government will back off until the law is reasonable and effective. Unfortunately, I will not predict how long that will take. So you must learn how to stay out of trouble.

The ADA is applicable to every business with fifteen or more employees. Thus, it covers millions of businesses. It is fundamentally an antidiscrimination law. It aids disabled persons in finding, keeping, and having equal opportunities for advancement in accordance with the contribution they can make. It requires that some very vague phrases be applied in making decisions that expose you to potential liability. We must look at what *is* a "disabled person."? What is an "essential function" of a job? What is a "reasonable accommodation."? And what is a "physical and mental impairment."? You will not be happy with the definitions, because there are simply no "bright line" tests.

DON'T *rely only on common sense to construe "disabled" in the ADA.*

Everything you think would constitute a disability does. Then add the physical disabilities that are not visible, but are still protected. But it is in the area of mental disabilities where the definition will surprise you. A "disability" according to Congress is an impairment "that substantially limits a major life activity." What is a major life activity? For Michael Jordan or Jimmy Regular? If Jimmy cannot play ball like Michael, does he have an impairment that limits a major life activity? Apparently, Congress meant a life activity that is carried on by us regular people. How about the slowest mental guy in class? Does he have a mental disability simply because he is the slowest? In my opinion, if you make a reasonable judgment to treat a person as not disabled and turn out to be wrong, you will not suffer some bureaucratic whipping.

Yet, it is in the area that you may be concerned with—drugs and alcohol—that common sense doesn't guide. Congress said that if a person *was* a drug addict or an alcoholic but they are fine now, they still have a record of impairment that protects them. You may not think of these problems as disabilities, but you must treat them as such—your common sense notwithstanding. However, a person who is *currently* on illegal drugs or on alcohol is *not* disabled and is *not* protected by the Act.

It is also the case that homosexuality or bisexuality is not a disability under the Act. However, in California, gays are protected by other discrimination laws.

DO *define what are the "essential functions" of a job in order to comply with the Americans with Disabilities Act.*

The ADA protects those disabled persons who can perform the "essential functions" of the job. Obviously then, you must know what these are before you can state that the disabled person is or is not qualified to do the job. You start with a job description. Then test whether every function in that description is actually done by the person that is currently doing the job. Then ask whether the job would really be a different job without that function; that is, is it "essential"? If so, then a disabled person is qualified (meaning you may not exclude him or her from consideration of the job) only if he or she can perform those functions.

Your own judgment as to whether that function is essential is evidence, but not conclusive. If your job description or ad does not include that function, it is definitely not essential. If other people doing the same or a similar job state that the function is essential, it is strong evidence. If the employee doing the same job spends most of his or her time doing that function, it is strong evidence. You do not have to do a formal job analysis as in large organizations to prove essential functions. The advice here again is to use common sense. Do not play games. If you run afoul of the law, you should get just a wrist slap.

The next step is to determine, if the person is *not* qualified to do the essential functions of the job, can he or she do them with the aid of "reasonable accommodation"?

DON'T *fail to consider if "reasonable accommodation" would render a disabled person qualified to do a job under the ADA.*

You have ascertained what essential functions must be performed to be qualified and therefore protected to do a job. You must go further and determine if the disabled person can do that job with assistance. This is called "reasonable accommodation." To state the obvious, if the person simply requires a change in hours to allow treatment of a medical condition once a week at an outpatient clinic, you must make this reasonable accommodation. You may also have to make changes in your facility to accommodate a wheelchair worker, or restructure a job if there is one essential function that the disabled person cannot perform. For example, a person's impairment may preclude driving; the mail clerk drives to the post office each day and the disabled person cannot perform that function; but a delivery driver is also available to do this function if assigned. You must do so. You may have to provide a reader for a blind person. You may have to have reserved parking for a wheelchair employee. You may have to change your job application form (or allow a person to have a reader to assist in filling it out). Many disabled persons are aware of the aids that could qualify them for a position and will suggest them. There are also support groups that can assist you in meeting this requirement. And there is a limit on how much you can be asked to do—the "undue hardship" exception. See **#124.**

124

DO *use only proper job standards for screening job applicants or promoting, selecting, and so forth, under the Americans with Disabilities Act (ADA).*

The standards that you set for selecting employees, or for promoting or making other job benefits available, cannot discriminate against disabled persons (see **#122** for a definition of disabled). This does not preclude you from setting job qualifications or standards that you feel are necessary to maintain production efficiency or quality. It does mean that the standard must be "job related" and "consistent with business necessity."

For example, a qualification requirement that is not job related is a spelling test for a production assembler. There simply is no basis for selecting on that criterion because spelling is not related to the successful performance of that job. If that employee was hired as a production worker and performed satisfactorily and applied for a lead person position that required a brief written weekly report, which would be difficult to read because it may be rife with spelling errors, you must ask if that report is an essential function of that job. Is it marginal or is it critical to success? If marginal, it is not "consistent with business necessity." On the other hand, if the person was applying for a position as a proofreader in the document and manuals department, spelling *is* a "business necessity" because this function is essential to that job.

There is also a "necessary for health and safety" standard that may be used for selection.

DON'T *see the "reasonable accommodation"*
standard of the Americans with Disabilities Act
(ADA) as requiring unreasonable expenses.

In **#123**, it was pointed out that a qualified person with a disability cannot be discriminated against based on that disability if the essential job function could be performed with "reasonable accommodation." How far must you go? The law does not require that you undergo an "undue hardship." If you have a two-story building without an elevator, and a wheelchair applicant applies for a job that requires daily visits to the second floor, must you install an elevator as a "reasonable accommodation"? Clearly the answer is no. But you must explore other options of accommodation. Can the job be restructured to eliminate that daily visit? If a meeting, could it be held on the first floor? If a report, could it be delivered by another employee?

What if there is no way to avoid some expenditure? Then there is at least some relief by allowing you a tax credit (a credit directly reduces your taxes; a deduction reduces your reported profit for taxes by a percentage determined by your tax bracket). This credit is available if you have less than thirty employees or revenue of less than $1 million per year. There is also a deduction of up to $15,000, for businesses of any size, if an accommodation requires an architectural or transportation barrier removal. And the Targeted Jobs Tax Credit Program also allows a credit for 40 percent of the first $6,000 of a disabled person's first-year salary.

125

DO *develop an employee selection process that*
does not violate the Americans with Disabilities
Act (ADA).

The ADA affects your employment selection process, as do many other of the antidiscrimination laws. The ADA prohibition is clear—you may not ask any questions regarding a disability until after making a job offer. This limitation includes job applications, interviews, and background checks. The danger of an inadvertent violation of the law is greatest in the interview; you have more company control over the application form and reference checking.

A table of prohibited questions based on all antidiscrimination laws is included in the Appendix. To put the ADA limits in perspective, understand that you may ask questions about an applicant's ability to perform specific job functions. Do you have a valid driver's license (if that function is job related)? If not, have you ever had epileptic seizures (assuming that this disability prevents a person from obtaining a valid driver's license in that state)? In a job-related question, the difference between the permissible and the prohibited is a matter of form, not substance. Alternatively, the person can be made a job offer conditioned on the possession of a valid driver's license. If he does not have the license, even because of a disability, the offer may be withdrawn. Any job offer may be made conditional on a medical exam or medical inquiries, but only if all entering employees are subjected to such an exam regardless of disability. All medical examination results must be kept confidential and segregated from employment records. Tests for illegal use of drugs, assuming they are valid under other laws in your state, are not "medical" exams under the ADA and may be demanded prior to the job offer.

DON'T *ignore the ADA restrictions; you can learn to operate within the law—good faith efforts will help keep you from sanctions.*

If a job applicant has a known disability (e.g., the person is missing an arm), the questions that may be asked under the ADA depend on whether the questions concern an "essential function" of the job. (See **#123** for a definition). If the function is essential, you may ask how the applicant will perform that function, with or without an "accommodation," even if you do not ask other applicants that question. But if the function is marginal to proper performance of the job, it may be asked only if you ask all other applicants the same question.

What are the lessons to be learned here? First, be sure that your application forms are legal. Most sources of job application forms will generally assure compliance; that may be one reason not to create your own. Second, do background checks and reference checks through persons who are familiar with these rules. Send them to a one-day course. Be sure they know how to access information from the ADA help line operated by the EEOC (800) 669-3362. And there is plenty of free material from the EEOC. Call the help line and order the Technical Assistance Manual on the Employment Provisions (Title 1) of the ADA. It is in the interview area that the real potential for violation lurks. The best policy is to use a dual interview. Have all formalities handled by your human resources person (whoever is trained as suggested above). Have your interviewing managers stick to questions regarding specific job qualifications and history. To be safe, provide them with guidelines.

DO *abide by the Family and Medical Leave Act (FMLA) of 1993 if you have more than 50 employees.*

Simply stated, the FMLA gives every employee the right to take up to twelve weeks of unpaid leave for (1) a personal medical condition; (2) a serious health condition of certain family members; and (3) the birth or adoption of a child. It provides not merely for the leave, but also requires that the employer maintain standard benefits for the employee during his or her absence. And upon return, the employee is entitled to certain reinstatement rights.

The family members who are covered by the Act include the employee's spouse (husband or wife as defined by state law), child (includes natural or adopted children under the age of eighteen or over that age if unable to care for themselves because of a physical or mental disability), or parent (includes a natural parent or one who acted as the employee's parent when young and does not include parent-in-law). The personal medical condition must render the employee unable to perform the essential functions of the employee's job. (This is another area of the law where the preparation of job descriptions will help clarify the applicability of benefits.) For family members, the "serious health condition" means one that requires inpatient care in a hospital (including any subsequent treatment required), or continuing treatment by a health care provider. "Health care provider" includes a doctor of medicine, an osteopath, a dentist, a psychologist, or nearly anyone who does not actively practice witchcraft.

DON'T *ignore the eligibility requirements for taking unpaid leave under the FMLA*

The first issue is to determine who is eligible to receive the benefits of the FMLA. (This book does not include state law provisions which may be more strict than the FMLA and will ordinarily require the employer to comply with the more severe of the two laws. You must check with your local officials, e.g., Workers' Compensation Board, to determine if such state law exists.) When an employee requests leave under the Act, you must determine two facts. Has the employee been employed for twelve months, which need not be consecutive? If so, then has the employee worked 1,250 hours during the last twelve consecutive months? For example, the employee may have worked for the company for seventeen months: twelve months in 1993, none in 1994, and five in 1995 as of June 1, 1995. The employee meets test one, but assuming that he or she works a standard forty-hour week (173 hours per month), the employee has worked only 865 hours in the last twelve months and is therefore ineligible. The employee must also meet certain notice requirements.

There are special rules relating to key employees with respect to reinstatement of such employees. (See **#128**). A key employee is a salaried, eligible employee who is in the top 10 percent compensation bracket for all employees. For a company with the minimum fifty employees, the key employee qualification will apply to the top five employees and is likely to include several of your top people aside from you, the owners. For additional eligibility, see **#127.**

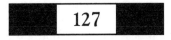

DO *examine the eligibility requirements of the FMLA before granting leave.*

The second requirement for obtaining leave under the FMLA is to give proper notice to the employer. If the need for the leave is foreseeable, then the employee must give at least thirty-days' notice. A need is foreseeable, for example, if the leave is being taken for childbirth or adoption. A medical procedure or treatment, such as a major operation, generally is planned by the doctor and patient in advance and so is foreseeable. If not foreseeable, then the notice requirement is softened to the maximum time practicable— at least one or two days before the leave is needed. If the proper notice is not given, the employer may delay the taking of the FMLA protected leave for thirty days. This should not be done unless the employee has no reasonable basis for claiming immediate leave.

The third requirement arises where the employer desires confirmation that the leave is required. The employer may demand that the employee provide a certification from a health care provider that the condition for the leave is indeed a serious health condition. It is recommended that you contact the Department of Labor which has an optional form for use by the health care provider to substantiate the condition. The employee has fifteen days to obtain the certification if the need for the leave is foreseeable, or a reasonable period of time if not. If you are skeptical of the need for the leave, you should inform the employee of what you will do in the event you are not satisfied with the certification.

DON'T *hassle the employee requesting unpaid leave under the FMLA but if you are suspicious, demand proper eligibility.*

If you don't believe the first medical provider's certification, you may require that the employee, at your expense, obtain a second opinion. If it differs, you must agree with the employee on a third provider whose opinion will be binding on both of you. If the employee fails to provide the certification, you may delay the FMLA leave, and if he or she never provides the certification, the employee loses his or her right to the unpaid leave.

You will see from the DOL form that reasons must be given by the medical provider for the leave and must be quite specific. They should include whether the condition is chronic, the length of time it is expected to last, and so forth. If the certification recommends a leave of over thirty days, the employer may require recertification after the stated minimum expected period has passed; that is, the doctor must again recommend a leave extension.

You may also require a fitness for duty report if the reason for the leave was the employee's own serious medical condition. You must inform the employee at the time the employee requests the leave that you will require this report. And to avoid any other discrimination charge, you must have a uniform policy as to the class of employees from whom you will require such a report.

128

DO *recognize your obligations under the FMLA to reinstate an employee who has taken unpaid leave.*

Reinstatement is different for regular employees and key employees. When a regular employee returns, you must offer the same position or an equivalent one. Equivalent means one with equal compensation, benefits, and other conditions of employment. If the employee is unable to perform the essential functions of the job, the employee does not have to be reinstated, but an obligation may arise under the ADA (see **#123**).

The difficult problem with reinstatement is that the employee is entitled to no more than the employee would have been entitled to had he or she not taken the unpaid leave. So that if the position has been abolished (not merely reshuffled to avoid the law), the employee is entitled only to an equivalent position. And if all the employees in a like position have had their benefits cut, the reinstated employee is entitled to more than the other employees.

Employees cannot waive their rights under the FMLA. However, if an employee is unable to assume the rigors of a prior position upon return, he or she may accept a position with lighter duties for a period of one year. And the right to restoration is available until the maximum twelve weeks have passed during the twelve-month period.

DON'T *forget that there are special rules applicable to the reinstatement of key employees that take unpaid leave under the FMLA.*

As defined above (see **#126**), a key employee is a special category employee as it relates to reinstatement. If an employer can show that reinstatement would cause "substantial and grievous economic injury" to operations, the reinstatement may be denied. It is difficult to say what such injury comprises, but it is generally thought that it is something more severe than the undue hardship used in the ADA (see **#124**). But there have not been enough court cases to determine the types and extent of economic injuries that would justify a refusal to reinstate.

The employer has the obligation (and forfeits the right to refuse reinstatement) to give notice at the time of the unpaid leave request that it will not reinstate the employee because there would be economic injury. If notice cannot be given immediately, then the employer must do it as soon as practicable. If the employer determines that reinstatement will cause the economic injury during the leave, the employer must serve notice (in person or by certified mail) and explain the basis for that conclusion. The employer also must give the key employee reasonable time to return, taking into account the situation of the employee and the employer's own needs. It is recommended that before you rely on the key person exception that you discuss this with a lawyer.

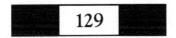

129

DO *recognize that the FMLA requires that you maintain employee benefits during the employee's unpaid leave.*

The law is clear that when an employee takes the unpaid leave to which he or she is entitled under the FMLA, the employee, or you, may elect to substitute other benefits that will pay for the time taken. For example, the substitution may be accrued vacation, sick leave, or personal leave, when the time taken is for birth/adoption or to care for a family member with a serious medical condition (see **#126** for a definition of a serious medical condition).

The matter of what the employee or you may elect depends on your medical/sick leave policy. If your sick leave policy does not allow time off with pay for a particular condition, then the employee cannot force you to *pay* for the time off taken under the FMLA, although the employee still has the right under FMLA for the time off. Your policy also controls the right to pay for time off for the care of a relative. If the employee elects to be covered by the sick leave policy, the employer must notify the employee that the leave is being counted as FMLA time.

The law is more clear on the issue of whether the employer must continue to provide benefits under the group health plan. The answer is yes. Assuming that neither party elected to have the leave treated as paid leave under the sick leave policy, the employer may require the employee to pay the insurance premiums for the period.

DON'T *fail to provide benefit coverage for persons taking unpaid leave under the Family Medical Leave Act (FMLA) that you provide for others.*

Other policies that you maintain for your employees must be continued for a person taking unpaid leave under the FMLA. Who is responsible for paying for those benefits that are purchased from outside suppliers depends on your policy with respect to other unpaid leave. Because an employer must reinstate an employee to a position with the same pay, benefits, and other terms of employment, the employer may be forced to pay the premiums on some benefits during the unpaid leave. For example, lapsed life insurance may require requalification by the employee and hence is not allowed. The employer may be forced to pay the premiums during the unpaid leave in order to avoid the requalification problem. If the employee never returns, the employer is allowed to recover from the employee that part of the premium.

Similarly, vacation that is accrued cannot be rescinded. But you need not accrue vacation or any other benefits if your policy with respect to non-FMLA leave does not provide for such accrual. In other words, you may not discriminate against any person who takes FMLA leave.

If you have a profit-sharing or pension plan, then the time taken under the FMLA cannot be deemed as a break in service for purposes of vesting or eligibility.

CHAPTER

8

CONTRACTS

DO *familiarize yourself with the fundamentals of contract law—many aspects of business law stem from these basic principles.*

Discussed here are the basic elements of a contract. The remaining information on contracts will be explained in the context of particular types of contracts used in small business. This approach will aid in your understanding and assist you in analyzing contracts and, with a little assistance, writing your own. While it does not cover as much ground, nor will you be able to startle your friends with recitations of the origin of the Statute of Frauds, you may finish the book rather than simply put it on the shelf to "read later."

You cannot hold someone to a promise unless you have given that person something of value to obtain the promise. The law calls this consideration. Some lawyers like to refer to the thing given as the quid pro quo—meaning something for something. What you give may be another promise or it may be something tangible, such as cash. In fact both persons can transfer something immediately to one another and that transaction is a contract. In other words, you cannot, unless you are under the age of ten, trade your ball for a bat and then demand back your ball for the bat you received. (If the bat was broken, unknown to you, you may have a warranty claim—but that comes later. See **#90**). What you give or promise to give must have value, but that value may be very small, even trivial. Remember, if you give someone something for nothing, it is more likely a gift than a contract.

DON'T *think that a contract can be formed only by a formal agreement in writing.*

A key element in every contract is mutual assent. It occurs when one party offers to do something in exchange for something else, and that offer is accepted by the person to whom it is made. This process is crucial to reaching a contract. The offer must be reasonably definite, otherwise it may be merely an invitation to negotiate. There are no magic words that one uses to make an offer. It is more a matter of whether it is definite in the circumstances. A great deal depends on what the parties are contemplating as a final step in the process. If the matter is of great concern, the parties usually contemplate a formal written agreement and the letters and documents preceding this are no more than negotiation. In other less material circumstances, the exchange of letters may be sufficient to create a binding agreement. The words are some indication. "Bid" is usually an offer. "Proposal" is often not. "If you will do . . . then I will do. . . ." is contract-type language.

A valid contract can only be formed by competent parties. In the case of individuals, this generally means that retail merchants may run across this problem if dealing with minors. Who is a minor is a matter of state law. Some states have two ages: one that allows a child to make a valid contract, but gives him or her the right to avoid the obligation; and one below which no valid contract ever can be formed. The more common business problem occurs with corporations and that has to do with whether the person has the authority to bind the company (discussed in **#78**).

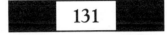

DO *understand the offer and acceptance process in contract formation.*

There are two more points to be made about the formation of a contract in addition to those made in **#130.** Once a definite offer is made, the other party may accept. The law requires such acceptance within a reasonable time. That reasonable time can be decided only by a judge or jury. You must protect yourself by always placing a limit on the time in which an offer may be accepted. If you make this an inviolable rule, it will also alert you to whether you are in fact making an offer when you are sending a letter mentioning what you want and what you may be willing to give for it.

You cannot accept part of an offer while rejecting the rest. There is no line item veto such as the President always wants and Congress has finally agreed to. It is all or nothing. If you respond that you will accept one part but not another, it is a counteroffer. If the other person then accepts your counteroffer, there is a contract on those terms.

Other terms you see in business contracts are "if" or "on condition" which mean just that—unless the event occurs first, there is no obligation to perform on the part of the person whose duty was conditional. "Represents and warrants" means that the person makes a statement based on facts and that if those facts are not true, there is a breach of contract. Warranties (see **#90**) should also be made conditions so that if the warranty/condition does not occur, you are relieved from your duty to perform.

DON'T *leave the question of what constitutes a breach to chance and be sure to include a term provision to your agreement.*

Most business contracts describe what constitutes a breach and have a provision as to what happens if there is one. If it is not specified, the law assumes that only something that is material can be a breach. Since the court may not consider the same conduct material as you do, you may wish to specify, for example, that " . . . a failure to perform as required in Paragraph X shall constitute a breach." It is also a way of calling the seriousness of the failure to the attention of the other party. Note also that the time of performance must be specified. If the timing is critical it is usually expressed by stating that "time is of the essence." But other language clearly stating the importance of time will suffice.

A contract should either have a specified term or length, or state specifically that it shall last until both parties have performed or shall continue on indefinitely. If a contract is indefinite in length, both parties should retain the right to cancel the contract after giving notice of a certain length. If a contract is of a definite length but the parties think they may wish to continue it if "things work out," make the contract automatically renewable unless one party gives notice of its intent to allow the contract to expire. Or make it renewable only if the parties agree before a certain date. If you allow a contract to automatically renew, be sure to put a reminder somewhere in your business files in case you wish to exercise your right. Use a refusal to renew as more of an invitation to renegotiate terms even if you do not desire to terminate; in other words, approach the other side a month before the contract expires and hint at nonrenewal.

132

DO *sign agreements with your sales channel representatives.*

Nearly all small businesses contract with salespeople to sell their goods. There are essentially three ways to engage sales representatives: direct (hired employee) salespersons (the most expensive initially), independent sales organizations (ISOs) or manufacturers' reps, and distributors. (In nearly all industries, large companies use direct salespeople, perhaps in combination with distributors and retailers.) Many small businesses confuse, or at least fail to understand, the legal significance of these three different channels. Yet it is simple because there is a key distinction. You sell to a distributor (wholesaler, jobber, stocking rep, etc.) and it is responsible to resell the goods. The distributor has total power over resale of the goods once it has completed purchase from the manufacturer. On the other hand, you do not sell to a manufacturer's representative, sales rep, ISO, agent, and so forth. You sell to the user (or other purchaser), and the sales rep simply is paid a commission for the sale.

This difference has two major impacts. First, the reseller is responsible for payment and it is *its* credit, not that of the ultimate customer, with which you must be concerned. The rep agreement is just the opposite. Second, you have lost pricing control once you sell to a distributor, but not so with the rep. In fact you can control *all* terms of sale with the rep and none with the reseller.

DON'T *present an unfair reseller or rep agreement to your business partner and you will find that signing and administering these contracts is easy.*

In many industries the sales channel to the next level (moving toward the ultimate customer) has been set historically, and if the industry is mature, it will circumscribe the options you have to sell your goods, unless the sales channel becomes the focus of your penetration strategy. You may also be hamstrung then with the discounts for resellers and the sales commissions for reps. Although, here again, you may decide to attempt to upset the industry leaders by using a deeper discount because you have found a cheaper method of manufacturing the product.

Always use a written agreement with your reps or resellers, at least the important ones. There are too many opportunities for future strife if you operate on a verbal understanding. Too often you want to try it out before you sign a formal agreement, but this just represents indecision. If the reseller is good, you are afraid to rock the boat; if bad, you say you don't really care and then they make a big sale and claim that on large orders you promised a bigger commission; either way you get grief. It is not difficult to sign or administer a written agreement program. The key is not to make a totally lopsided agreement that no reseller with sense would sign. This reseller or rep is your business partner. There is no need to give away the store, but there is no reason to seek every edge either. Lawyers like to draft lopsided contracts because they don't usually "live with them" after the negotiations are concluded. If the most important thing in your life is getting the edge, I suggest you move out of New York City for awhile.

DO *develop and implement a sound reseller agreement.*

The reseller or distributor agreement should cover a number of points that are unique to the relationship, while also including the basic terms of any sales transaction. It is recommended that your standard sales terms be included by attaching a copy of your sales form (see **#87**) to the agreement, incorporating it by reference in the main body of the agreement.

The agreement must first address the issue of whether the appointment will be exclusive or nonexclusive. This is not a legal decision but one based on your marketing strategy. From a legal point of view it is recommended that you state the status that you wish to implement simply to avoid future disputes. If the agreement is exclusive, it is important to define carefully the territory and the products. Also, it is important to define whether you will allow one reseller to sell from its territory into the territory of another, with or without some recompense. What about selling into an uncovered territory? Allow that only at your pleasure. What if a reseller has multiple offices and not all are within the territory? Redefine your territory if possible. Remember that if you give an exclusive territory, the term of the agreement and the cancellation rights (see below) become much more critical.

Other duties that you may wish to obligate the reseller to perform include providing competitor information, attending training sessions, attending trade shows in the territory, and so forth. These may legally be less important than establishing your mutual expectations.

DON'T *allow your reseller to expand your warranty; protect your trademark and tradename; and prohibit sale of competing products if desirable.*

In your reseller agreement, make clear that the reseller has no right to vary the warranty that you offer. Salespeople have been known to "puff" while selling and you should not be saddled with any warranty terms that you do not want. Also, you must protect your trademark and trade name. A new distributor may wish to use your corporate name followed by "of Colorado" or the state in which it intends to operate. This is permissible if you make it very clear that if the contract ends the distributor will completely and immediately change its name on all literature, store front, and so forth, including a change in corporate name as registered in the state in which it is doing business. See also **#67**.

Decide if you wish the reseller to be able to sell competing products. There is no flat prohibition in the antitrust laws that make a total prohibition illegal, unless you dominate the market for the product (an unlikely circumstance for a small business). Some people have the mistaken notion that you can demand exclusive dealing only if you are granting an exclusive reseller arrangement. The law does not so proscribe you; but it will be a bit difficult to convince a reseller that you may appoint other resellers in the territory but that they can sell only your goods. Be certain to broadly define the competing goods so you do not get into a dispute over what can be sold. If a particular competitor is your nemesis, state that the reseller cannot sell any of its goods, competing or not.

DO *not lock yourself into a long-term relationship with a reseller; define the break-up process.*

In **#133** we discussed that you must carefully consider the term and right to terminate a reseller agreement if it is exclusive. If nonexclusive, you can always appoint another reseller if things are not working out right. But if exclusive, the term becomes very important—you could be tied to this reseller and lose valuable sales. So never make the term indefinite unless you can terminate without cause. However, termination without cause is not likely to be satisfactory to a reseller that is seeking an exclusive relationship. As an alternative, keep the term short with automatic renewals unless one party gives notice (during a specified period immediately prior to expiration) that it intends to terminate. Use this threat to renegotiate terms, such as the minimum annual volume to retain exclusivity. Include the right to terminate the agreement for cause and spell out the particular obligations of the reseller at risk of cancellation.

Define what happens on termination for whatever reason the agreement is terminated. Must the reseller return its inventory to you within a specified time? Must you purchase it? (It may be to your advantage to purchase the inventory if you are appointing a new reseller.) You may wish to fill orders received after termination. If you acknowledge orders, you will be bound to fill the orders unless you specifically override the sales form acceptance provision. The point is to think out these alternatives in advance and draft your agreement accordingly.

DON'T *lose control of the credit situation with a reseller; implement a reasonable but firm inventory maintenance policy.*

Protect yourself with respect to credit terms in the reseller agreement. First, set forth your credit terms clearly. Then state that late payment must be accompanied by a late fee. Charge the late fee and allow it to remain on the statement of account. If it accumulates and you decide not to press for payment, it may be a valuable card to play at some later time. You should retain a right to delay shipment if payment is not current. This may be used for leverage in obtaining payment for past invoices.

If you require a distributor to maintain a certain inventory, or you demand a stocking order at the time you enter into the agreement, consider that the distributor may demand return or rotation rights; that is, the right to return inventory items not selling and exchange them for others. If you agree, limit the number of times that this may be done per year, and the maximum time since purchase.

Be sensitive to the problem of allocation of production. This is usually more critical for the reseller relationship than the ultimate customer (as set forth in the sales form) because the reseller is more aware of the situation. Make it clear that orders from resellers are subject to acceptance as stated in the sales form. This is another way to control the credit situation. It can also be used to enforce a minimum-order-size policy.

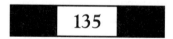

DO *use a sales rep agreement and control the efforts of the sales rep as your own; an exclusive with a territory in which each sale is paid for is best.*

The sales rep (manufacturer's representative, agent, independent sales organization, etc.) relationship is more like having a direct salesperson than a reseller arrangement that is more like a customer relationship. You can exercise more control over the activities of the sales rep. For one, you can set the price and the rep may not vary that price. This should be made clear in the agreement. You will be expected to prevent the rep from representing any other manufacturer with similar products. But you should again make this explicit in the agreement. The rep agreement also has a territory defined so that the sales on which commissions are paid can be identified. Commissioned sales are those for which the goods are shipped directly into the territory; but see the discussion below of commission splits.

As in the reseller agreement, you may work on a nonexclusive or exclusive basis. Your marketing strategy should determine which relationship is better for you. The exclusive arrangement means that you will pay the rep a commission for sales in the rep's territory regardless of the rep's involvement in the sale. You are paying the rep to cover the territory, not to make every sale. If you cannot abide this concept, the exclusive rep agreement will not work for you. If the agreement is nonexclusive a number of sticky issues arise immediately. Since you will not be paying commissions for every sale to the nonexclusive rep, you must identify how you will define the sales for which you do. All of the ways are complicated and are sure to give rise to conflicts. Think over the nonexclusive agreement carefully.

DON'T *let the rep sit on the territory—define its duties and enforce them; use a customer or product/territory approach to pay commissions.*

You should require the rep to carry out other marketing and sales-related tasks for you if exclusive. The sales rep should be obligated to attend sales meetings, buy (preferably) samples to carry and show to prospects, communicate the status of leads, and forecast sales for the territory. Some products require that the rep have a showroom or other place where customers can see and try samples. If this is desired, spell that out, including whether you are expected to cover costs.

You must also define carefully the products that are covered by the agreement. Identify them by product line name or if sold under a particular trademark. One common method is to attach a copy of your price list and circle or mark the products that are (or are not) included.

You may also use a customer approach rather than by product or territory to identify sales eligible for commissions. This approach is typical when the rep is small. The customer may dominate virtually all of the time of that salesperson. Handling commissions becomes a snap. The problem that may arise is when the customer has many locations, each with its own buying authority. Reps in other territories that have called on the same account will feel that they have earned the commission. It is best to exclude the customer from all other rep contracts.

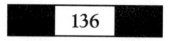

DO *specify when commissions are earned and paid in a sales rep agreement.*

Most small companies suffer from inadequate cash flow. Therefore, it is important that you structure your sales rep agreement so as to pay the rep only after you get paid. Understand the difference between the obligation to pay and payment. When the sale is booked or shipped, the obligation to pay should arise since the rep has completed its task. But you do not want to pay then, so you book a credit to the rep's account. The agreement should provide that you will pay when you are paid, or more specifically, X days after you receive payment. If there are many small orders, you may wish to pay in the aggregate, perhaps before the tenth of the month following the month of sale.

There are many variations of commission schedules. They may escalate based on cumulative monthly or annual sales. Or the commission may be geared to the size of a single purchase order—the larger the order, the higher the commission rate. Or a rate applies to increments, with the rate for each successive increment in the size of an order decreasing. You must always carefully consider what signal you are sending to the rep when you design a commission plan. Many manufacturers also use occasional commission "kickers" to stimulate sales, or use a bonus for a new product introduction. Because you may wish to change commissions from time to time, it is advisable to place the commissions in an exhibit to the agreement rather than in the main body.

DON'T *treat a sales rep the same if it terminates the sales rep agreement than if you terminate it.*

Rep agreements may terminate for a variety of reasons. If the rep is not performing to your expectations, and you have a right to cancel without cause, you may terminate the agreement. If there is a performance requirement, and the rep fails to meet it, you may terminate. Generally, either party may terminate once a year. If a rep terminates to take on a line with another manufacturer, he will be soliciting the customers he was previously selling your products to. In such event you should give no quarter to the rep in the posttermination period. On the other hand, if you decide to hire a direct salesperson to replace the rep, you may feel that the rep should be treated particularly fairly. These thoughts color the posttermination clause.

First, a commission is usually paid on any order booked prior to termination. If the notice period is long, for example ninety days, then any orders booked after termination may be noncommissioned. There should also be a period stated during which the order may be shipped in order to earn the commission. This protects against the entry of a large scheduled order with deliveries that may go far into the future and may be canceled. Reps will often want to be protected on certain accounts that have been worked and are ready to order. That is a matter for bargaining. But if you agree, obtain the account names in writing, cull the "hopes," and set a time for expiration. If you have a new rep coming on board you may wish to deny any further rights. Do not include protection in the agreement.

CHAPTER

9

COMPUTERS

DO *understand what is meant by computer law.*

The term computer law is a little confusing, since there is no area of the law that has been created strictly for computers. Instead, it is more like oil and gas law or admiralty law in that it is an area of human activity for which lawyers believe the subject matter (oil and ships) is sufficiently distinctive to merit a special category. They gather the various classic divisions of the law (contracts, torts, employment, etc.) relating to this subject matter into texts and areas of practice expertise that is based on an intimate knowledge of the subject matter.

Computer law involves contract law, tort law, privacy law, commercial business law, intellectual property (IP) law, and even criminal law. It is distinguishable because it requires some grasp of computer hardware and software. Yet, the intellectual property laws apply to computers, with some twists and turns, like any other subject matter. Purchasing a computer involves a commercial transaction to which the Uniform Commercial Code applies just like purchasing an automobile. Most of the difficulties in applying contract, tax, or IP law stem from the uniqueness of software—it is in itself a unique human endeavor. The following discussion will cover some of the quirks in applying standard legal concepts to computers. (See Intellectual property, **#143**; Procurement, **#144**; Crime, **#141**.) There are special problems such as state sales tax on software: a product subject to tax, or a service not subject to tax in some states. To classify the subject matter of a software development contract as goods or services may be impossible.

DON'T *think that laws do not apply to cyberspace (the Internet).*

Aside from the annual Super Bowl, there are few events in recent memory that have generated more hype than the Internet, aka, the Information Superhighway. (Hype and the word *super* are handmaidens.) The universal availability of inexpensive information and communication services will undoubtedly have a major impact on our society, but its impact on the law, after some settling down, will be minimal. Some areas bear mention. Privacy on the Internet is discussed at **#139**.

Crime begets punishment, usually. Breaking and entering, and stealing or destroying property are crimes. Some like to see the hackers as the modern analog of Robin Hood. Unfortunately, the analogy is flawed simply because Robin Hood was a fictional character who did no serious wrong in tweaking the nose of the establishment. Hackers do. We now have at least one case where a hacker was convicted and sent to jail.

The Internet is creating new problems for intellectual property protection. Valuable software files can be transmitted internationally in seconds from the comfort of your den. The responsibility of Internet access providers is not yet clear, though it is reasonable to predict that they will be saddled with some duty to refrain from posting copyrighted material for others to download. To copy a copyrighted software program and transmit it to a friend or associate is no different from copying it on a disk and handing it to him or her. It is theft. See **#140.**

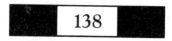

138

DO *inform your employees about your voice mail and E-mail policies.*

The use of voice mail and E-mail for both internal and external communications has raised the Big Brother bugaboo over privacy rights. Unlike a telephone conversation that is transitory, and therefore not likely to be monitored by the company, voice mail and E-mail messages are stored purposely or inadvertently. In a dispute concerning sexual harassment, for example, recorded messages of solicitation by the manager, or invitations by the employee, may provide damning evidence for one side or the other. Can this information be used? And do you want your employees to work in an atmosphere of surveillance?

The new federal Electronic Communications Privacy Act gives employers the unqualified right to access the electronic messages recorded by the employee. The applicability of the law to internal communications probably is airtight. There is simply no right of privacy in the Constitution, however broadly interpreted, that allows the employee to claim any personal right to the information, and therefore any right to protection of it. The application to external communications, whether by private E-mail, such as MCI Mail, or over the Internet, is not so clear. It may depend on what is the reasonable expectation of privacy in the circumstances. See **#139** regarding external privacy rights. So publishing your policy may be the primary determinant of the employee rights. This requires a balance of the right to access with a respect for your employees' sensitivity to privacy issues.

DON'T *give the wrong signals to your employees regarding their voice and E-mail privacy rights.*

If you have a policy that forbids employees from accessing the voice mail or E-mail messages of other employees, it may imply that these messages are private, even with respect to your access. So, if you feel that such access is or may be necessary, you must specifically point out in such policy that the company reserves the right to access the stored messages, even though other employees do not. This must be coupled with identification of those individuals who may access the messages. (Limit this to one or two people who have the human resources responsibility.)

Employees may infer that because they have passwords limiting access to their computer files or voice mail that theirs is a right of privacy against the company. Your policy should warn the employees that passwords are easily evaded by computer-literate people or other technical types. You should strongly proscribe any deferred eavesdropping by your technical telecommunications support and maintenance personnel.

If you have no policy, before you invade these files, even for legitimate business reasons, consult legal counsel. Limiting access to a few select people under commitment to nondisclosure and immediately informing the employee may be advisable.

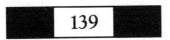

139

DO *realize that when you operate on the Internet, you have privacy rights, but there are exceptions in the law, and possibly in your on-line contract.*

At #138, the law of privacy is discussed with respect to E-mail and voice messages that employees send and receive on the company's internal network. What privacy can one expect on a public network, such as the on-line service providers and the Internet? The Electronic Communication Privacy

Act (ECPA) sets the rules. The ECPA covers voice and E-mail. It breaks out the proscribed acts into two categories.

The first deals with interception, what in voice parlance would be referred to as wiretapping. It is illegal to do so or to use or disclose the contents if you know that the information came from an illegal interception. Consequently, a system provider may not disclose the content of a message that you sent to it for retransmission to another. There are a number of exceptions to this rule for the service provider, such as allowing it to intercept in the course of providing the service. There are also exceptions if one of the parties to the communication consents to the interception. But it is the contract that you sign with the provider that probably is more restrictive on your privacy rights with respect to the provider. Your consent waives all the rights under the ECPA.

Nor do you have any privacy from law enforcement officials if they comply with certain conditions, usually a court order. The service provider is not even obligated to inform you of the interception, indeed they may be precluded from doing so.

DON'T *attempt to conduct industrial espionage on the Internet or you may be subject to large penalties for illegal access.*

The second aspect of the ECPA is the prevention of unauthorized access to information stored on a computer system. In other words, it makes hacking illegal. While the hackers may be concerned with punishment meted out for destruction or damage of information, you must be sensitive to the punishment for simple access (which includes access beyond authorized access, too) that is done for "commercial advantage." In other words, industrial espionage on the Internet is illegal. The penalty for this type of illegal access is quite severe: a fine up to $250,000 and up to one year in jail, or both. This is much greater than if you are caught physically trespassing. And access is not illegal if it is accidental, (i.e., the person did not intend to invade the privacy of the other person). Intent is always difficult to prove; although one court has held that the use of surreptitious means is evidence of intent.

Here again *your* privacy rights are limited with respect to law enforcement officials, just as they are limited with respect to search and seizure of your property. And as with interception, consent will waive your privacy rights to the messages that are stored, for example, by a system operator. If someone invades your rights, you may sue that person for damages. So if you are the victim of an unauthorized access, you may inform police but you may also bring suit for the illegal access. You can collect actual damages (for example the theft of a trade secret may result in lost sales and profits), as well as costs and attorneys fees.

DO *obey the rules for protecting copyrighted matter on the Internet.*

The copyright laws (see **#74**, etc.) are alive and well on the Internet. Despite the ease with which a work may be downloaded and copied (compared to obtaining a book and photocopying all of the pages), it is unlawful to do so. What are the rules? First, understand the limits of fair use (see **#76**). If you are downloading for your own personal use, you are in a much safer area. But if you operate a bulletin board or think others may be interested and you post material, you are certainly flirting with illegality. This was brought home to a operator who was posting images from *Playboy* magazine: the magazine sued and recovered $500,000 in damages.

What about software available on the Net? Commercial software on-line is protected just like software purchased in a store. You cannot legally obtain commercially licensed software on the Net without a license. Many publishers are waiting for on-line security problems to be resolved so that payment may be made directly to the maker (or an authorized distributor), but it is not available yet. Shareware is a creature of the Internet. It is a throw-it-at-the-wall-and-hope-some-will-stick marketing scheme. You post the program and a license for a limited period of use. Anyone who copies the program and finds it useful is expected to pay. They may not. It is based on trust. As a practical matter the author cannot do anything about it. There is also public domain software that is truly free. But not every program without a copyright notice is in the public domain. See **#74**.

DON'T *misuse the E-mail of others and understand your own rights to messages you post on the Internet.*

Another aspect of proprietary rights on the Internet is ownership of E-mail. As noted in the discussion of copyrights at **#74** and the following discussion, the author's rights come into being as soon as the work is fixed in a tangible medium. As soon as someone places that E-mail message in a storage device it is fixed and a copyright is established. If you sign a contract with an on-line service provider, though, you may be waiving your copyright to the messages. And do not think that if your E-mail message incorporates some other person's writing or image, that your copyright includes that writing or image. You are not the author. Further, if you are creating an E-mail at your work place, the E-mail copyright is not owned by you. See **#75** for the work-for-hire doctrine.

If you belong to a user group where messages are posted, your copyright prohibits reproduction or distribution without your permission. Particularly in larger systems where there is a moderator, the system operator may own a compilation copyright (see **#76**) for the message collection. Each message sender still owns the copyright in the particular message, and the system operator cannot violate any of the sender's exclusive rights. But it can prevent anyone from copying the entire collection and reposting it to another system—for example, a free one. If you want others to copy and disseminate your message, simply add a statement that you claim no rights in the message. Or you may condition the right.

141

DO *not trifle with the criminal laws that prevent computer crime.*

It would not be fair to minimize the seriousness of computer crime. On the other hand, it is sometimes difficult to suppress the image that the Software Publishers Association (SPA) is the modern Carrie Nation protecting society from itself. Whether the spate of laws condemning computer crime is simply the usual reaction of Congress and state legislatures to that self-appointed judge and jury of society—the media—or a worthy effort to nip a new crime in the bud may be in the eye of the beholder. But there is some real law dealing with computers, and more precisely, communication crime.

The Electronic Communication Protection Act (ECPA) is discussed at **#138**. It applies to private communications; that is, messages between two parties not intended for public dissemination. The Computer Fraud and Abuse Act (CFAA) deals with the use of the computer to commit fraud on one or more persons. It is aimed at hackers, a group once known for a fanatic obsession for solving computer problems—now known as a shorthand expression for illegal accessers. It explicitly protects government databases and computer files. It also proscribes illegal access to financial, credit, or credit card information. It additionally prevents the trafficking in passwords. Like many criminal statutes, it requires intent to be guilty of a felony (felonies, as opposed to misdemeanors, are serious). But in the famous Internet Worm case, it was held that there need not be criminal intent, merely intent to gain access. Repeated tries could constitute intent to gain access.

DON'T *think that the Internet is a new mechanism for carrying out fraudulent schemes; old laws, as well as new, protect consumers.*

If the Internet effects a significant change in society, conducting commerce on the Net without wholesale fraud will depend on a system of credit purchasing. Now, however, the question is whether the Net does not facilitate credit crime rather than enable commerce through credit purchasing. Specifically, the use of the Net to transmit information about stolen cards and to exchange card information is a threat to the entire structure of credit purchasing. In addition to the CFAA there are specific laws that prohibit the production, use, or trafficking in—knowingly and with intent to defraud—of counterfeit credit devices. Since many of the techniques for obtaining an access card or code are through software programs that sample sources, the mere production of an access code by such methods, or the possession of a bank of such codes, is illegal.

The telephone is an instrument that facilitates the perpetration of fraud. Defrauding people of their money through telephone scams is an established fact. In response, Congress has enacted a Wire Fraud Act. While perhaps redundant in view of the CFAA, it is as applicable to computer-based fraud as well as telephone fraud. It is probably true that the provisions of the Federal Trade Communications Act, which widely regulate telephone solicitation, are applicable to the Internet. In short, if an activity is illegal when using the telephone or mail, it is most likely to be illegal when using the Internet.

142

DO *obtain protection for your software if you are in the software development business, and even if you are not.*

Software is protectable in several different ways, at vastly different costs, and with considerably different breadth. But who should consider software protection?

Of course if you are in the business of developing software for commercial applications, you must consider protection—this may be one of your most important assets. If you are a system integrator, or sell hardware with industry-specific software that you create from scratch, or that you tailor for specific applications, by all means seek protection. You should also consider protection of software that you create, or have created for you, for your internal use, as it may be valuable to others. Others may have problems for which you found a unique solution that could be licensed. It may even be to your advantage to license a competitor—the royalties a competitor pays constitute an additional cost to its product. You do not need to hire a cast of software programmers to create the software; you can contract out the actual code development (see **#145**). Nor need you take on the marketing task and divert your efforts from your core business. One of my clients created a licensed product by pairing his special industry knowledge with the computer skills of a freelance programmer. By protecting their new product, they each made money on the license.

DON'T *be confused by the various methods of protecting software.*

In the realm of intellectual property law, software is odd. It may be protected by three methods: trade secret (see **#70** for a discussion of general principles), copyright (see **#74** for a discussion of general principles), and patent (see **#143** for a discussion of the differences between patent and copyright protection for software).

Trade secret rights are used to provide perpetual protection by closely guarding the software with a license that demands confidentiality, or by maintaining the source code secret. A confidentiality agreement is used where the number of users/licensees is limited, perhaps to a few hundred. Each license is negotiated and a licensee signs an agreement to pay royalties in exchange for a nonexclusive license. The license provides that the licensee shall not disclose the software or documentation to any third party. A breach of this obligation would give rise to a suit based on the contract. Because the number of licensees is limited (a practical, not legal requirement), the license is signed, and the prohibition against disclosure can be monitored and enforced. The secret remains and protection is effective.

If the software is for the mass market, such as a word processing program, it is not practicable to obtain a confidentiality agreement from every single user. Even if you did, you could never enforce it. You may attempt to protect the program by maintaining the source code in confidence, but that allows others to develop a program with identical features without violating your trade secret. Additional forms of protection are recommended.

DO *use copyright law to protect software that you create.*

As explained in **#142,** software is protectable by trade secret, copyright, and patents. Each method of protection has unique uses and opportunities.

Software has been explicitly recognized as copyrightable since the Computer Software Copyright Act of 1980. But what is protectable? Source code, object code, operating system, applications, databases, games, utility programs, and so forth, are all protectable. Software may be stored on floppy disks, hard disks, firmware (ROM or microcode), tape, microfilm, or plain old ordinary paper. (It is easiest to think of software in relation to copyright as a source code printout; when embedded in a microprocessor as microcode, it seems more like a machine element than a "writing"—but courts have held that the storage medium is irrelevant.)

It is not necessary to register the copyright, though there are advantages in doing so (See **#74**). Nor need you use a copyright notice, though it is highly recommended that you do. The notice may appear on the hard copy and on the opening screen (look carefully at any application program you start up). Registration is not complex and is extremely inexpensive—a $20 filing fee. You can fill out the TX form obtainable from the Copyright Offices yourself. To assist you, I highly recommend *How to Copyright Software,* Salone (1989) from Nolo Press, 950 Parker Street, Berkeley, CA 94710.

DON'T *fail to consider patenting software if it is unique and valuable.*

In addition to protection through trade secret law, **#70,** and copyright law, software may be patented. This area of the law is unsettled. The Supreme Court, after some vacillation, appears to condone software patents, but the parameters are still in doubt. Compared to protection by other methods, a software patent is considerably more expensive—probably $5,000 at a minimum. So reflection on the value of protection is required.

The advantage of patenting is that even if the infringer was unaware of the patent on your product, the patent may be infringed. Compare copyright where it must be proved that the infringer "copied" (which includes access to your product) your software. However, a software patent is obtainable only if you can prove to the United States Patent and Trademark Office (PTO) that your program is patentable over the prior art (see **#51**).

One objection to patenting software is that it is a mental process and therefore not within one of the allowable classes of patents. You will be more successful if the program is part of a machine or apparatus; for example, if the software program is embedded in the controls of a machine. The patent is really a machine patent, not strictly speaking a software patent. But some software patents have been allowed where the program runs on a garden variety personal computer and the core of the invention resides in the code. The boundary of patentability lies somewhere near the prohibition against patenting a mathematical algorithm, but the line is fuzzy. Unlike copyright protection, expert help is required here.

144

DO *negotiate a sound development contract for software if you are the developer.*

If you are in the business of developing software, you need a standard contract to cover your needs. The discussion here takes the position of the developer. See **#145** for the position of the customer.

The typical contract calls for the developer to create software that meets certain expressed needs of the customer and to transfer that program to the customer in exchange for payment. You need to specify what is to be created. This is not simple. If the customer is sophisticated, it may have the wherewithal to prepare a specification that describes in detail the software required. A statement of work is recommended so that the customer cannot later complain that something different (more) was intended. The customer wants an airtight delivery schedule. You need to keep this requirement as loose as possible to cover unforeseen problems. You want payment as early as possible; the customer wants the opposite. The recommended approach is to create a schedule with milestones of completion and a payment accompanying each. Keep as many rights to the software as possible if it has the potential for sale to others. One approach is to transfer title and to take back an exclusive license that allows you to license others (except direct competitors of your customer), perhaps with a royalty paid to the customer. Or try to retain all of the rights if you want to sell a proprietary version.

DON'T *expose yourself to unlimited liability in developing software for a customer.*

An area of contention in negotiating a development agreement for software with a customer is the warranty and indemnification provisions. As the developer you will want to eliminate all warranties by selling the software as is. But this is not usually achievable. The next best position is to give an express warranty that the software will conform to the specification in the statement of work and will be of good, workmanlike quality.

In conjunction with the express warranty, there should be a limitation on implied warranties. The UCC reads in certain warranties in every commercial contract. One is an implied warranty that the software will meet the description of goods in an offer letter, advertisement, or the claims made by salespeople. This implied warranty can be limited by the express warranty as stated above. Of great importance in a software development agreement is the implied warranty of fitness for a particular purpose. In brief, if the customer has informed the seller of the use to which the program will be put, this warranty says it must meet that stated use. Again, limiting the warranty to conformance with the specifications attached will avoid the problem. Then, you must expressly disclaim all other warranties, express or implied. This language supersedes applicability of the UCC. Especially significant is that it defeats the UCC provision for consequential damages from a breach of warranty. But it is recommended that you state this limitation of damages in explicit language. A good start here is to look closely at the warranty and disclaimers on standard computer program licenses. Microsoft has already paid its lawyers to solve your legal problem.

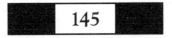

145

DO *try to live with standard software for your in-house operations.*

In the days of mainframe and minicomputers, much software was designed for or by the user. In the current world of the ubiquitous PC, most software is purchased off the shelf at a local computer store in a shrink-wrapped package. Quite aside from the enormous difference in price this change has made, the standardization has resulted in higher quality, if for no other reason than because the millions of users more quickly uncover errors.

If the software does not operate properly on your computer what is your remedy? Like most consumer products, not much. There are standard warranty disclaimers (see **#90**) and limitations for consequential damages in nearly every software application program license. If so, take it back or throw it away and vow never to deal with that supplier again. But it is probably not the software itself anyway. It will be an incompatibility with your computer configuration (the software and add-on hardware you have had installed). For this cure, your remedy may lie at the door of your computer dealer, particularly if it installed all the software and hardware on your system. If you were told that the package being purchased would work with your configuration, this is a warranty. Unless you were informed that the warranty was limited before purchase, your warranty guarantees proper operation. Do not accept less.

DON'T *be at the mercy of a software developer if you need custom software.*

You may find that the software that is commercially available for your application does not meet your unique needs. A typical example is the procurement of manufacturing/inventory control packages. The vendor may offer to tailor the software to your existing system. Fine. But be sure that you get what you want. The objectives of the developer in this type of contract is explained in part in **#144**. Here we look from the customer's perspective.

An irritating but accepted fact is that software is sold with bugs—small defects, which to the user are not so small. If this were an automobile, you would be back to your dealer for immediate action and he would respond post haste (at least since the Japanese have landed). But at best your software developer will be concerned, and at worst they'll be cavalier. You need a strong provision for the fixing of bugs *in a reasonable time frame and as many as occur.* Major survival-threatening system software should classify bugs, and the most critical class should demand immediate and unremitting repair. If necessary, hold back payment until X days of successful operation beyond acceptance. Or buy a maintenance contract that adjusts the price of the software by any maintenance. Do not agree that if bugs cannot be fixed the software developer may simply return the money; it likely will be gone and surely will be inadequate. If the software can be procured in modules, buy one first, see that it and the developer are fine, then buy the others.

CHAPTER

10

BUSINESS SUCCESSION PLANNING

DO *plan for succession of your family business and start by familiarizing yourself with the basics of the federal estate and gift tax.*

When you decide that it is time to start thinking about your family-owned business after you retire and pass away, you must learn the basics of the federal gift and estate tax. Frankly, this is really boring stuff. But if you are at the age where this subject is of interest, you must have learned by now that not everything in life you must learn is pleasant. So, let's get on with it.

The basic rule is simple. You have a credit (not a deduction) of $192,800 (the equivalent of a $600,000 exemption of assets) that you may use for all the substantial gifts made during your life and transfers upon death. If you are married, you and your spouse both have a separate credit. After that you pay a federal estate and gift tax that starts at 18 percent and increases to 50 percent for amounts in excess of $2,500,000. The lower rate is misleading. If your estate is over $600,000, the bracket rate applicable starts at that value; that is, the rate applicable to $600,001, which is 37 percent.

The following basics underlie some important tax planning techniques that you must grasp. First, all plans should result in your using up your $600,000 of tax-free asset transfer. To give away a part of your estate without using the credit is a waste, and it means you have paid too much tax somewhere else. A credit not used is lost forever.

DON'T *start planning on the best way to structure the succession to your business until you grasp the basics.*

Second, the term substantial gift means one that is over $10,000 per person per donee (the gift recipient) per year. If you have three children, you and your spouse may give away $60,000 per year without using the credit.

Third, you have an unlimited deduction of all property that you leave to your spouse. This rule provides another significant tax-planning advantage. See **#147**. It is circumscribed only by the exception that a terminable interest is not allowed a deduction unless it is a qualified terminable interest property (QTIP). (A terminable interest is, for example, a life estate—the house is yours so long as you live.) The reason that you may wish to give your spouse a life estate in your half of the estate is that you may wish to control disposition of the property (for example, to children of a previous marriage, or to a charitable institution). The transfer to your spouse may be by will, joint tenancy with right of survivorship, or life insurance.

Fourth, there is an ugly little tax called the generation skipping transfer tax. It precludes you from leaving gifts or testamentary (at death) transfers to your grandchild, thereby skipping the tax that would be levied if you left the money to your child, who would in turn leave it to their child, just as you intended. A grandchild is only one kind of skip person. A spouse, regardless of the age difference, is never a skip person. The good news about the GST tax is that there is a $1 million lifetime exemption which may be allocated between any transfers.

147

DO *evaluate the bypass trust for saving estate taxes in the succession of your business.*

Nearly all estate planning for married persons starts with the opportunity afforded by the unlimited marital deduction (see **#146**). The marital deduction offers the chance to defer estate taxes (not avoid, but defer) until the death of the second spouse. During the second spouse's life, there are opportunities to reduce the estate to avoid the second tax. But first, you must remember to use that $600,000 exemption before taking advantage of the unlimited marital deduction. You can do that by leaving the first $600,000 of your estate (let us assume it is a total of $2,000,000) directly to your children. But if you wish to allow your spouse to utilize that amount, you may leave it in trust with the income to them for life (you can even invade principal at the trustee's discretion) and the remainder to your children. Thus you can achieve your assurance that the money will reach your children regardless of your surviving spouse's desires, utilize your exemption, and still assure your spouse that he or she will have income if necessary. Because the money (and all appreciation thereon) bypasses the surviving spouse's estate and goes to the next generation, the trust is called a Bypass Trust.

Should you put more than $600,000 in the bypass trust? The answer is not as clear and requires an evaluation of the whole estate. But if you are in a noncommunity property state, you should always balance the assets between the spouses before death through tax-free gifts so that whichever spouse dies first, the $600,000 can be used.

DON'T *fail to use gifts to minimize taxes in passing on your business, with the caveat of maintaining control and financial security.*

The other common alternative to planning to minimize estate taxes at the time of death is to use a gift program during your life and during that of the surviving spouse. The power of a gifting program stems from the effect of compounding. If you could give a gift of $10,000 today, live twenty years and realize a modest return on that amount of 6 percent per year, you would die with $40,000 in funds. This amount would be taxed at least at 37 percent if your assets are over $600,000. When you realize that you may do this for each child each year, the amount you may pass to your children without tax is considerable.

The amount need not be given in cash. You may give stock in the family corporation each year with a value of $10,000. Over a period of years you will have transferred a significant portion of your stock thereby minimizing your estate tax. You must realize that if the asset is appreciating; that is, your business is growing, time is your enemy because your estate increases and so does your tax. So early gift giving has the maximum effect. And if you don't use the yearly exclusion of $10,000 it is lost forever.

The problem you have surely recognized is that this policy of gifting depletes your own assets, control, and financial security. No program for minimizing taxes should ever jeopardize your security. So the remaining discussion of succession planning focuses on various techniques for saving taxes but without sacrificing control or security.

148

DO *face up to the fact that you will owe some estate tax when you die regardless of the deferral techniques used—how will you pay it?*

The techniques discussed above can defer tax until the last spouse dies or at least reduce the tax on the first to die, but eventually the surviving spouse will owe an estate tax. This tax will be due in nine months and payable in cash. At 50 percent, and even assuming that the family business after twenty or thirty years is worth only $3 or $4 million, how can the estate pay in cash a $1.5 or $2 million tax bill? Unless preparations are made, it probably can't. There are two possibilities for deferring the tax built into the tax code.

First, there is the possibility that if you can show the IRS that a cash payment will result in a forced sale or financial disaster, the IRS may allow the estate to pay the tax in ten installments, the first due in nine months and the remainder due in nine payments over the next nine years. This is a loan and you must pay steep interest. The good news is that the interest payments are deductible by the estate as a cost of administration with each payment being deductible when paid.

The second relief in the code is at your election. You may pay your estate taxes over fourteen years (four years interest only; ten years full amortization) with no payment due in nine months after death. A few of the qualifications include that the business be closely held, be an active operation, and that the business in the estate must be greater than 35 percent of the total. You must take advantage of this.

DON'T *pass up the advantages of life insurance to fund the estate tax on your business so that it may remain in the family.*

A common way to meet the estate tax cash obligation is to use life insurance. The matter is complicated, however, because the life insurance proceeds are taxable, too, if the policy is owned by the deceased. The solution is to place ownership in a trust with directions to use the proceeds to pay the estate taxes. Furthermore, there is an interesting type of trust with the odd name of Crummy trust (named for the taxpayer in the case approved). We have learned that you may give a gift each year to each child, and a like amount for your spouse, up to $10,000 without tax. Suppose you make the gift to a trust instead of directly to the child. It is a gift tax rule that a gift is completed only if the gift was a "present interest," meaning that the recipient had an immediate right to the money. In a trust designed only to pay taxes, there is no present interest. But suppose the trust allowed the child to take the money paid for only a period of thirty days after the gift is made. The gift satisfies the present interest rule. But what if the child does take it? Well, no more gifts! But if the child passes, then the funds may be used to pay the annual premiums each year, and upon your death, it can be used to pay the estate taxes. Not only does this work, but it is quite widely used. It permits the steady purchase of the necessary insurance, including any occasional increases to meet the changing value of the business.

DO *grasp the concept of an "estate freeze" as it relates to business succession planning.*

Basic to all business succession planning is the concept of an estate freeze. As explained in **#146,** when you die the government demands its share of your created wealth. Suppose you have built a successful business that is worth several million dollars. You wish to retire and to achieve some liquidity of this asset. Suppose further that you have one or more children that may be involved in the business with you and your spouse. You may sell the business, pay the capital gain on the proceeds, and share some of this money with your children by gifts (or intend to leave the money to them on your death). There is no business remaining and the estate will be taxed as a cash estate. On the other hand, suppose you wish to have the business taken over and run by your children. This family-business succession can be planned to minimize estate taxes.

Although you wish to leave the business to the children, you need liquidity and you do not want the business value to increase while in your estate (since this will result in larger estate tax). In other words, you would like to freeze the value of your interest in the business to the present value. This is achieved by dividing the ownership interests in the business into two classes or categories. One with high present value but little or no appreciation potential; the other with just the opposite. You take the first, the children take the second.

DON'T *get tripped up in the estate tax bramblebush when doing business succession planning.*

In a corporation, the older generation's interest is structured as a preferred stock (see **#37**) with no voting rights but high dividend payout (depending on the cash flow of the business). The children receive common stock with no dividends at all but complete ownership of the business. Since the common stock pays no dividend, it has a low present value. Therefore the value is low for the purpose of determining gift tax. In fact, if you transfer a little bit each year, your gift may be come nontaxable because of the annual gift tax exclusion. When you die, the preferred stock in your estate is worth no more than at the time of the restructuring (or recapitalization). It may even be possible to reduce further the preferred share value through a buy-sell agreement with restrictions on the right to transfer. (Restrictions reduce value because they reduce liquidity, and illiquid assets are always less valuable.) Everyone is happy, right? Oh, we forgot Uncle Sam.

The IRS convinced Congress that these techniques were distorting the law of estate taxation. So Congress enacted Chapter 14 of the code which restricts the valuation that may be placed on a family transfer of an interest in their business. The application of these restrictions is complicated but will be simplified for purpose of explanation. However, you must have legal advice in this planning area—it is simply too complex to do alone.

150

DO *your planning of the succession of your business at death in light of the IRS restrictions.*

As noted in **#149,** the IRS has placed restrictions on the techniques for passing the interest in a family business with minimum estate taxation. These restrictions apply if two conditions are met. First, it applies to any transfer from a controlling owner to a family member. Control means an interest of more than 50 percent of the voting rights, or 50 percent of the stock value. Family means spouse, children, or grandchildren of the owner or the owner's spouse, or any son- or daughter-in-law of such child or grandchild.

Second, it applies if the owner retains an interest in the business. This interest includes any stock that has a right to a dividend that is superior to the right of the transferred interest. In other words, it covers any retention of preferred stock that pays a dividend. If the retention is of common stock, it is not an interest—but then such retention defeats the purpose of restructuring. Furthermore, you may not retain the common stock and accompany the retention with an option in your family to purchase the stock at some time in the future. (If you could do this, one could argue that value is affected in some way by that option, thus decreasing value and achieving the same result as if you retained preferred shares). However, if such option was for a specified amount at a specified time, this would not turn the common stock into the proscribed interest. (Because this type of option *can* be valued, if the option was cheap the retained value would be dear, and the transferred value would be large, and the hoped for effect would be dashed.)

DON'T *abandon any business succession plan because the IRS has made it more difficult—it is still a favorable estate tax–saving method.*

As explained above, the IRS has restricted the methods available to minimize estate taxes when passing on a family business. But all is not lost.

If the interest retained by you when you restructure the company ownership is one of the proscribed interests, the value of the retained interest will be zero. (See below for a method that avoids this result.) The effect is to place all of the value of the business on the common stock interest that is transferred to the family. That means there will be a large gift tax due at the time of the transfer. There are various ways in meeting this tax obligation, including use of the unified gift and estate tax credit (see **#146**). However, while this may have reduced the full benefits of the estate plan as set forth above, it still allows the freeze of the value of the business; that is, the *future* appreciation of the business will not be taxed in the owner's estate.

The effect of the retained interest rule is avoided if there is a legitimate installment sale to the family. This requires a sale agreement between the owner and the family providing for fixed amount payments on fixed periodic dates with missed payments to accrue. This relieves the gift tax burden and allows the family to buy out the business from earnings; it does not offer the flexibility of noncumulative preferred stock dividends, which, if missed, do not accrue. In short, an installment sale is not as favorable as a preferred stock freeze.

151

DO *structure the succession plan for your business so that it takes advantage of discounts.*

Some of the basics of estate planning for leaving your business to your family are covered in **#149** and **#150.** There are limits on reducing the value of the business when you transfer it to your family although that is the primary objective of all estate planning. But all valuations of corporate stock take into account restrictions that are placed on the shares. In other words, if the marketability of shares is less, relative to shares traded on a stock exchange, they are reduced in value. These discounts on value can be substantial; if the restrictions are not seriously disadvantageous, they should be considered.

There are two common discounts that are available. First, is the lack of marketability for shares not traded on a securities exchange. Obviously it is harder to sell stock that is not freely traded. This lack of liquidity is reflected in a lower value for the shares. After many cases in which economists and financial experts have testified, there is a de facto discount of 15–30 percent of the fair market value of the same shares if traded on a stock exchange.

The other discount commonly applied to share valuation is whether the block of stock held is a minority or majority interest. A minority interest may have a discount of 15–50 percent; a controlling block may have a premium value that is at 20–50 percent above a traded stock. Other discount factors may apply.

DON'T *fail to cover all of the discounts that may be available when valuing your business for succession planning.*

If you are the first generation owner of your business, the chances are that you personally are the most important asset of the business. In small businesses, personal relationships are critical to growth and stability. No one can soothe a disgruntled customer like you can, no one understands your market like you do, and no one has his or her finger on the pulse of the industry like you. Your value is apparent: the firm is where it is because of you. When you die, or leave, the company may be losing its most valuable asset. Many courts have applied a generous discount for this loss. On the other hand, if you have been prudent enough to purchase key man insurance on yourself, this will be deducted from any discount that you would otherwise be entitled to. However, the insurance is a safer bet.

Less well recognized as a discount factor is unrealized gains. If a corporation has a large capital investment in a highly appreciated asset, the business value will reflect that. But if that asset is sold, there is a large capital gain on the transaction and a large tax to be paid. It can be argued, at least in some situations, that the asset should be discounted by the tax. If the company is being liquidated, there is no question that such discount will apply. But it is less recognized in an estate valuation.

Finally, because of the enormous potential liability for environmental damage in some businesses, an existing claim, if not the threat, should be applied as a discount.

DO *use the ESOP as a favorable retirement tool for you and the employees of a non-family-owned business, but beware complexity.*

As noted in **#117**, the Employee Stock Ownership Plan is one form of retirement plan, but also much more. If you have a family-owned business, then the ESOP is not a planning tool, because it distributes stock widely to the employees, not to a small group. But if your business isn't family owned, and you are looking for a liquidity device, the ESOP is unparalleled. Congress has been very sweet on the ESOP. There is no more favorable tax vehicle for making your business assets more liquid. As noted above, however, the downside is that it is complex and requires a battery of accountants, appraisers, and attorneys to keep within the rules.

If you establish an ESOP, you can contribute stock in the company or cash that is used to purchase the stock. The stock is held in trust for each employee, and there is no tax to the employee at the time of contribution. When an employee retires, the trust distributes stock in the company, or cash, or the trust may purchase listed securities of equal value and distribute these. The plan may provide for a "put" from the employee to the firm; that is, the right to force the company to purchase the employee's stock upon their retirement. This provides a liquidity device to the employee, although they must immediately pay tax on cash received.

The advantage to the owner, in addition to the incentive to the employees, is liquidity and tax advantages.

DON'T *fail to consider the ESOP as a liquidity tool in your estate planning for your small business if you can afford the cost.*

As seen in the preceding DO, there is a nice advantage to an employee in an ESOP. For the owner, he may sell his shares to the trust for cash. Since the owner has a large block, the amount of cash may be substantial, more than the trust has or the company can contribute. Where is this cash to come from? Again, Congress was sweet on the ESOP. The ESOP trust can borrow the money from a bank (if the corporation has adequate cash, it could also borrow from the corporation). And when the corporation declares a dividend in the future payable to the trust-shareholder, to pay the interest on the trust loan, the dividend is deductible. Of course, the bank must be comfortable that the corporation has the financial capacity and stability to pay down the loan. Banks being notoriously conservative, it may still be difficult to get a loan. Once more, Congress to the rescue. If the ESOP owns more than 50 percent of the company, and the employees have full voting rights in their ESOP-owned shares, the bank may deduct up to 50 percent of the interest income when computing its taxes. If the company is stable, the deduction may be negotiated into a lower rate of interest to the trust.

Finally, the owner who sells his shares to the ESOP (if he has owned the shares for three years and the ESOP trust owns the shares thereafter for three years) can take the cash and invest it in listed securities without tax payment until these securities are sold. However, the ESOP must end up owning 30 percent of the stock of the company, but you may own the rest.

153

DO *look at the drawbacks of using an ESOP for estate liquidity of your small business.*

At #117 and #152 it was noted that the chief drawbacks for the ESOP were the complexity and cost. The reasons for this are several. First, the IRS rules for an ESOP plan are complicated and ambiguous in some areas. If the plan is improperly drafted, the results are disastrous because all of the tax benefits are lost and a large tax is due immediately. In such circumstances, attorneys place a premium on their billings to protect against liability. And the papers that must be filed regularly must be reviewed not only by attorneys but also by accountants. More cost. Then the accounting itself is quite complex, again because of the possible ways of construing various rules. Still more costs.

Finally, there is the valuation problem that is unique among retirement benefit plans, and more onerous than in other plans. When the corporation is deducting contributions of its stock to the ESOP trust, it wants the appraisers to place a high value on the stock to maximize the deduction and lower corporate taxes. But if the employees have a put to sell their stock back to the trust upon retirement, then the company does not wish to pay more for the shares. If the appraisal differs to suit the purpose, there is a potential liability for a breach of honesty and fair dealing with the employees. And because this possibility exists, the appraisal must be very careful. So, multiple appraisals may be necessary, and the liability threat means that the price will be high. Discuss the ESOP with your advisers. They may discourage use for pragmatic reasons.

DON'T *allow the tax advantages of the ESOP to distort your succession plan.*

ESOPs as an estate planning tool highly favored by Congress must not be misunderstood in the context of the closely held family company. An ESOP, like a stock bonus plan, results in the widespread distribution of the company stock in the rank and file employees. It is not possible to fully take advantage of the ESOP and still maintain control in a small group. This is the price that Congress exacts for the tax benefits extended. There is also the matter of equity dilution; that is, as the stock is distributed, the ownership interest of the family decreases. Since the original owner may not be able to divest himself or herself of the large amount of stock in his or her estate by gift or other tax-saving devices (as discussed at **#149**), this may be inevitable. But if continued ownership of the principal asset of the next generation is intended to be the business, the family jewel, then the price of stock distribution to save taxes may be too high.

This is not to say that a plan cannot be devised to minimize these consequences. The trust for the ESOP generally is controlled by the owners of the company. There is no requirement that the company continue to contribute cash to the trust. Nor is there any requirement that the trust purchase company stock with cash contributed. So the amount of dilution can be limited. Or the purchase of company stock may be used only rarely—in the event of an estate tax liquidity problem.

154

DO *plan for the retirement or death of yourself or one of the other key partners or shareholders in your closely held business.*

In **#149** we discussed some of the problems in business succession planning that are specific to a family-owned business. But there are also problems that should be dealt with in the closely held business between nonrelatives that own substantial shares. The problem also relates to the retirement, not just death, of one of the key people.

The problem of control of the closely held business was discussed above (see **#14**). But we recognized that the problem on death of a closely held company shareholder presented unique problems calling for use of a buy-sell agreement. In a buy-sell, each shareholder (actually the heirs of the shareholder) agrees to sell his or her shares in the event of death to the other owners of the business who in turn must purchase those shares. The chief problem with the buy-sell is pricing; unlike the right of first refusal restriction, which automatically places a valuation on the shares, there is no third-party offering a set price. There is also a procedural problem—should the corporation or the other shareholders be obligated to purchase the shares? The former is referred to as a stock redemption agreement and raises statutes regarding the necessity of the company to have certain funds before it can buy back shares. However, if the company is successful, the stock redemption requirements do not present a problem. (The laws are designed to protect creditors from the shareholders who may redeem stock rather than pay debts.)

DON'T *select a pricing mechanism for a buy-sell agreement in a closely held business without a full consideration of the relevant factors.*

There are literally hundreds of ways to price the stock at the time of the shareholder's death. Just as different stock analysts value a public company's shares from different perspectives, here too there are conservative and technical approaches. Book value certainly is conservative, but it may be the most appropriate for certain businesses at certain times. There is a price-earnings ratio that may be based on earnings over a short or a long period of time, or a moving average, or various assets such as insurance proceeds or real estate may be valued separately and their earnings excluded from other calculations, for example. Or, rather than a formula, the shareholders may agree to meet annually and set a price based on a majority vote. Or the shareholders may throw the entire valuation problem to an appraiser that they agree on—or to be chosen.

The payout may be selected in a variety of ways depending on the individual financial condition of the shareholders. The downpayment, usually required to fund estate taxes (if there is a buy-sell, no deferral is allowed) may be funded through insurance. But a difficult problem is the security for the installment payments. If the corporation becomes financially troubled, the security will probably fail to serve its purpose. If the company enters bankruptcy, the creditors surely will challenge the valuation as too high and demand repayment of the amounts paid. This leads to tax problems.

155

DO *use stock incentives for key employees in a closely held company, but be careful regarding transferability of the stock.*

Stock options in a corporation were discussed in **#13** and recommended for providing the proper incentives for key employees. But we also noted in **#14** that stock of a closely held business should be subject to restrictions to prevent the stock from getting into the wrong hands. These two objectives are not necessarily in conflict. A stock option may be given with the transfer limited to a resale of the stock to the company when the employee wishes to cash out. However, the formula for repurchase must be fair to provide the desired incentive. Furthermore, if the stock must be resold to the company, why use stock at all? The value of the stock, as determined by the valuation formula, is simply a measuring tool in the appreciation of the company as reflected in the stock valuation formula. So keep the formula, and dispense with the stock. This is referred to as phantom stock.

The nice thing about phantom stock is that it does not involve all the complicated rules relating to real stock. On the other hand, phantom shares are no more than a contract right, and a breach of that contract by the company could involve a real litigation hassle for the employee. On the other hand, if the corporation goes into bankruptcy, you may be as well off as an unsecured creditor as a stockholder. A phantom stock plan is more like a deferred compensation plan. Note also that the phantom stock plan avoids the problem of a second class of shares in an S Corp (see **#6**).

DON'T *ignore the desire of nonfamily key employees for stock in a closely held corporation—consider restricted stock.*

Another way to meet the needs of key employees you do not want to make full "partners" in the closely held business is to transfer shares to them that are restricted. The principal reason for using restricted stock is that you wish to give the employee a bargain on the purchase price. You cannot do that with qualified stock options which must be priced at the fair market value. Like an option, restricted stock usually is subject to immediate return if the employee leaves, except that a portion of the stock vests (becomes irrevocably the employee's) over a period of years. So the employee is motivated to stay. Like other restricted stock, even after vesting, the stock must be resold to the company if the employee leaves, retires, or dies. If the value has gone up, the employee is rewarded.

There are some mean tax rules for restricted stock, however. The IRS allows you to sell (or give) the stock at lower than fair market value only because the stock is at a "substantial risk of forfeiture." That is, if you do not stay the required time, you must give up the stock. But when the stock vests, you must pay the tax due on the difference between the amount paid and the value at the time of vesting. At that time, you have income without cash to pay the tax. But because the company has a deduction equal to the gain you received, it may be willing to pay a cash bonus sufficient to pay your tax bill. Of course, because the cash bonus is also taxable, the bonus must be enough to cover the tax on the bonus. See an advisor here.

APPENDIX

Confidential Disclosure Agreement

XYZ Corporation ("XYZ") is willing to disclose to you certain confidential information, including trade secrets and other proprietary information of XYZ relating to the Widget ("Widget Information") that we have designed and developed and are commencing to manufacture. The purpose of this disclosure is to allow you to [evaluate the Widget design for the purpose of investing in XYZ or entering into a business relationship with XYZ] [review the Widget design to enable you to bid on one or more components or subassemblies of the Widget] [evaluate the Widget with a view toward purchase of 10,000 units of the Widget in the event it meets your requirements (but this agreement is not an agreement for purchase of the units)] [evaluate the performance of the Widget in your operating environment in return for your agreement to provide XYZ with a report on such performance].

You agree that ABC Company ("ABC") and the employees of ABC (you agree that you will disclose this Widget Information only after such employee has entered into an agreement to maintain such Widget Information in confidence) will maintain the Widget Information in strict confidence and will not disclose it to others, nor use such it for any purpose other than the purpose set forth above for a period of five (5) years from the date of this agreement.

The information included in Widget Information shall not include information that you have in your possession as of the date of this agreement as evidenced by documents dated prior to the date of this agreement, information that enters the public domain through no fault of yours, or information you receive from a third party after the date of this agreement who has no obligation to maintain the information disclosed to you in confidence.

If you agree to the above terms and conditions, please execute the enclosed copy of this agreement and return it to XYZ prior to _____, 1996.

ABC Company   XYZ Corporation

_____   _____
Darryl ABC, President   Harry XYZ, President

Dated: _____   Dated: _____

GENERAL PREEMPLOYMENT INQUIRIES

If You Need to Know	Ask/State	Don't Ask
NAME (including other names the applicant may have used)	"What is your name?" "We would like to check your past employment and your educational record. Have you used any name other than that you have given to us?"	"What was your maiden name?"
ADDRESS	Residential address. Name and address of person to be notified in case of emergency	"Do you own or rent?"
AGE	"Are you over 18 years of age?" "If so, we will need proof of your age *after* you are hired. If not, we will need a work permit *after* you are hired."	"What is your age?" "What is your birthdate?" "When did you graduate from (high school, college)?" [Or other questions that, when answered, would indicate that the applicant is over 45.]
SEX/MARITAL STATUS	If less than 18 years of age: "What is the name and address of your parent or guardian?"	"What is your sex?" "Male?" "Female?" "What is your sexual orientation?" "Are you married, divorced, single, etc.?" "Do you have any children that live with you?" "If so, how many?" "What age are they?" "Do you have child care?" "Are you pregnant now or are you planning to have children (or any query regarding child bearing)?" "Do you live with anyone else?"

GENERAL PREEMPLOYMENT INQUIRIES (Continued)

If You Need to Know	Ask/State	Don't Ask
LEGAL RIGHT TO WORK	"After you are hired, you must show proof of your legal right to work in the United States. If you cannot, we will terminate your employment."	"Are your a U.S. citizen?" "Do you have a green card?" "Where were you born?" "Where were your parents born?" "What nationality are you?"
LANGUAGE SPOKEN	If job related, i.e., the company job description requires, or considers desirable that the employee speaks another language: "What other languages can you speak, read, or write?"	"What language do you speak at home?" If applicant indicates "Yes" in response to the question in the adjacent column re additional languages: "How did you learn to speak this other language?"
WORK AVAILABILITY	State policy with regard to regular hours and overtime (including scheduling notice). If employees (e.g., in retail sales establishments), are assigned hours weekly and may include Saturdays, Sundays or holidays, or evenings, state company policy and ask: "Can you meet these requirements?"	"Does your religion (or "personal beliefs," etc.) preclude you from working Saturdays?" "Sundays?" "Do you require time off for your religious holidays?"

GENERAL PREEMPLOYMENT INQUIRIES (Continued)

If You Need to Know	Ask/State	Don't Ask
HONESTY, MORAL CHARACTER, FINANCIAL CONDITION	After explaining that a positive answer will not necessarily disqualify the applicant, you may ask: "Have you ever been convicted of a felony?" If the position requires bonding, state that a bond is a condition of hiring.	"Have you ever been arrested?" "Have you ever been refused bonding, or has any bond on you been canceled?" "Were you ever in military service in the United States or any foreign country?" "What type of discharge did you receive?" "Have you ever had your wages garnished?" "Been in bankruptcy?" "What is your current financial condition?" "Credit record?"
ASSOCIATIONS, CLUBS, ETC.	"If you feel that belonging to any club, organization, or association is related to the job you are applying for, tell me the names. However, omit the names of any such club, organization or association that may show your age, sexual preference, religion, race, disability, etc.)."	"Give the names of all clubs, organizations or associations to which you at one time belonged or to which you now belong."
REFERENCES	"Give the names of references with whom we can check the facts you have given us."	[Do not ask the references any of the questions that you are prohibited from asking the applicant directly.]

PREEMPLOYMENT INQUIRIES UNDER THE AMERICANS WITH DISABILITIES ACT (ADA)

(Prior to a Conditional Offer of Employment)

Area of Interest	Ask/State	Don't Ask
GENERALLY	After describing the essential and marginal job requirements: "Can you perform the functions of this job, with or without reasonable accommodation?" "Please describe or demonstrate how you would perform these functions?"	"Do you have a disability that would interfere with your ability to perform this job?" "Can you walk?" "Can you stand?" [These questions are identified as impermissible questions in the EEOC Enforcement Guidance—honestly!]
ATTENDANCE	After stating company policy with respect to attendance: "Can you meet these attendance requirements?" "Did you have any unauthorized absences from your job last year?" "How many days were you absent from work last year?" "How many Mondays or Fridays were you absent?"	"How many days were you sick last year?" "Were you sick?" [May not be asked as a follow-up question to the permissible question in the next column].

PREEMPLOYMENT INQUIRIES UNDER THE AMERICANS WITH DISABILITIES ACT (ADA)

(Prior to a Conditional Offer of Employment) (Continued)

Area of Interest	Ask/State	Don't Ask
STRESS	"How well can you handle stress?" "Do you work better or worse under pressure?" "This job requires the employee to prepare written reports containing detailed factual summaries and analyses. These reports must frequently be prepared within tight time frames. Can you perform this function, with or without accommodation?"	"Have you sought treatment for your inability to handle stress?" A series of questions such as: "Do you ever get ill from stress?" "Does stress affect your ability to be productive?" "Have you ever been unable to 'cope' with work-related stress?"
VISION	"Do you have 20/20 corrected vision?"	"What is your corrected (or uncorrected) vision?" [May not be asked as a follow-up question to the permissible question in the next column]. "Do you have AIDS?"
AIDS		A series of questions such as: "Do you have open skin sores? Do you have boils? Do you have fever? Do you have dark urine? Do you have jaundice?"

PREEMPLOYMENT INQUIRIES UNDER THE AMERICANS WITH DISABILITIES ACT (ADA)

(Prior to a Conditional Offer of Employment) (Continued)

Area of Interest	Ask/State	Don't Ask
CONDITION OR STATUS OF A KNOWN OR DISCLOSED DISABILITY	After disability becomes known and the job requirements are described: "Describe or demonstrate how you would perform the functions of this job."	"How did you become disabled?" "What effect does being in a wheelchair have on your daily life activities?" "Do you ever expect to walk again?" "Is your diabetes (or other disease) under control?" "Does your diabetes (disease) interfere with your ability to work?"
WORKERS' COMPENSATION HISTORY		"Have you sustained any job-related injuries in the last 5 years?" "Have you ever filed a workers' compensation claim?"

PREEMPLOYMENT INQUIRIES UNDER THE AMERICANS WITH DISABILITIES ACT (ADA)

(Prior to a Conditional Offer of Employment) (Continued)

Area of Interest	Ask/State	Don't Ask
DRUGS	"Are your currently using illegal drugs or illegally using prescription drugs?" [Permissible even if applicant is in fact a drug addict.] "Have you ever illegally used drugs?" "Have you used cocaine (or other controlled substances) in the past two years?" "Have you ever been convicted on a drug charge?" If an applicant tests positive on a drug test: "What medications are you taking that may have resulted in a positive drug test result for a controlled substance?" "Are you taking this medication (as indicated by the drug test) pursuant to a lawful prescription?"	"What medications are your currently taking?" "Have you ever taken AZT (or other prescription drugs)?" "How often did you use illegal drugs in the past?" "Have you ever been addicted to drugs?" "Have you ever been treated for drug addiction?" "Have you ever been treated for drug abuse?"

PREEMPLOYMENT INQUIRIES UNDER THE AMERICANS WITH DISABILITIES ACT (ADA)

(Prior to a Conditional Offer of Employment) (Continued)

Area of Interest	Ask/State	Don't Ask
ALCOHOL	"Do you drink alcohol?" "Have you ever been convicted for driving while intoxicated?"	"Do you drink every day?" "How many times a week?" "Alone?" "Have you ever been treated for alcoholism?" "Are you an alcoholic?" "Does alcohol interfere with your daily activities?" "Do you belong to Alcoholics Anonymous?"
LICENSES/CERTIFICATION	"Do you have a valid California state driver's license?" "Please provide a DMV printout of your driving record that was run within the last 3 months." "Do you have a DOT certification to drive a truck interstate?" "Do you intend to obtain one?" "Why not?"	
HEIGHT, WEIGHT, EATING HABITS	"What is your height?" "Weight?" "Do you regularly eat three meals a day?"	"Do you need to eat a number of small snacks at regular intervals throughout the day in order to maintain your energy level?"

INDEX

Advisory jury, 64
Affirmative covenants in loan documents, 45–46
Age Discrimination in Employment Act (ADEA), 140
Agency law, 111
Aliens, 142–143
Alternative Dispute Resolution (ADR), 60–61
American Arbitration Association (AAA), 62, 130, 177
Americans with Disabilities Act (ADA), 172–177
   preemployment inquiries under, 227–231
   See also Disabilities, persons with
Arbitration, 62–63
Articles of Organization, 26–28
At-will employment, 143–144

Bank financing
   collateral and, 43
   committing assets and, 43
   covenants and, 45–46
   default and, 47–48
   loan agreements, 41–43
   personal guarantees and, 37–38
   representations and, 44–45
   revolving loans and, 42
   true interest and, 42–43
   warranties and, 44–45
Bank loans. *See* Bank financing
Bankruptcy, 112–113
   actions as a creditor, 115–116, 117
   bankrupt trustee, 113–114
   chapter 7, 115–117
   chapter 11, 115–118
Bankruptcy: A Feast for Lawyers (M. Evans & Co., Inc.), 112
Blue sky laws, 13
Board of directors, 10
Businesses, types of, 2. *See also* Corporations; Limited liability companies; Partnerships; Sole proprietorship
Business succession planning
   Bypass trust and, 209
   Crummy trust and, 211
   discounts and, 214–215
   ESOP and, 216–218
   estate freezes and, 149
   estate tax and, 208–209, 210–214
   gifts and, 208–210
   IRS restrictions on, 213–214
   marital deductions and, 209

   retirement or death of substantial shareholder, 218–229
   rewarding key employees, 220–221
Buying and selling goods
   changes in terms, 126
   control of terms, 124–125
   delivery terms, 126
   indemnification against patent infringement, 128
   property rights and, 122–123
   purchase orders and terms, 119–122, 125–126
   sales transactions, 123–124
   warranties and, 127–128
Buy-Sell agreement, 20
By-laws, 11, 13
Bypass trust, 209

Capital leases, 38–41
Carnet, 136
C corporations, 5, 8
   compared with S corporations, 7–8
   definition of, 7
   fringe benefits and, 165
   fringe benefits with, 22
   See also Corporations
Centralized management and LLCs, 24
Chapter 7 bankruptcy, 115, 116, 117
Chapter 11 bankruptcy, 115, 116–118
Child Labor laws, 140
Close corporations, 15
   employee shareholder compensation and, 20–22, 22–23
   maintaining, 19–20, 35–36
   retirement or death of a shareholder in, 218–229
   See also Corporations
COBRA (Consolidated Omnibus Budget Reconciliation Act), 140, 156–158
Coined trademarks, 87
Collateral, 43
Common stock, 3, 17
Computer Fraud and Abuse Act (CFAA), 200
Computers, 195
   computer fraud, 200–201
   cyberspace, 195–96
   E-mail, 196–197, 199–200
   illegal access, 198
   Internet, 195–201
   privacy rights, 196–198
   software protection, 201–206
Computer Software Act of 1980, 203

Phantom stock, 220
"Piercing the corporate veil," 16
Piggyback rights, 57
Preferred stock, 9, 17, 52–54
Prior art search, 73, 74
Privacy rights, 196–198
Pro forma invoice, 132
Proprietary rights, 122–123
Public offerings, 55
Purchase orders, 119–122, 125–126

Qualified incentive stock options, 19
Qualified terminable interest property
(QTIP) and estate taxes, 208

Ratchet clause and venture capital, 52
Reasonable accommodation, 174–176
Redemption clause and preferred stock,
56–57
Registration rights and "going public," 58
Religious discrimination, 147–148
Restricted stock, 220–221
Retirement plans, 162–167
Revolving loan, 42
Rules of the American Arbitration Association, 62

Safe harbor, 151
Salaries. *See* Wages
Sales representatives, 186–187, 190–193
S corporations
definition of, 7–8
potential tax problems with, 9
qualification for, 8–9
See also Corporations
Selling goods. *See* Buying and selling goods
Settlements, 67
Sexual Harassment, 167–172
Shareholders, 10
retirement or death of, 218–220
sale of stock by, 13–14, 19
See also Corporations; Stock
Shareholders agreement, 11
Software
protection of (for developers), 201–206
purchasing custom, 206
standardization of, 205–206
Sole proprietorship
positive aspects of, 2–3
transferring to a corporation from, 14–15
Stock
common, 3, 17
convertibility of, 54, 55

options, 18–19, 220
phantom, 220
preferred, 9, 17, 52–54
pricing after a shareholder's death,
218–220
restricted, 220–221
restricting transfers of, 19–20
sale of, 13–14, 19
types of, 16–17
See also Corporations
Suggestive trademarks, 87
Supplier credit, 48–49

Tariffs, 135–136
Taxes, 2
employee shareholder compensation and,
20–22, 22–23
estate, 208–209, 210–214
gift, 208–209
withholding, 5, 140, 159
Temporary employment, 155–156
Term sheets and financing, 50, 51
Terms of purchase, 119–122, 124–125
Testing, employee, 146–147
Title VII, Equal Employment Opportunity
Act, 140, 143, 146, 147
Trade dress, 101–2
Trademarks, 72, 84–85
applying for registration, 85–86, 92
determining uniqueness of, 85
federal registration of, 89, 91–92
in foreign countries, 137–138
infringement and, 88–89
intent to use (ITU) applications, 93–94
maintaining rights, 90–91
protection of, 91
symbol for, 89
secondary meaning, 97–98
strong, 87
weak, 86
Tradenames
corporate name protection, 94–96
fictitious names, 96
personal names, 96–97
Trade secrets, 98–99
ex-employees and, 101
preventing misappropriation of, 100–101
protecting, 99–100
software protection, 201–206
Trials, 68–69

Uniform Commercial Code (UCC), 27, 125,
128